No More Rules

California Institute
of the Arts   School of Art

24700 McBean Parkway Valencia California 91355

805 255 1050

No More Rules

Graphic Design and Postmodernism

Rick Poynor

Laurence King Publishing

LAURENCE KING

Published in 2003 by
Laurence King Publishing Ltd

71 Great Russell Street
London WC1B 3BP
United Kingdom
Tel: +44 20 7430 8850
Fax: +44 20 7430 8880
e-mail: enquiries@laurenceking.co.uk
www.laurenceking.co.uk

A catalogue record for this book is available
from the British Library

ISBN 1 85669 229 9

Designed by Kerr|Noble
Edited by Nell Webb
Picture research by Helen McFarland
Additional photography by Nigel Jackson
Printed in China

Text set in Eureka by Peter Bil'ak, Pop by Neville Brody
and Pop modified by Kerr|Noble. Cover: Sign Painter Ad Art by House Industries

Frontispiece: Edward Fella. Poster for Jeffery Plansker lecture at California
Institute of the Arts, 1994

Contents

Preface

No More Rules has its starting point in a close engagement with graphic design of the postmodern era that began, for me, in the early 1980s. It deals with recent events in design history, but it is not a history as such. It doesn't set out to argue that there shouldn't be any more rules in graphic design, only that during this period many designers, including some influential ones, have proceeded as though this were the case. Contemplating the mass of material and reviewing how it has been treated in other accounts, often by individual designer and by stylistic tendency, it seemed most useful to identify some key themes in design's rule-defying relationship with postmodernism – origins, deconstruction, appropriation, technology, authorship and opposition – and organize the book on this basis. Some of the examples shown and considered here, and some of the ideas and arguments discussed, were selected because they played a central role in design thinking during this period. Any critical survey that did not include them would be making a serious oversight. Others feature because they are representative of approaches that became typical.

What made these years so stimulating for someone observing and writing about graphic design was the high level of discussion that the work generated, particularly in the late 1980s and early 1990s when many of these ideas were novel and unfamiliar in design circles and the technology was changing rapidly. I am especially indebted to a number of designers and design writers who, in different ways, have played a significant role in the development of my own thinking about this material: Ellen Lupton, J. Abbott Miller, Robin Kinross, Neville Brody, Peter Saville, Rudy VanderLans, Michael Rock, Steven Heller,

Katherine McCoy, Edward Fella and Jeffery Keedy. It would amaze me if I have said nothing in these pages with which they want to disagree strenuously. My thanks to these colleagues and my thanks also to all the individuals and organizations that have shown their support for the fundamental principle of free discussion by permitting their work to be reproduced in this book.

Warm thanks must also go to Laurence King and Jo Lightfoot at Laurence King Publishing; to Nell Webb, the book's tirelessly conscientious editor; and to Amelia Noble and Frith Kerr, its designers, who kept faith with the project from the start.

Rick Poynor

Introduction

Twenty years after the term started to be used widely, postmodernism remains a difficult, slippery and, for some, infuriating topic. There is already a vast literature devoted to every aspect of postmodernism and new books arrive all the time. By the late 1980s, it was common to see the word used in newspapers and magazines and some publications ran whole series of articles attempting to explain what it meant. Sometimes they just ridiculed it. For a while it was voguish to drop this clever-sounding buzzword into cultural conversations and it even started to show up in television commercials. The widespread assumption now, outside the academy, is that postmodernism has gone the way of so many other intellectual fads. Many people never understood what it was supposed to mean and even the most knowledgeable observers are sometimes inclined to treat it with suspicion. For Judith Williamson, author of *Decoding Advertisements*, interviewed in a design journal, the term is too vague to be useful in anything other than a stylistic sense.[1] Richard Kostelanetz, author of *A Dictionary of the Avant-Gardes*, is even blunter: 'My personal opinion holds that anything characterized as postmodern, whether by its author or its advocates, is beneath critical consideration, no matter how immediately popular or acceptable it might be.'[2]

So why write a critical survey of postmodernism and graphic design at this point? First, because no matter how awkward, problematic and uncertain the concept of postmodernism might appear to be, it is now so well established as a way of thinking about our time and our 'condition' that it cannot be simply ignored. Second, because despite a certain amount of discussion in design magazines and chapters about postmodern graphic design in a few books, there has, surprisingly, never been a book devoted to the

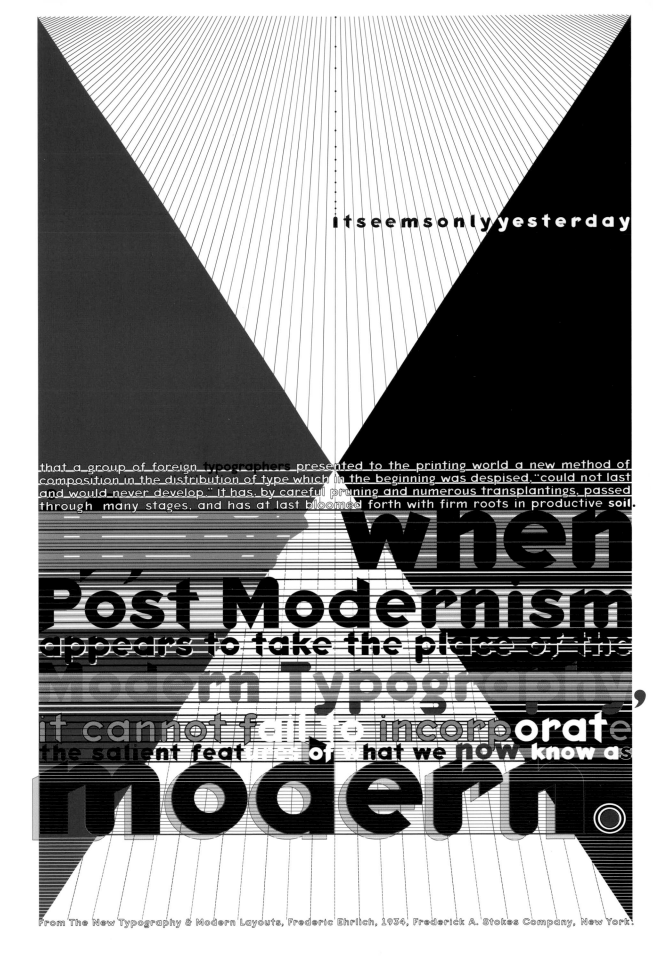

itseemsonlyyesterday

that a group of foreign **typographers** presented to the printing world a new method of composition in the distribution of type which in the beginning was despised, "could not last and would never develop." It has, by careful pruning and numerous transplantings, passed through many stages, and has at last bloomed forth with firm roots in productive **soil.**

when Post Modernism appears to take the place of the Modern Typography, it cannot fail to incorporate the salient features of what we now know as **modern**

From The New Typography & Modern Layouts, Frederic Ehrlich, 1934, Frederick A. Stokes Company, New York.

Jeffery Keedy. Emigre Type Specimen Series Booklet No. 4 : **Keedy Sans,** typographic illustration, Emigre, USA, 2002 topic. I say surprisingly because it could be argued that graphic design, as currently practised, is a prime example of a popular, accessible medium exhibiting symptoms of postmodernism. In the last 15 years, graphic designers have created some of the most challenging examples of postmodernism in the visual arts. For the most part, though, despite their cheerful embrace of 'low' popular culture, cultural studies commentators have overlooked these communications and products. Critical introductions to postmodernism and the arts routinely deal with literature, architecture, fine art, photography, pop music, fashion, film and television, but they show little sign of even noticing, still less attempting to 'theorize', any form of design, despite its obviously central role as a shaper of contemporary life.[3]

For their part, few graphic designers have been eager to define their output as postmodern. Those who have laid most positive and even argumentative claim to the label have tended to be American. Many of the designers, American and non-American, who are identified in *No More Rules* as producing work which relates to postmodernism and its themes would reject the term vehemently. For many others, the word would be no more comprehensible as a description than it would be to ordinary members of the public. Graphic design as a profession has long had an aversion to theory and many of the key postmodernist texts are highly demanding even for those who possess a basic sympathy for their arguments and intentions. For other designers, postmodernism is too closely identified with a particular historicist style of architecture current in the 1980s and it is consequently rejected on grounds of æsthetic taste as much as anything. As chapter 1 argues, this essentially stylistic view of postmodernism by some design commentators has inhibited an understanding of the way in which postmodern tendencies continued to influence design throughout the 1990s.

It is not this book's purpose to provide an overview of postmodernism and all attempts at summary inevitably run up against the multitude of sometimes conflicting interpretations that postmodernism has generated. (Some suggestions for further reading are given in the bibliography.) A few key postmodernist ideas can, however, be sketched here and some of these will be developed in the book as they relate to graphic design. Postmodernism cannot be understood without reference to modernism. While the 'post' prefix might seem to suggest that postmodernism comes after modernism, or that it replaces or rejects it, many commentators point out that postmodernism is a kind of parasite, dependent on its modernist host and displaying many of the same features – except that the meaning has changed. Where postmodernism differs, above all, is in its loss of faith in the progressive ideals that sustained the modernists, who inherited the eighteenth-century Enlightenment's belief in the possibility of continuous human progress through reason and science. The Enlightenment project, writes David Harvey in *The Condition of Postmodernity*, 'took it as axiomatic that there was only one possible answer to any question. From this it followed that the world could be controlled and rationally ordered if we could only picture and represent it rightly. But this presumed a single mode of representation which, if we could uncover it … would provide the means to Enlightenment ends.'[4] For postmodern thinkers, it is no longer possible to believe in absolutes, in 'totalizing' systems, in universally applicable values or solutions. They view with incredulity the claims of grand or metanarratives – as Jean-François Lyotard termed them in *The Postmodern Condition: A Report on Knowledge* – that seek to explain the world and control the individual through religion, science or politics.[5]

The products of postmodern culture may sometimes bear similarities to modernist works, but their inspiration and purpose is fundamentally different. If modernism sought to create a better world, postmodernism – to the horror of many observers – appears to accept the world as it is. Where modernism frequently attacked commercial mass culture, claiming from its superior perspective to know what was best for people, postmodernism enters into a complicitous relationship with the dominant culture. In postmodernism, modernism's hierarchical distinctions between worthwhile 'high' culture and trashy 'low' culture collapse and the two become equal possibilities on a level field. The erosion of the old boundaries allows new hybrid forms to blossom and many changes seen within design in recent years, as it took on some of art's self-expressive characteristics, only make sense in these terms.

The dissolution of authoritative standards creates fluid conditions in which all appeals to universality, expertise, set ways of doing things and unbreakable rules look increasingly dubious and untenable, at least in the cultural sphere. As many cultural critics have noted, the products of postmodern culture tend to be distinguished by such characteristics as fragmentation, impurity of form, depthlessness, indeterminacy, intertextuality, pluralism, eclecticism and a return to the vernacular. Originality, in the imperative modernist sense of 'making it new', ceases to be the goal; parody, pastiche and the ironic recycling of earlier forms proliferate. The postmodern object 'problematizes' meaning, offers multiple points of access and makes itself as open as possible to interpretation.

No More Rules' central argument is that one of the most significant developments in graphic design, during the last two decades, has been designers' overt challenges to the conventions or rules that were once widely regarded as constituting good practice. Towards the end of his life, the modernist poet T.S. Eliot observed that 'It's not wise to violate rules until you know how to observe them' and the commonly held view that one should master one's discipline before seeking to disrupt it also held true for design.[6] In *Typography: Basic Principles* (1963), John Lewis, a British designer and graphic design teacher, includes a chapter titled 'Rules are Made to be Broken'. 'Before you start breaking rules,' he writes, 'you should know what they are. Once one knows what are the correct procedures one can look at them critically and see whether by deliberately flouting them anything can be added to methods of communication.'[7] Lewis believed that there was even a place for illegibility, for mixing up fonts and mutilating letters, if it would serve the message by adding some excitement. However, when it came to book design, no interference between author and reader could ever be justified. 'The book page is not a medium for self expression,' he decrees.[8] For this generation of designers, the rules of page layout and typographic craft distilled from 500 years of printing history provided an essential framework, though knowing when and how to break them was acknowledged as vital to creative design. In 1981, the American designer Bob Gill summarized the thinking behind his 25 years as a designer with a two-sentence book title that was virtually a manifesto in itself: *Forget All the Rules about Graphic Design. Including the Ones in this Book.*[9] Graphic designers have continued to invoke the need first to absorb, but then to resist and transcend the rules of professional design. 'Rules are good. Break them,' Tibor Kalman urged colleagues, as recently as 1998.[10]

By this time, as Kalman well knew, the idea of rules had become highly contentious. The late 1980s and early 1990s had seen a huge body of work, much of it created by young designers, in which every principle and ordinance heeded by earlier generations had been subjected to continuous assault. As chapter 2 shows, this process began mainly at Cranbrook Academy of Art, under the influence of writing by postmodern theorists. Edward Fella, an American designer then in his late forties, has a pivotal place in these developments. Fella, like Kalman, was essentially self-taught, but his rule-breaking method was grounded, as T.S. Eliot had advised, in a thorough acquaintance with design's conventions. David Carson, probably the most widely adulated designer to emerge in the 1990s, took a different view, arguing without embarrassment that it was his ignorance of rules, with all their prescriptions and constraints, that allowed him to produce designs that seemed to many to resemble nothing ever encountered before in commercial print media. 'I never learned all the things you're not supposed to do, I just do what makes the most sense ...' Carson explained. 'There's no grid, no format. I think it ends up in a more interesting place than if I just applied formal design rules.'[11]

For many young designers, this was a hugely beguiling idea. In Carson's case, it produced extremely striking and visually exciting results, seeming to some, at least for a while, to confirm the total irrelevance of rules: the designer trusts to his intuitive sense of what will work, what feels right, and everything falls into place. 'By unmooring the page from the grid, each design element operates through an associative illogic, arresting the eye and pulling attention into an adventure of the senses across the open field of the page,' enthused one reviewer in a British style and fashion magazine.[12] Such an approach was enough to provoke several years of soul-searching in the design schools, since every foundational principle they taught now seemed open to question.

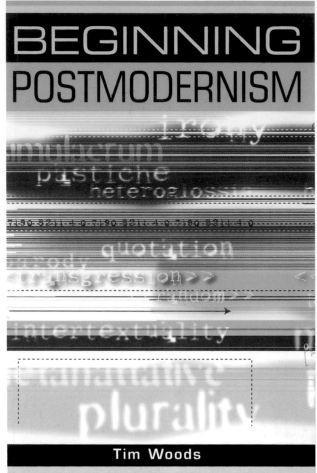

Phillip Castle. Mythologies by Roland Barthes, book cover, Granada Publishing, UK, 1976

[Right] **River Design Company. Beginning Postmodernism** by Tim Woods, book cover, Manchester University Press, UK, 1999

It soon became clear, looking at the work pouring from legions of imitators, that without a very particular kind of talent, 'associative illogic' was most likely to lead to work that was simply a mess. Intuition alone was not enough, but there was no doubt that appeals to this mysterious internal guidance system, which was the unique property of the individual designer or viewer, reflected a wider reluctance in society to submit to any form of imposed, external authority. Was this sufficient, though, to explain the widespread enthusiasm for signifiers that, in the new atomized digital typography, no longer signified in any established, collective sense? The literary critic Fredric Jameson notes how in schizophrenia – a term that he uses as description rather than as diagnosis – as temporal continuities and spoken language break down, 'the signifier in isolation becomes ever more material ... As meaning is lost, the materiality of words becomes obsessive, as is the case when children repeat a word over and over again until its sense is lost ... a signifier that has lost its signified has thereby been transformed into an image.'[13] Something similar seems to be at work in much of the rule-defying design produced during this period, as the materiality of typographic form takes precedence over linguistic sense.

One only has to look at cover designs of books about postmodernism to see how, from the mid-1990s, the unmoored

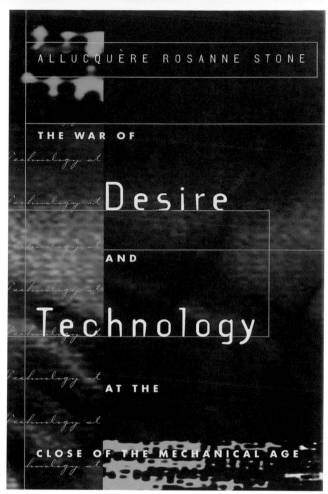

Steve Rawlings. Umberto Eco and Football by Peter Pericles Trifonas, book cover, Icon Books, UK, 2001

[Right] **Mimi Ahmed.** The War of Desire and Technology at the Close of the Mechanical Age by Allucquère Rosanne Stone, book cover, MIT Press, USA, 1995

page and its nebulous, associative space became the defining trope when representing this subject matter. In the 1970s, montage – a modernist device – was still the most contemporary-looking way of depicting the collisions and fusions of the postmodern cultural landscape. In Phillip Castle's airbrush illustration for a paperback edition of Roland Barthes' *Mythologies*, conventional reference points are becoming unfixed and jostling each other in new configurations, suggesting the possibility of new cultural relationships, but each shiny element is distinct in itself, retaining its own clear boundaries. In fully postmodern representational space, all that is solid often melts into an intoxicating, semi-abstract blur. *Beginning Postmodernism* (1999), an introductory text aimed at students, dissolves postmodern keywords such as irony, pastiche and intertextuality into a hyperactive field of shooting horizontal lines. On covers for the 'Postmodern Encounters' series of essays, dealing with topical themes in the work of Foucault, Baudrillard, Eco, Derrida and others, the thinkers' heads meld with a tempestuous electronic space, boiling over with logos, images and word fragments, as though the Zeitgeist itself is gushing from their brains. On the cover of Allucquère Rosanne Stone's *The War of Desire and Technology at the Close of the Mechanical Age* (1995), the title type, contained by a precise-seeming but arbitrary framework of pink rules, hangs above foggy images in which nothing definite can be perceived.

Since the mid-1990s, there has been a retreat from the total repudiation of rules, not that this ever held much appeal for most established practitioners. David Carson looks increasingly like a coruscating one-off, rather than the harbinger of a new school of untutored designing driven by raw talent and unfettered intuition. Graphic designers did not need to look far to see that, whatever its merits as a critique of design, the argument that no special know-how was needed to become a designer would encourage anyone who felt like it to buy a copy of QuarkXpress and a few fonts and set up as competition. Designers who have spent several years and run up large debts acquiring a college education have every reason to believe that there are many aspects of being a designer that can only be properly absorbed through study.

If there were sound commercial reasons to preserve the idea of design as a craft, the nature of craft was also undergoing intellectual reassessment. In a perceptive analysis of what it means to possess craft knowledge, published in 1994, the British critic Peter Dormer argues that the 'constitutive rules' that govern a particular kind of craft activity are not external to it. These rules are the activity: they give it its own internal logic, which the practitioner must follow, and, taken together, they add up to a body of knowledge. To divorce them from the activity would be to destroy it.[14] Graphic design without any rules would cease to be graphic design and this is even more the case with typography. As this introduction was written, signs of a growing backlash against rule-less design were starting to emerge from the typographic establishment. A book titled *About Face: Reviving the Rules of Typography*, published in 2002, contends that 'Rules can be broken but never ignored' and this phrase from its introduction is emblazoned in large letters across its title spread, as a guiding principle.[15] The text reiterates conventions of effective typographic practice with which every guide-writer from Jan Tschichold to John Lewis would concur. There is no discussion of postmodernism in the book (ours is a 'modernist society', claims the author) and the typographic experiments of the last 20 years go largely unmentioned.[16]

Yet this period has seen an explosion of creative activity in visual communication, as designers re-examined existing rules and forged new approaches. Graphic design is a much more open, diverse, inclusive and, perhaps too, inventive field as a result of these challenges. Inspired by a revised conception of authorship, which ran counter to postmodern assumptions, graphic work became more self-assertive, idiosyncratic and sometimes extreme, as many examples in this book clearly show. Design now embraces a broad range of stylistic possibilities, from informal approaches inspired by the vernacular – admired for its energy and anti-professionalism – to virtuoso forms of digital image-making that push graphic technology to the limit. The complexity of construction that has been a feature of postmodern design from the start, leading, at the high point of rule-breaking zeal, to the paradox of meaningless complexity finds expression today in spectacularly detailed designs that radiate a commanding sense of expertise.

As a professional activity, graphic design faces an uncertain future now that new technology has opened up graphic production and expression to many more people. Its role in postmodern society is, however, likely to remain central. Postmodern graphic designers are deeply implicated in a consumer culture that makes ever more ingenious use of design as a beacon of identity and a tool of seduction. At the same time, they are freer than ever to question, oppose and perhaps begin to reframe design's future role.

1 Origins

When postmodernism first began to be mentioned in connection
with graphic design, the search, among commentators, was for a
definable style that could be labelled 'postmodern graphic design'.
To an extent these observers succeeded in their aim and by the end
of the 1980s, when this 'style' had seemingly run its course, it was
possible to believe that postmodern design was over and that other
stylistic approaches had taken its place. Most surveys and histories
of graphic design covering this period continue to take this view.
While there was a kind of graphic design that bore some relation to
trends in architecture also labelled 'postmodern', the use of
postmodern graphic design as a contained stylistic category
is misleading because it implies that the design that succeeded it
in stylistic terms no longer has a relationship with postmodernism.
Yet if there was, and is, a cultural condition that can be called
postmodernism, there is no reason for believing that it came to
a sudden halt around 1990 and proponents of postmodernism as
a graphic style do not argue that it did. They don't have to, since
their analysis confines itself mainly to questions of æsthetics;
having defined the style, it is enough that it stops. The cultural
factors that gave rise to postmodernism did not disappear in the
1990s and it could be argued that many of them have intensified.

One of the earliest uses of the term 'postmodern' in
relation to design in a general sense appeared in 1968, in the
British magazine *Design*. A year earlier, art historian and critic
Nikolaus Pevsner had described certain tendencies in architecture
as postmodern, and design critic Corin Hughes-Stanton proposed
to apply the description to 'freewheeling' forms of design thinking
previously labelled 'Pop'.[1] The tendency's later eclecticism was
already apparent in its use of Art Nouveau, 1920s moderne and

pseudo-space age imagery. Hughes-Stanton laments postmodern design's lack of originality and the fact that it has not produced its own contemporary style. He welcomes it, however, not as a rejection of modern design, but as a logical step in its development. 'As an attitude, it is closer to people and what they want: it is prepared to meet all their legitimate needs without moralising about what those needs should be. Its roots are thus deeper embedded in society than those of the Modern school.'[2] He predicts the continuing breakdown of modernist boundaries in design, suggests that design will become more æsthetically adventurous and sees a dawning integration of pleasure-giving and ergonomic factors.

In the 1970s, the term 'postmodern' continued to be applied to architecture by various critics and architects, but it was Charles Jencks who did most to establish the idea, with his book *The Language of Post-Modern Architecture* (1977). Postmodern architects, he argues, are still partly modern in terms of sensibility and use of technology. Consequently, the postmodern style is 'hybrid, double-coded, based on fundamental dualities'.[3] This could entail the juxtaposition of old and new, or the witty inversion of the old, and it nearly always meant the architecture had something strange and paradoxical about it. For Jencks, postmodernism represented the demise of modernism's avant-garde extremism and a partial return to tradition. It was an acknowledgement, too, that contemporary society is composed of different groups with different tastes. Postmodern architecture's hybrid, double-coded forms attempted to communicate both with the elite professional class, able to decipher the references, and the general public, which would enjoy the playful elements. If the dynamiting of the modernist Pruitt-Igoe housing scheme in St Louis, Missouri, on 15 July 1972 spelled the death of modern architecture, as Jencks liked to argue, then, in his view, Michael Graves' controversial, competition-winning Portland building (1982), with its giant, decorative keystone, was postmodern architecture's first major monument.[4]

In graphic design, Wolfgang Weingart was a seminal figure in the development of the 'new wave' that came, in time, to be called postmodernist. Weingart trained as a typesetter in Basle, Switzerland, and from 1968 he was a tutor at Basle's

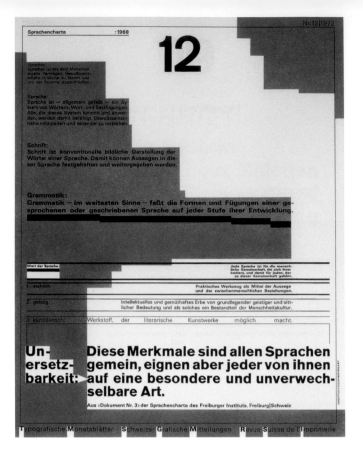

Wolfgang Weingart. Typografische
Monatsblätter, no. 12, magazine cover,
Switzerland, 1972

Kunstgewerbeschule. As a typesetting apprentice, he had been
obliged to memorize and regurgitate dozens of 'correct' answers
to design problems set out in teaching manuals for typography.
'It seemed as if everything that made me curious was forbidden:
to question established typographic practice, change the rules, and
to reevaluate its potential,' he writes. 'I was motivated to provoke
this stodgy profession and to stretch the typeshop's capabilities to
the breaking point, and finally, to prove once again that typography
is an art.'[5] In 1964, in an article for the trade journal *Druckspiegel*,
he wrote that 'Phototypesetting with its technical possibilities is
leading today's typography into a game without game rules.'[6]
The editors declined to publish his text in full, fearing they would
lose their readers. Weingart was determined not to be constrained
by the reductive conventions of Swiss modernist typography,
which in his view had hardened into orthodoxy and formula.
Using lead type and letterpress, he began to investigate basic
typographic relationships, such as size, weight, slant, and
the limits of readability. He was fascinated by the effects of
letterspacing and he stretched words and lines until the text came
close to being unintelligible. In 1972 and 1973, he designed a series
of 14 related covers for *Typografische Monatsblätter* magazine, which
introduced his challenging ideas to Swiss and international readers.

Weingart's work was spontaneous, intuitive, deeply infused
with feeling and it had a significant influence on American design.
In 1968, soon after Weingart started at the Kunstgewerbeschule,
Dan Friedman began his studies at the school, and from 1970 to 1971,

Dan Friedman. Typografische Monatsblätter, no. 1, magazine cover, Switzerland, 1971

[Right] **Dan Friedman.** Space, promotional poster for a picture newspaper, USA, 1976

April Greiman also undertook postgraduate work. In 1972, at Friedman's instigation, Weingart toured the United States, speaking about his work in Philadelphia, Columbus, Cincinnati, Princeton, New Haven and Providence.[7] Two early pieces by Friedman show how his own approach evolved during this period. A minimalist poster based on the letter 'N', created in 1968 for a film showing at the Hochschule für Gestaltung in Ulm (where Friedman also studied), is, in his own words, 'simple, restrained, orderly, static, exclusive, abstract, pure, reduced, harmonious, systematic, and integrated'.[8] By contrast, a 1971 cover for *Typografische Monatsblätter*, in which a series of letterforms found in Times Square, Manhattan, float above the city, is 'complex, excessive, chaotic, dynamic, inclusive, vernacular, contextual, expanded, dissonant, random, and fractured' – qualities that would be seen, with growing frequency, in the years ahead.[9] After they met in 1972, Friedman and Greiman had a considerable impact on each other's approach to design. In a 1976 poster by Friedman for a new picture newspaper, *Space*, to be published by the Institute for Vision and Energy, found images such as a sofa, a typewriter and a pair of lovers float and revolve around each other like so much debris adrift in deep space. It was a sign that design was beginning to break from its moorings, question its commitment to rationalism and determinacy and take on increasingly unfixed and open-ended new forms.

Wolfgang Weingart. Kunstkredit 1976|77, exhibition poster, Switzerland, 1977

[Right] **Wolfgang Weingart.** Kunstkredit 1978|79, exhibition poster, Switzerland, 1979

In the late 1970s, Weingart started to receive commissions to design posters for museums and other cultural organizations and his work changed direction. The collage-like 'Kunstkredit' exhibition poster (1977) was contructed from separate pieces of film layered together and fixed to a film base, then transferred directly to the offset litho printing plate. Weingart's complex pictorial spaces, unprecedented at the time, fused typography, graphic elements and fragments of photographs on equal terms. He exposed sections of the grid, violating its purity with jagged outlines, torn edges, random shapes and imploding sheets of texture, as in the second 'Kunstkredit' poster (1979). Weingart ruptured, twisted and layered his surfaces into multifaceted cubist geometries that embodied a new kind of self-referential graphic space. His photomechanical expressionism, discovered in the darkroom and at the lightbox in the process of working, acted on the viewer's senses and emotions to show that, in the right hands, graphic design could sometimes be a medium for autonomous artistic expression.

An early use of 'postmodernism' specifically in reference to graphic design occurred in 1977, when the American designer Wilburn Bonnell curated an exhibition titled 'Postmodern Typography: Recent American Developments' at the Ryder Gallery in Chicago.[10] Bonnell's decision to label the work 'postmodern' was

[Right] **April Greiman and Jayme Odgers.** Wet, magazine cover, USA, 1979

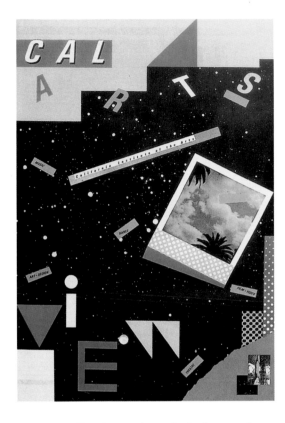

April Greiman. CalArts Viewbook, cover of tabloid-sized overview, California Institute of the Arts, USA, 1979

inspired by the term's use in architectural writing. The show featured work by Friedman, Greiman, Steff Geissbuhler, Willi Kunz, Bonnell himself, and others, although its participants did not necessarily regard themselves then (or later) as practitioners of postmodern design, tending to see the term as too limiting or too vague. As so often with design work of an experimental nature, their clients came mainly from the cultural and educational sectors and there seemed little chance at first that it would be taken up in the corporate sphere. Greiman's covers for the *CalArts Viewbook* and for an issue of the West Coast magazine *Wet* in 1979 exemplify many of the characteristics of the new work. Her eclectic visual language draws from Surrealism, Art Deco and ornamental pattern-making. For *Wet*, Greiman and Jayme Odgers, a regular collaborator at this time, collage the various elements together to form an angular, richly detailed graphic setting – a kind of shrine – for the picture

of pop singer Ricky Nelson at its centre. In a poster|brochure for
California Institute of the Arts, which has become emblematic of
the period, Greiman and Odgers present a paradoxical interior
space in which gravity is suspended, relationships of scale are
overturned and the illusory nature of the panorama is underlined
by the presence of a hand, holding up the scene for inspection.
A woman's face, gazing out of this world at the viewer, suggests
that this rule-free zone should be understood as a mental space
with boundless possibilities. Greiman's reflections in interview
highlight the subjective concerns of her early designs. 'I'm a feeling
person. Obviously the optimum situation is to have a balance
between mind and heart and between body and spirit. ... I think
culturally we're seeing that the forms being expressed in New Wave
are very female.'[11] Greiman contrasts the mystery, irrationality
and unexplainable aspect of her work with the masculine linearity
of Swiss design; her aim, though, was to build additional layers on
this sense of order and structure rather than to abandon it.

A poster by Willi Kunz, created in 1978 for an exhibition of
photographs by Fredrich Cantor, was also hailed as a quintessential
example of postmodern design. Kunz, too, had studied at the
Kunstgewerbeschule in Basle before moving in 1970 to the United
States. At first sight 'Strange Vicissitudes' is much closer to the
linearity that Greiman resisted. It is certainly highly organized:
the large type used for the photographer's name contrasts with
the tiny type used for the picture's title, which hinges from the
'F' in a vertical white band. The main photograph of actor Marcello
Mastroianni plays against the smaller image of an anonymous
woman and the black bars at either side lock the two images in
place. However, the red title, letterspaced across the main picture,
introduces an element of subtle disturbance and the grid of dots
(an allusion, Kunz notes, to the lights in the Mastroianni picture)
also reads as somewhat arbitrary and strange.[12] The woman looks
out from under her fringe with a single eye – a rogue dot that has
escaped from the grid – while Mastroianni's eyes are shut tight.
In Kunz's poster, the idea of the grid, which had been so central to
Swiss design in the 1950s and 1960s, is simultaneously acknowledged
and subverted. The vertical cut in the corner of the Mastroianni

Fredrich **Cantor**

strange VICISSITUDES

June 17
July   8
■78

FOTO
492 Broome Street
New York, NY 10013

Willi Kunz. **Strange Vicissitudes,**
exhibition poster, USA, 1978.
Photographs by Fredrich Cantor

image gives the composition a destabilized 'stepping' movement
often seen in the work of Weingart and other exponents of
typography's new wave.

To appreciate the new wave's impact on design in the
United States, it is necessary to understand how constrained
prevailing conceptions of design had become. An issue of *Print*
magazine devoted to communication design in the 1970s is
titled 'The Triumph of the Corporate Style' and there is a striking
homogeneity in the examples of design and advertising it shows.
Company literature produced by corporations such as Mobil,
Exxon, North American Rockwell and Aristar was orderly, well
structured, undeniably clear, but totally predictable and lifeless
in its use of watered-down modernist forms. 'The 1970s was marked
by the rise of the Corporate Style in communications design and
the subsequent enfeeblement of imaginative activity,' concludes
the issue's introduction. 'It was a period in which security and
safety replaced risk as the dominant selling tool.'[13] The writer
wonders whether anything can be done to bring about a
transformation of attitudes in the 1980s, though, as we have
seen, such changes were already under way. However necessary
these changes might have been, early responses to the new wave
were often negative. Older designers, accustomed to rigorously

suppressing the personal, registered concern at the eruption of wayward subjectivity and resisted the idea, expressed by Weingart and Greiman, that design might be a form of art. These critics saw the new wave's stylistic elements and effects as obstacles to the lucid transmission of the client's message and they dismissed these experiments as a passing fad. An early article about the new wave, titled 'Play and Dismay in Post-Modern Graphics', quotes a senior New York designer: 'I don't consider graphic design to be an opportunity to advance art forms. It has to advance the client's interest.'[14] For the critic Marc Treib, postmodernism's assault on the eye with pages of blips, slits, dots and zits was initially enjoyable, an exhilarating relief from ordinary design, but rapidly became exhausting and tedious. 'It is like listening to six radios playing at once, each with a different station. This is not charged complexity; it is noise.'[15]

Yet the cultural ideas surfacing in the work of Friedman, Greiman and others had been around for some time, even if they were unfamiliar in graphic design. In his book *Complexity and Contradiction in Architecture*, first published in 1966, Robert Venturi presents a 'gentle manifesto' for an architecture that would reflect the richness and ambiguity of contemporary experience. Architects, he argues, can no longer allow themselves to be intimidated by orthodox modern architecture's puritanical injunctions and restrictions. Among other preferences, Venturi favours elements that are hybrid rather than pure, distorted rather than straightforward, ambiguous rather than articulated, accommodating rather than excluding, redundant rather than simple, and inconsistent and equivocal rather than direct and clear. Architecture, he declares, should evoke many levels of meaning; it should be possible to read it and use it in several ways at the same time. 'I am for messy vitality over obvious unity,' writes Venturi. 'I include the non sequitur and proclaim the duality.'[16] More, he concludes, inverting the well-worn modernist axiom, is not less. In their famous study *Learning from Las Vegas* (1972), Venturi, Denise Scott Brown and Steven Izenour applied some of these ideas to a detailed, illustrated analysis of the Las Vegas Strip, which they addressed non-judgementally purely as a phenomenon of architectural communication.[17] The attention they gave to brash roadside signs usually dismissed by the cultured as debased and ugly encouraged graphic designers to look more sympathetically at vernacular design as a way of breaking free from modernism, particularly at Cranbrook Academy of Art (see chapter 2).

When measured against the radical challenges directed at architectural practice in Venturi's manifesto, much of the graphic design first labelled 'postmodern' now looks far from shocking. In the late 1980s and early 1990s, designers would go much further in their attempts to create multilayered communications that captured the complexity and ambiguity of modern experience. Despite Weingart's experiments with text setting, most early postmodern designers accepted the established rules of intelligible typographic delivery and they concentrated their attention on what happened around the edges of the text rather than on new ways of handling text itself. This distinction can be seen in *Fetish*, a magazine started by Jane Kosstrin and David Sterling, former students of Cranbrook Academy of Art and founders of Doublespace, based in New York. The shortlived, large-format publication, aimed at metropolitan sophisticates with a fascination for material culture, was a postmodern proposition in its own right. A special issue on synthetics, published in 1980, features articles about plastics, pocket cameras, astro turf, Barbie dolls, and synthesizer music. Picture material, feature titles and pull-quotes underscored by heavy rules are set on the slant and irregular chunks of striped pattern punctuate the issue; one spread features swathes of zebra pattern. A feature titled 'Machine Music' employs some of the new wave's most familiar typographic gestures – letterspacing, mixed type weights – and an inventive repertoire of devices and symbols evokes the unfamiliar notation and sounds of contemporary electronic music. While the pages are busy with activity and 'noise', the main text is presented in five conventionally set, sanserif columns. In an interview with fashion designer Betsey Johnson, seven narrow text columns, treated as a graphic component of the spread alongside other elements, descend in a series of roughly equal steps, but the unconventional text block still retains a high degree of clarity.

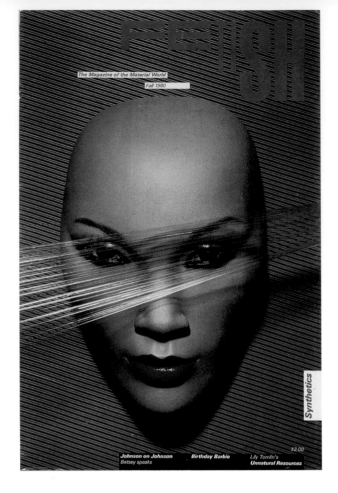

[Right & opposite] **Doublespace.** Fetish, no. 2, magazine cover and spreads, USA, 1980. Cover photograph by Jere Cockrell. Betsey Johnson photograph by Stephen Ruehr

[Top & bottom] **Christoph Radl.** Memphis logos, Italy, 1982 and 1983

[Middle] **Valentina Grego.** Memphis logo, Italy, 1983

In *Fetish*, graphic design is the medium of a new sensibility: informal, playful, ironic, synthetic, pluralist, referential, and confident in the intrinsic interest and value of everyday popular culture. In late 1980, this emerging global sensibility saw the birth of a three-dimensional design phenomenon that would have far-reaching international influence, even in the sphere of graphic design. The Memphis design group founded in Milan by Ettore Sottsass, Michele De Lucchi and others took its name – according to Memphis chronicler Barbara Radice – from the Bob Dylan song 'Stuck Inside of Mobile with the Memphis Blues Again'. Memphis objects were most striking for their use of plastic laminates printed with a wild variety of colourful patterns. Like roadside neon signs, laminates were identified with ordinary, 'undesigned' environments: coffee shops, ice cream parlours, milk bars, fast-food restaurants, and kitchens and bathrooms in the home. Memphis applied this cheap-looking material to luxurious pieces for the living room that were as wilful and bizarre as they were æsthetically compelling. Memphis designs, Radice observes, are 'assemblages, agglomerates ... deposits of decorations that overlap, intersect, add up and flow together ...'[18] She goes on to explain: 'The whole Memphis idea is oriented toward a sensory concentration based on instability, on provisional representation of provisional states and of events and signs that fade, blur, fog up and are consumed.... Communication – true communication – is not

MACHINE MUSIC

by Mark Abbott, Brian Doherty, William Hohauser, and Doug Snyder

You've heard of Tuxedo Moon, seen that name listed somewhere, it's a new-wave-clothing boutique in San Francisco or something; Stockhausen, that's a familiar name—(he's a German philosopher, right?); you're vaguely aware of the Throbbing Gristle, sure, that's an English version of Screw magazine; you haven't listened to disco music since "Rock the Boat" and a friend of yours once put on a Steve Reich album, and, though it sounded almost pretty, it was mostly "beeps" and "boops." Machine music? Not into it. You pass right by the bins marked "Electronic" at your local vinyl vendors and head straight for the rock-and-roll alphabet-card sea.

But here's a fact—if your taste represents even the most mundane M.O.R. or grass-roots anti-trendiness, you still own records bubbling with covert electronic innovation, like it or not. You don't have to be able to grasp the essence of Robert Fripp's explanatory tape-loop raps, or be a regular at any SoHo side-street laboratory-cum-coffee house, or know who Wendy Carlos is (or was)—you don't have to go looking for machine music—it has already found you. From elevators crawling with Muzak to synthesized drums on the latest country and western albums, Fetish asked the four members of Sick Dick and the Volkswagens, a successful, New York-based experimentally-inclined electronic/mathematical/musical expedition, to gently guide us through a history of what is now a profoundly omnipresent creature—machine music. What unfolded was an alluring network of tales ranging from the starkly seminal to the sublimely complex, and including a great mass most of us are harboring on our very own shelves right now—the commonplace subliminal.

The synthetic sounds found in today's pop music (disco and new wave) have deep-founded roots in classical experiments with mechanized sound starting in the beginning of this century. People wanted to create new instruments to play in ensembles, or like Edgar Varese, used sirens and other sound effects as supplements to traditional chamber music. The novelty of a strange sound incorporated with conventional instruments has worn off—but the method has been developed through the years, and in current academic music it is common to find a piece scored for instruments and tape. The tape cues into the performance with totally new sounds, imitating other instruments not in the ensemble (sometimes strange or hard-to-find instruments), or supplying different figures played earlier by the same performer. In pop recordings, it is also not unusual to find sound effects, some purely electronic, and others, such as airplanes, telephones, cars, etc. But the most powerful development in recent pop music has been the popular assimilation of the synthesizer as an instrument.

Early music machines

Tracing the development of the synthesizer, one could probably start with early experiments on an instrument called the Trautonium built by Frederick Trautwein of Berlin in 1928. Like the organ, the Trautonium had a keyboard, but instead of just switching to a different set of pipes and keeping the scales constant, each key could be set to have its own sound and pitch. In one sense, it could be considered the first electronic sound effects machine.

Electronic organs followed soon, but their pitches were usually preset in chromatic relationships (with minor tuning capacity). At about the same time, sound generators of all sorts were being invented. One such device was the Intonarumori, built in 1913 by Luigi Russolo and used that year in Milan in the "Art of Noises" performance, a symphony concert in which a group of Dadaists performed all sorts of unexpected instruments, not excluding a bicycle. Many instruments like the Intonarumori were constructed and used in performances. While not electronic, these innovators looked very much like the large horns used in P.A. systems today, and produced very unique, non-traditional sounds. The array of early electronic instruments that ensued, most of which appeared before 1950, had sci-fi names: Dynamophone, Theremin, Rumorarmonie, Russolofono, Sphaerophon, Mellochord, Mixturtrautonium, Elektromuzon.

The logistics of producing electronic music were greatly aided by the introduction of integrated systems of sound producers and modifiers (modulators) in the form called synthesizers (first marketed by R.A. Moog in 1964), and later by computer-controlled sound generators. Some composers, however, didn't like the aesthetic results of these instruments, since most of the sounds and organizations were too identifiable, and since at first really complex sounds could not be synthesized. So some composers used machines merely as extensions of the classical sound generators (oscillators, etc.), where the resultant sounds were methodically pieced and layered together by means of the conventional studio techniques already known to them.

The development of synthesis systems

Originally, R.A. Moog and Don Buchla independently developed systems in the U.S. Studios around the world also developed their own synthesis systems, and eventually other systems, such as the Putney VCS-3 from England or John Eaton's Synket, were marketed worldwide. One of the most notable users of these new synthesizers was Wendy (formerly Walter) Carlos, who was first introduced to electronic music at Columbia, and then later gained an appreciation of the classics. She immediately turned her particular taste into a hit with her Moog versions of "Switched on Bach," in 1968. Since that time, Keith Emerson (of Emerson, Lake and Palmer) has worked in performance versions of the Moog in pop recordings, as has David Rosenboom with the Buchla system.

In addition to manually controlled synthesis systems, computer systems have greatly advanced the flexibility of sound synthesis. Early work by Max Mathews at the Bell Telephone Laboratories has produced obtrusive long-range (eg. Music IV) for digital sound structure. Mathews has also been fundamental in the development of real-time computer sound synthesis systems, where sounds are produced live via digital numbers that represent amplitudes, pitches, etc.) to analog (what a speaker uses to produce sound) conversion, so that sounds can be heard spontaneously.

Early production studios

While initially there were three major studios producing electronic music in the early 50's, later in Paris under the direction of Pierre Schaeffer and Pierre Henry; one in Cologne, directed by Herbert Eimert with principal achievements being made by Karlheinz Stockhausen; and one at Columbia University in New York, directed by Vladimir Ussachevsky and Otto Luening)—now there are virtually hundreds all over the world. In the early days, each studio had its own approach to sound construction. The early French works relied on organic constructions of recorded sounds. These methods were rejected by the Germans who established a more purist approach in which they started with sine tones and built up layers using new pitch relationships not possible on conventional instruments. In America, both of these approaches were incorporated into a broader spectrum of styles that included conventional instrumental sounds, leading to the coexistence of tape and instruments. Examples of work from this period are Henry's "Astrologie" ('52), Stockhausen's "Studie II" ('54), and Ussachevsky's "Piece for Tape Recorder" ('54).

The Producers

The music producer has also had a great deal to do with the increase of electronics used in today's pop music. Some of the earlier individuals like Brian Eno and John Cale came from more serious academic backgrounds where they were exposed to music by the new breed of classical composers like Cage, Stockhausen, Berio, Kagel and Young, and brought with them into the studio a strange aesthetic for processed sound that has resulted in drastic transformations of performing artists' sounds on record from their live efforts. Cale's work with Nico and Eno's work with Cale, Ultravox, Genesis, as well as his own works, are prime examples. Some of these techniques have even been kept and used in live performances after being recorded on discs.

Synthe-rock

Among the earliest examples of electronics used in rock or popular music were The Chipmunks, in "The Chipmunk Song" ('58), The Beatles' Sergeant Pepper's Lonely Hearts Club Band, Pink Floyd's "See Emily Play" from The Piper at the Gates of Dawn, The Beach Boys' use of the Theramin in "Good Vibrations," and the Rolling Stones' use of reversed piano in "2000 Light Years From Home" from the Ip Their Satanic Majesties Request—not to mention works by The Grateful Dead, and of course, Frank Zappa and his group The Mothers of Invention. Zappa, perhaps the most serious composer of the early rock genre, let his influences be known and even went so far as to ask well-respected soprano Cathy Berberian to appear in his "200 Motels." So, perhaps the age of psychedelia really marked the first heavy use of electronics, later to achieve freaky space-outs in the pop era.

Some of the most unusual contemporary synthesized music is the dance-oriented "rock/electronic" coming primarily from the U.S.A. and England. Among the English groups are musicians of classical, "art" rock and folk rock backgrounds who are using fresh ideas that have resulted from transforming the new technologies and popular forms. Some of these new groups have experimented with rhythmically-pulsed electronic bursts and blends. Perhaps the strangest and darkest group, Throbbing Gristle, has steadily advanced its use of electronic gadgets in performance through the transformation of only one large mixer and P.A. system into a stereo wall of active synthetic convoluted sound. Their popularity through their adventurous elitism of electronic violence and bleakness has permitted other artists of similar focus to organize a new order of music. Groups and individuals such as The Leather Nun, Monte Cazzona, Thomas Leer and Robert Rental are all breaking existing barriers with their warped sensibilities. Other British groups include Cabaret Voltaire, Experleres, Human League, Orchestral Maneuvers, Durutti Column, Protex, This Heat, General Strike, and the Flying Lizards. All play a heavily electronic rhythmical music.

Here in the U.S. groups like Tuxedo Moon, Units (S.F.), Non, Sick Dick and the VW's, Dark Day, B-people, Suicide, Martin Rev, Implog, Dew, WKG8, Information, etc., are relying upon electronics for freshness. Other groups like Mars, Teenage Jesus, Rhys Chatham, Glenn Branca, Theoretical Girls, DNA, and Borbetomagus, use amplification for the power needed to take ideas and reshape them into sonic revelations.

Germany has also spawned a healthy pop/electronics scene, with Tangerine Dream, Kraftwerk, and Can; France with Metal Urbain and Magma; Holland with the Minny Pops; and Japan with the Plastics.

One reason for this advance in electric eclecticism is the accessibility of keyboard synthesizers. Another is the influence of earlier popular groups such as The Grateful Dead, Roxy Music, Genesis, Soft Machine, solo-line projects, and perhaps even John Lennon's work after meeting Yoko.

Future trends

The devices now found in recording studios would make some of the first producers of electronic music very jealous. Music that once had to be contained on four tapes or more can now be put on one, and the bulky knobs and equalizers and the like now fit comfortably around one board which two or four hands can control with ease. With computer memory presently able to record the most expensive units, even more hands can be "remembered" during the mixing and processing. With devices such as digital reverb and delay, phase shifters, frequency shifters, harmonizers, various filters, ring modulators, vocoders, flangers, reverb chambers, tape echo, speed change, reversing, wave shapers, and electronic switches, producers and musicians now have limitless possibilities to turn the straightest sounds into the most way-out space noises.

How much further can the present technology take us? With the advent of digital recording we can look forward to better systems that use computers to process sounds instantaneously. Soon, the only limitation will be the speed of the computer in conducting the massive calculations necessary for any sort of high-frequency musical sound. (A complex sound in stereo would require about 80,000 pieces of information—in the form of numbers—for just one second.)

With the recent developments in microprocessors, the home micro-computer has become yet another tool of the composer. In fact, the non-composer, too, can now experiment with the new devices and get sonic rewards. And for the non-musical, consider the work of musician Laurie Spiegel, who has plans to market a microchip containing a program of her music, instead of a record or tape—just plug into your home computer system, get up, and dance to the beep.

Top Ten Picks

Synthe-sound faves of Sick Dick and the VW's

Harold Budd, The Oak of Golden Dreams, Advance.
Fripp and Eno, No Pussyfooting, Antilles.
Philip Glass, Einstein on the Beach, Tomato.
Mimaroglu, Wings of the Delirious Demon, Finnadar.
Minny Pops, Drastic Measures, Drastic Movement, Plurex.
Tony Oxley, February Papers, Incus.
Reich, Maxfield and Oliveros, New Sounds in Electronic Music, Odyssey.
Karlheinz Stockhausen, Song of the Youths, Deutsche Grammophon.
Edgar Varese, Music of Varese, Angel.
Michel Waisvisz, Crackle, SAJ.

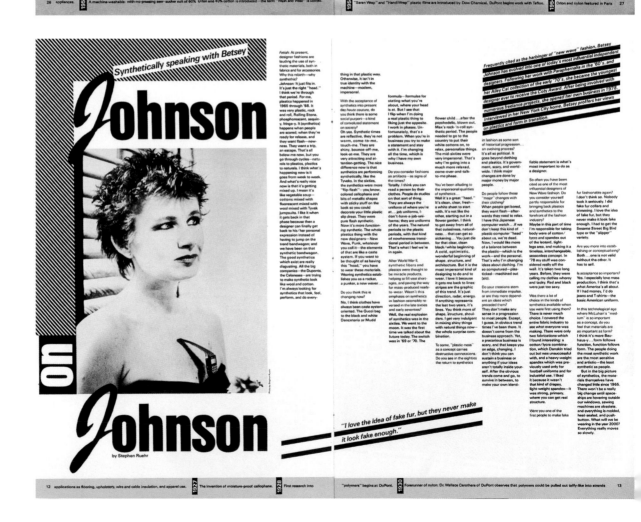

Synthetically speaking with Betsey Johnson

Johnson on Johnson

by Stephen Ruehr

Fetish: At present, designer fashions are lauding the use of synthetic materials, both in fabrics and for accessories. Why this rebirth—why synthetics?

Johnson: It just fits in. It's just the right "head." I think we're through that period. For me, plastics happened in 1965 through '68. It was very plastic, rock and roll, Rolling Stone, phosphorescent, sequin-y, fringe-y. It (synthetics) happens when people are scared; when they're ready for release, and they want flash—now. They want a trip, an escape. That's all below me now, but you go through cycles—naturals to plastics, plastics to naturals. I think what's happening now is it goes from week to week. And what's really new is that it's getting mixed up. I mean it's like vegetable soup—cottons mixed with fluorescent mixed with wool mixed with Tyvek jumpsuits. I like it when it gets back in that phase because then a designer can finally get back to his/her personal expression instead of having to jump on the trend bandwagon; and we have been on that synthetic bandwagon. The good synthetics which exist are really disgusting. All the big companies—the Duponts, the Celaneses—are trying to make synthetic look like wool and cotton. I'm always looking for synthetics that look, feel, perform, and do everything in that plastic way. Otherwise, it isn't in true identity with the machine—modern, impersonal.

With the acceptance of synthetics into present day haute couture, do you think there is some social purport—a kind of convoluted statement on society?

Oh yes. Synthetic times are reflective, they're not warm, come-to-me, touch-me. They are shiny, bounce-off-me, look-at-me. They are very attracting and attention-getting. The nice difference now is that synthetics are performing synthetically, like the Tyveks. In the sixties, the synthetics were more "flip-flash"—you know, colored cellophanes and bits of metallic shapes with sticky stuff on the back so you could decorate your little plastic slip dress. They were pure flash synthetic. Now it's more functioning synthetic. The whole plastics thing with the new designers—New Wave, Punk, whatever you call it—the elements of that are like a caste system. If you want to be thought of as having this "head," you have to wear these materials. Wearing synthetics establishes you as a rocker. Now I think clothes have always been caste system oriented. The Gucci bag to the black and white Danceteria or Mudd formula—formulas for stating what you're about, where your head is at. But I see that I flip when I'm doing a real plastic thing to liking just the opposite. I work in phases. Unfortunately, that's a problem. When you're in business you try to make a statement and stay with it. I'm changing all the time, which is why I have my own business.

Do you consider fashions as artifacts—as signs of the times?

Totally. I think you can read a person by their clothes. People do studies on that sort of thing. They are always the uniform of where you're at...job uniforms, I-don't-have-a-job-uniforms; they are uniforms of the years. The natural periods to the plastic periods, with that kind of nowhereness transitional period in between. That's what I feel we're in again.

After World War II, synthetic fibers and plastics were thought to be miracle products, helping to fill vast short-ages, and paving the way for mass-produced ready-to-wear. Wasn't this emphasis on synthetics in fashion ostensibly reversed in the late sixties and early seventies?

Well, the real explosion of synthetics was in the sixties. We went to the moon. It was the first time we talked about the future today. The switch was in '69 or '70. The flower child... after the psychedelic, blown out, Max's rock-'n-roll synthetic period. The people needed to go to the country to put their white cottons on, to relax, personalize things. The mid-sixties were very impersonal. That's why I'm going into a much more relaxed, come-over-and-talk-to-me phase.

You've been alluding to the impersonal qualities of synthetics...

Well it's a great "head." It's clean, clear, fresh—a white sheet to start with. It's not like the other, starting out in a flower garden. I think to get away from all of that coziness, naturalness...that can get so sickening... You just die for that clear, clean black/white beginning. A cold, optimistic, wonderful beginning of shape, structure, and architecture. But it is the most impersonal kind of designing to do and to wear. I love it because it gets me back to lines: stripes are the graphic of this trend. It's just direction, radar, energy. If anything represents the last two years, it's lines. You think more of shape, structure, shoulders. I get very indulgent in mixing shiny things with natural things now—the whole surprise combination.

To some, "plastic-ness" as a concept carries destructive connotations. Do you see in the eighties the return to synthetics?

From immediate impulse, or are they more dependent on ideas which preceded them?

They don't make any sense in a progression to most people. Except, I guess, in obvious trend times I've been there. It doesn't come from the business approach. Yet, a precarious business is scary, and that keeps you on edge, changing. I don't think you can sustain a business or anything if your ideas aren't totally inside yourself. After the obvious trends come and go, to survive in between, to make your own identi-fiable statement is what's most important to do as a designer.

So often you have been cited as one of the most influential designers of New Wave fashion. Do you consider yourself partly responsible for bringing back plastics and synthetics to the forefront of the fashion industry?

Maybe in this part of time I'm responsible for taking body wore of cotton/lycra and spandex out of the leotard, tight-legs area, and making it a timeless, interchangeable, seasonless concept. In '78 my stuff was considered really off the wall. It's taken two long years. Before, they were calling my clothes whorey and tacky. Red and black were just too sexy.

Was there a lot of choice in the kinds of synthetics available when you were first using them? There is never much choice. I covered the entire fabric industry to see what everyone was making. There were only two fabrications which I found interesting: a cotton/lycra combination, which Danskin tried out but was unsuccessful with, and a heavy-weight spandex which was previously used only for football uniforms and for industrial use. I liked it because it wasn't that kind of drapey, light-weight spandex—it was strong, primary, where you can get real structure.

Were you one of the first people to make latex fur fashionable again? I don't think so. Nobody took it seriously. I did fake fur collars and trimming. I love the idea of fake fur, but they never make it look fake enough. I had my eye on the Sesame Street Big Bird type or the "slipper" variety.

Are you more into establishing or conceptualizing? Both...one is not valid without the other. It has to sell.

Is acceptance so important? Yes. I especially love mass production. I think that's what America's all about. If I had money, I'd do jeans and T-shirts—the basic American uniform.

In this technological age where McLuhan's "medium" is so important as a concept, do you feel that materials are as important as form? I think it's more Bauhaus-y... form follows function, function follows form. The people doing the most synthetic work are the most sensitive and artistic—the least synthetic as people.

But in the big picture of synthetics, the materials themselves have changed little since 1965. There won't be a really big change until spaceships are hovering outside our windows, sewing machines are obsolete, and everything is molded, heat-sealed, and push-button. What will we be wearing in the 2000? Everything really moves so slowly.

Frequently cited as the harbinger of "new wave" fashion, Betsey Johnson has evolved into one of today's most influential independent designers. Following her work with Paraphernalia in the 60's, she became the youngest designer ever to receive the Coty Award. After being involved with numerous freelance projects, she opened her own business in 1978. Interviewed in her New York City home, Betsey proffers her views on plastics and form in transition.

"I love the idea of fake fur, but they never make it look fake enough."

Designer unknown. Memphis: The New
International Style, book cover, Electa,
Italy, 1981

[Right] **Jim Cherry.** Claro Que Si
by Yello, album cover, Vertigo, West
Germany, 1981

simply the transmission of information … Communication always
calls for an exchange of fluids and tensions, for a provocation, and
a challenge. Memphis does not claim to know what people "need,"
but it runs the risk of guessing what people "want".'[19]

Memphis graphics spoke in the same provisional, polyglot
style as the furniture and objects. The cover of the first Memphis
catalogue (1981) presents a jagged collision of sheets of pattern
and Memphis logos are similarly patterned, angular and block-like,
anticipating the geometrical typefaces drawn by Neville Brody
for *The Face*.

It was not surprising then that the startling forms and
imagery of postmodern architecture and furniture design should
inspire graphic commentary from designers and image-makers.
In a 1981 album cover design for the Dadaist Swiss electronic pop
group Yello, provisionality is the guiding theme. Jim Cherry's
sleeve shows two peculiar, synthetic figures, possibly intended
to be members of the band, constructed from a loose collection of
elements that reference modern architecture, domestic appliances
and the world of consumer luxury. One figure's conical head has
a narrow modernist window slit where its eyes would be and a
projecting partition for a nose; the other's left eye looks like a
ventilation panel. Both are decorated with Memphis-like areas
of pattern or texture and the typography of the group's name is
a heterogeneous mix of styles. The cover's mood is retro, though

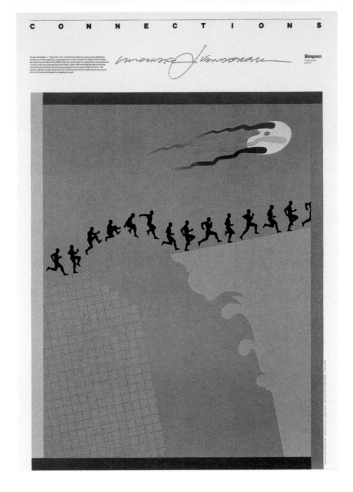

Michael Vanderbyl. Connections,
promotional poster, Simpson Paper,
USA, 1983

it avoids specific quotation, while suggesting that in the playground of consumer culture almost anything has the potential to be plucked from its original context and used as material for semiotic manipulation and bricolage.

In San Francisco, Michael Vanderbyl, a leading member of the Californian new wave, created a number of pieces in response to new tendencies in architecture and design. In a 1983 promotional poster for Simpson Paper, a stream of figures leaps from a modernist skyscraper symbolized by a grid, across a void, and on to the top of a classical column – a clear, if somewhat literal, appeal to the value of pre-modern cultural forms. The decoratively exposed grid recurs in a 1983 poster for the American Institute of Architects, to announce a series of lectures on the theme of the city, where it assumes the outline of a skyscraper skyline surrounded by open, organic space. The postmodern city can seemingly exist in harmonious balance with the surrounding landscape only so long as clear limits to growth – symbolized by a warning sign stamped across the open area – are observed. In a series of promotional mailers for Simpson Paper, Vanderbyl celebrated the work of fashion designer Issey Miyake, architect Michael Graves, and the Memphis group. The Memphis mailer, designed in 1985, indicates the degree to which the new wave's once controversial stylistic innovations had by that time achieved acceptability for commercial clients. Memphis-style texture within the word 'Innovation' helps to give

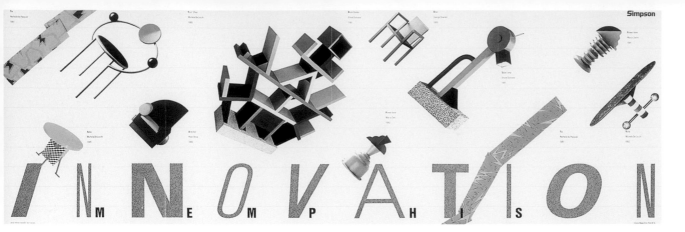

Michael Vanderbyl. Innovation,
promotional mailer about Memphis,
Simpson Paper, USA, 1985

William Longhauser. The Language
of Michael Graves, exhibition
poster, USA, 1983

cohesion to the widely spaced letters rendered in alternating styles
and weights, and the letterspacing finds structural reinforcement
in the diagonally spaced catalogue of Memphis furniture and
objects. A similarly exuberant response to the formal possibilities
of postmodern architecture and design can be seen in a 1983 poster
by American designer William Longhauser for a Michael Graves
exhibition. Each letter of Graves' surname refers to some aspect
of his architectural language, most notably the 'V' modelled on the
Portland building's oversized, painted keystone. As if this powerful
expression of acclaim were not enough, the growing cult of the
postmodern architectural superstar can be gauged by the fetishistic
use of Graves' first name to compose a repetitive grid of dots.

In Britain, postmodern tendencies in graphic design took
a different form. Where American critics were concerned from
the movement's earliest days to establish a category of design that
could be labelled 'new wave' or 'postmodern', in Britain there were
no attempts at this stage to define the existence of a new wave in
reaction to modernism.[20] This was probably because modernism had
never been the dominant force in British graphic design that it was

in Europe, or that it was, in a more corporate sense, in the United States. Much more than in the US, Britain's new wave was identified with youth culture and popular music and these designers tended to position themselves outside of design's professional mainstream, a quest for identity that could be read as a postmodern gesture in itself. While many designers, using a conceptual approach established in the 1960s, professed to produce communications that could speak univocally to all viewers, some of the most influential British designers of the late 1970s and early 1980s chose to address audiences close to their own concerns. Graphic design was in this fundamental sense an aspect of subculture, a creative tool by which young people communicated among themselves.[21] Their designs were not intended to be meaningful for those on the outside, including designers positioned in the mainstream, and the design profession was consequently slow at first to acknowledge the significance of work that seemed frivolous and marginal to the concerns of visual communication as an ever-expanding business. Nor was this work especially visible to American designers, unless they were music fans. Although some Americans read *The Face*, Neville Brody's large body of work did not become widely known in the US until the late 1980s when *The Graphic Language of Neville Brody* was published. The output of another significant designer, Peter Saville, has never featured in surveys of postmodern design by American writers, even though it is more fully postmodern, in a cultural sense, than much of the decorative work routinely cited as exemplifying early American postmodernism.[22]

If these British designers did come to be termed a 'new wave', it was largely by association. The appellation belonged, in the first instance, to the style of rock music that emerged in the late 1970s after punk rock (see chapter 2 for a consideration of punk graphics) and the key figures – Barney Bubbles, Saville, Brody and Malcolm Garrett – all produced designs for new wave musicians. A song book for Ian Dury designed by Bubbles in 1979 suggests the degree to which Bubbles was aware of international design trends. One version of the book's cover overlays a damaged grid with an informal, ink-drawn portrait of Dury complete with punkish splotches and squiggles, an image close in spirit and style

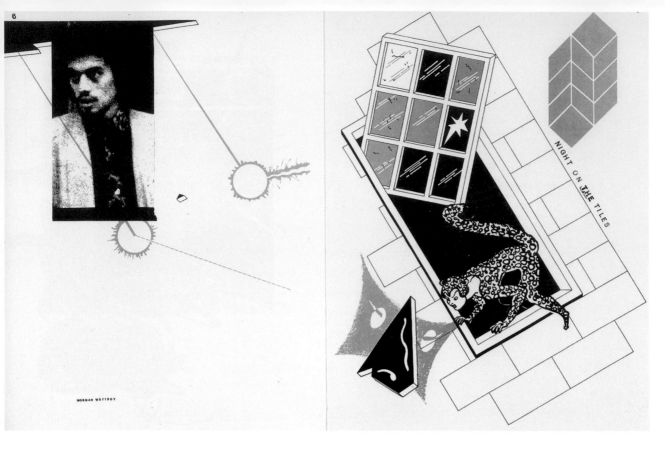

NORMAN WATTROY

NIGHT ON THE TILES

Barney Bubbles. The Ian Dury Songbook,
spread, Wise Publications, UK, 1979

to 'Swiss Punk', the label sometimes applied to Weingart's late 1970s posters and to designs by Friedman from the same period. Inside, Bubbles provides a series of enigmatic portraits of individual band members, which combine surrealistic image-games with a dynamic command of graphic space. Only Greiman at this stage produced designs so heavily charged with subjective symbolism.

For the most part, however, British new wave design bore little resemblance to parallel developments in the US. The work produced by these designers followed no consistent pattern. It was eclectic in inspiration and pluralistic in its application of style. If it was sometimes a response to 'pioneering' modernism, this manifested itself more as historicism and homage than as a desire to subvert what later modernism had become. Sometimes it was hard to pin down specific visual sources for British new wave designs, but this only served to emphasize their break from graphic communication's prevailing norms and tropes. Malcolm Garrett's cover for Magazine's album *The Correct Use of Soap* (1980) combines conventional typographic and decorative elements – serif typefaces, box rules, two ellipses – to form a symmetrical device as sharply defined in appearance as it is inscrutable in purpose. It is much too elaborate to be called a logo, yet it has the air of being a sign intended to encode and express the essence of its contents. In what way does this device relate to 'the correct use of soap'? The question is clearly unanswerable. The cover says something about the uncompromising personality of the band, but it also asserts the designer's freedom to 'make a statement' using his own tools,

Malcolm Garrett. The Correct Use of Soap
by Magazine, album cover, Virgin Records,
UK, 1980

[Right] **Malcolm Garrett.** Someone
Somewhere (In Summertime) by Simple
Minds, 12-inch single cover, Virgin Records,
UK, 1982

on his own terms. Garrett often cited André Breton and one might
read this strange sleeve as a form of typographic surrealism.

Even when the graphic style employed was radically
different, this quality of strangeness remained. Early releases by
the British band Simple Minds had a hard, precise, robotic beat
and Garrett reflected this mood in cover designs consisting largely
of abstract shapes. When the band's sound became more expansive
and lyrical, he changed direction. For the title of a 12-inch single,
Someone Somewhere (In Summertime) (1982), he used an ornamental
typeface with script-like terminals, which evokes medieval
illuminated manuscripts. Unusually, the lyrics are presented
on the front cover within the frame of a book page, though there
is no attempt to make this look realistic. The pale background
approximates to the texture of parchment, the book's typography
clashes with the title below, and the photograph has the crude
grain – exacerbated by the use of harsh colour – of an old text
book image. In short, the design fulfils all the requirements of
Jencksian postmodernism: it is hybrid, double-coded and
represents a partial return to tradition, though its disjunctive
quality ensures that it can only be read as the product of a
playful, contemporary design sensibility.

In the work of Peter Saville, early British postmodern
design found its most sensitively attuned and rigorously reductive
exponent. Where Garrett and Brody, like Weingart and Greiman,
tended to assert the presence of design, to supercharge their
work with expressive devices and compel viewers to pay attention,

·CLOSER·

ATROCITY EXHIBITION
ISOLATION
PASSOVER
COLONY
A MEANS TO AN END

PRODUCED BY MARTIN HANNETT AT BRITTANIA ROW
ENGINEERED BY MARTIN HANNETT AND JOHN CAFFERY
ASSISTED BY MICHAEL JOHNSON

Peter Saville and Martyn Atkins. Closer
by Joy Division, album cover and inner
sleeve, Factory Records, UK, 1980.
Photograph by Bernard Pierre Wolff

Saville achieved the same effect by subtraction. He was an
instinctive rather than theoretical postmodernist who understood
the new cultural mood from his first sight, in 1978, of Philip
Johnson's proposals for the AT&T building, a postmodern New York
skyscraper with a broken classical pediment for a crown. 'Within
12 months, neo-classicism and the influence of architectural
postmodernism were everywhere,' Saville recalls. 'People in
New York were buying columns to put in their apartments.
My contribution was the graphic equivalent. It was always an
emotive feeling and after a year or so I began to trust in my
senses.'[23] No matter how arbitrary Saville's intimations and
borrowings might have seemed, they often struck a chord. In 1980,
for the cover of *Closer* by the doom-laden Manchester rock band Joy
Division, Saville and his collaborator Martyn Atkins used the bare
minimum of elements. The predominant feature of both 12-inch
sleeve and inner sleeve is whiteness. Each of the four surfaces
carries the same elementary frame constructed from a single rule.
The placement of type inside this frame and the lapidary type style
itself is likewise consistent on all four surfaces. The only image,
positioned on the cover, is a black and white photograph by Bernard
Pierre Wolff, showing four figures in robes mourning a dead man. It
is not clear whether this represents Christ or someone else and the
image is ambiguous in an even more fundamental sense. Does the
photograph show a sculpture recessed in a niche, or a painting? The
scene is lit in such a way that it could be either. Here again, the

design is a hybrid. Its typographic manner is revivalist, its imagery is a neo-classical quotation, its atmosphere is historicist, but its effect comes from the fact that none of these constituent elements would normally find use in combination on a rock album cover. Saville's postmodern devices frame and memorialize the content – music of exceptional emotional power – in a way that was entirely unfamiliar at the time.

These record covers were created at a moment when design was beginning to assume increasing importance in consumer society. Their emphasis on sometimes quite luxurious visual values anticipates the coming decade's economic boom, in which the increasing democratization of design, and a view of design as hedonistic pleasure, would play a central role. Designers were visual interpreters of the emerging mood and they made the assumption that their audiences were sufficiently literate, in a visual sense, to decipher and enjoy a broad range of graphic signals that were often extremely subtle. It may be that, precisely because it was so successful in capturing attention, early postmodern design carried the spores of its own cooption and failure. From the outset, it embodied an implied critique of design's norms, values and limitations. As the 1980s unfolded, designers began to apply postmodern theory to a more self-conscious deconstruction of design's inbuilt assumptions and of its persuasive power as public communication.

2
Deconstruction

From the 1960s onwards, there are many examples of graphic design
created by non-designers ignorant of the rules of professional craft;
self-taught form-makers who effectively made things up as they
went along. Such work is not usually allowed into surveys and
histories of design, which are generally based on professional
understandings of what constitutes good practice. The profession's
aim, expressed through its organizations and in its publications,
has been to assert the validity and necessity of its methods as a way
of ensuring continuing work for its members. In the postmodern
period, restrictive, rule-bound thinking and 'totalizing' tendencies
of any kind have been challenged by thinkers in many disciplines.
Writing about scientific method, the philosopher of science Paul
Feyerabend concludes that 'The only principle that does not inhibit
progress is: *anything goes.*'[1] Deviations and errors, he suggests, are
essential preconditions of progress; from sloppiness and chaos
arise the theories on which the growth of knowledge and scientific
advance depend. More generally, postmodern theorists have
repeatedly questioned the boundaries between high (valuable) and
low (inferior) forms of culture, pointing out the ease with which
audiences move between different types of cultural experience –
from chart pop to classical music – without pausing to wonder
whether this is in some way unacceptable. In such a climate, it
becomes increasingly difficult to defend the idea that there are
right ways and wrong ways of going about visual communication.

In the 1970s and early 1980s, graphic artists associated with
punk rock mounted a sustained assault on professional design's
orderly methods and polite conventions, revelling in deviation
and chaos and refusing to acknowledge any such category as 'error'.
Jamie Reid was a key figure in this movement and his anti-design

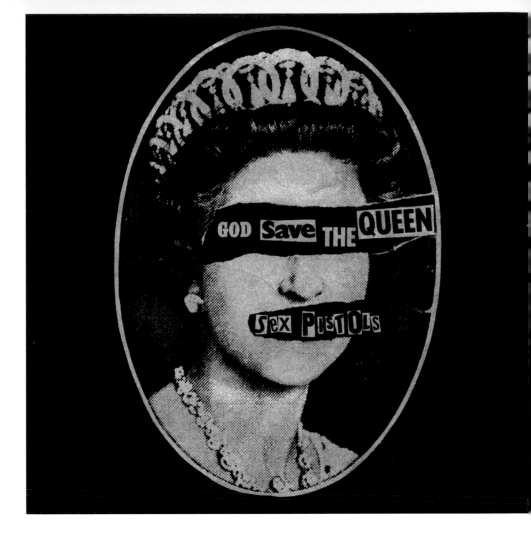

Jamie Reid. God Save the Queen by the
Sex Pistols, 7-inch single cover, Virgin
Records, UK, 1977

inventions came to define the graphic look of punk, as its angry,
musical insurrection took hold overseas. In the mid-1960s, Reid
studied painting at Croydon Art School, south London, where he
met Malcolm McLaren, who was later to manage the Sex Pistols.
In the early 1970s, still based in Croydon, he undertook the graphics
for six issues of *Suburban Press*, a community magazine that mixed
texts by the Situationists, an international radical movement which
had made an incisive critique of modern society, with muck-raking
stories about local politics and council corruption. Reid learned
many techniques by experimenting with a Multilith 1250 office
duplicator. He found the Situationists' theoretical texts verbose
and sought ways to simplify these ideas into aggressive graphic
form. Like the designers and artists of the 1960s underground press,
he ransacked articles and scissored headlines from establishment
newspapers and attempted to *détourne* the media – to 'turn it back on
itself' – by applying its communications in new contexts. He created
a series of stickers printed on fluorescent paper in the style of sales
promotions, announcing 'Save petrol, burn cars' and 'Special Offer.
This store welcomes shoplifters', which was plastered over shops
on Oxford Street, London.

    McLaren's invitation in 1976 to become involved with the
Sex Pistols, which became the very archetype of a punk rock band,

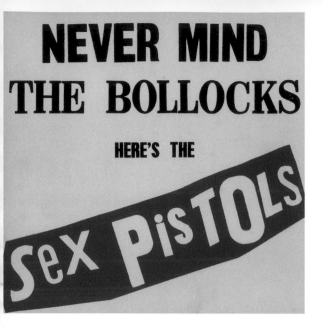

Jamie Reid. Never Mind the Bollocks Here's the Sex Pistols by the Sex Pistols, album cover, Virgin Records, UK, 1977

presented Reid with an opportunity to apply these ideas to a much more visible public project. On the picture sleeve for the single *God Save the Queen*, released in May 1977 to mark the British monarch's silver jubilee celebrations, he masked the Queen's face with rough strips torn across her eyes and mouth to form voids that carry the title and band name in cut-up, 'ransom note' lettering. The cover of the Sex Pistols' first album, *Never Mind the Bollocks Here's the Sex Pistols* (1977), delivered its verbal affront – considerable, at the time – in crude, butcher block typography on an acidic yellow background that was the antithesis of harmonious, tasteful, professional design and would have been viewed as an unpardonable æsthetic offence by many practising designers. The song titles, pieced together from found letters in the now familiar anarchic style, were scattered randomly across the back of the sleeve. Reid continued in this vein through the band's subsequent record releases, stickers, tour posters and promotional materials for the Sex Pistols' film, *The Great Rock 'n' Roll Swindle*. 'We wanted to make [the audience] think for themselves, always with that element of questioning the status quo and what is considered normal,' he explained.[2]

Reid was an artist improvising with graphic techniques for political purposes, rather than a paid-up member of the design profession, and this detachment from ordinary professional assumptions and concerns was typical of punk's amateur designers and image-makers. In the US, in the late 1970s and early 1980s, punk scenes thrived in cities such as Los Angeles, Seattle, New York and Boston, and for these underground communities, street posters played a critical role. 'For the nascent, developing punk scene – isolated from the media and the mainstream promoters – the street poster was the only means of announcing a show. It was *the* medium of communication, a punk community billboard back in the days when even college radio wouldn't play the music,' recalls Robert Newman, a Seattle writer and punk.[3] Posters by band members and friends were Xeroxed, 'instant printed' or silkscreened in garages and basements, then flyposted on telephone poles and walls. As Newman notes, these scratchy images, an urban folk art with a sinister edge, reflected a belief that anyone could do it and that any graphic style or level of skill was acceptable. Fine artist Frank Edie's

Frank Edie. Concert poster, USA, 1978

[Right] **Cliff Roman. The Weirdos are Loose,** concert poster, USA, 1977

largely typographic poster for The Dils, Negative Trend and other groups, created for The Bird club in 1978, is built from an intricate jigsaw of frequently violent text fragments clipped from newspapers to form an agitated alphabetic backdrop from which the main gig details emerge with powerful clarity. Words slide together and break apart, but a high degree of graphic organization underpins the apparent chaos. The same spiky tension between control and disorder can be seen in a 1977 concert poster by Cliff Roman, a student at California Institute of the Arts and member of The Weirdos. Distorted collage portraits of the group and urgent, hand-drawn lettering – a cheap solution often used by punks – erupt from the Los Angeles street map. The device serves a practical purpose, showing people where to go, while declaring ('The Weirdos are loose ...') the presence in the city of an almost combustible punk spirit.

Punk design in its rawest forms was barely recognized by the professional mainstream at this point, let alone accepted as a valid form of design, but by the start of the 1980s some designers were making sustained use of similar devices and strategies. In 1980, Terry Jones, former art director of British *Vogue* and designer of one of the first books about punk, *Not Another Punk Book* (1977), launched his own magazine, *i-D*, to document trends in popular culture and

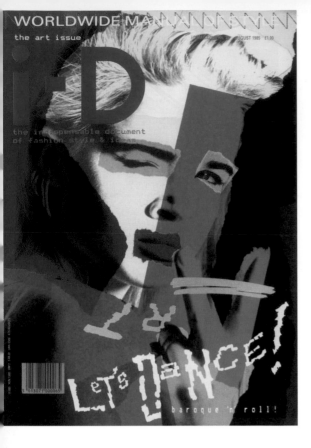

Terry Jones. i-D, no. 28, magazine cover, UK, 1985. Photograph by Nick Knight

[Right] **Hard Werken.** Hard Werken, no. 1, magazine cover, The Netherlands, 1979

styles of street fashion. Jones coined the term 'instant design' to describe his restless, speedy, journalistic way of working and, in a 'manual' about his career published in 1990, he catalogues the graphic techniques used to achieve these rapid transcriptions of the passing scene: handmarks made with stick, pencil, pen or brush; stencils and rubber stamps; manual and electric typewriters; computer lettering (at this point still crude and 'low-tech'); montage; photocopying; blocks containing type or logos; and print effects, often developed from mistakes. In the course of the 1980s, all of these devices were used in i-D, which went through many changes of graphic style, paper and page size. 'There was a stage when everything was so æsthetically beautiful,' Jones said in 1988. 'What I'm going through now is an anti-style phase. And I think we've got some way to go with the anti-style, the anti-layout and the anti-art before it gets assimilated.'[4]

In Rotterdam, similar ideas were explored in the magazine *Hard Werken* ('hard work'), which between 1979 and 1982 published ten large-format issues. Its editors were also responsible for its design and by 1980 several members of the team had decided to band together to

Hard Werken. Hard Werken, no. 3, magazine spread, The Netherlands, 1979

form the Hard Werken Association, among them Rick Vermeulen and Tom van den Haspel (both designers) and Henk Elenga and Gerard Hadders (originally trained as fine artists). They were joined in 1983 by Willem Kars, who had run the graphic workshop where *Hard Werken* magazine began life. Hard Werken, like Terry Jones, occupied a space much closer to mainstream perception than the first wave of punks. They consciously rejected the functionalist tradition, exemplified by Wim Crouwel and Total Design, which had ossified into unadventurous dogma in less supple hands, and their raucously eclectic, supposedly 'anti-typographical' manner was viewed with deep suspicion by more classically inclined colleagues, who labelled it 'ugly'.

'We don't have a collective style,' Hard Werken explained. 'Some of us work intuitively, others more deliberately and controlled, but we're all different. A lot can be used, though. In that sense we are fairly aggressive. It looks as if we combine every conceivable colour and typeface. On the magazine we don't bother very much about sticking to the rules, or about what is proper. Nor are we concerned with functionality or legibility, but rather with the total picture, even if that picture is illegible at times …'[5]

In its first phase, from 1980 to 1985, working mainly for clients in the cultural sector – arts organizations, theatres and publishers – Hard Werken produced some of the most challenging designs of the period. A poster by Van den Haspel for 'The Year of Japanese Film' (1981) anticipates by several years the deconstructed design of the late 1980s. Its free-floating typographic elements and irregularly shaped zones of texture form loose, provisional groupings that suggest instability and flux and seem to have only the most tangential, and certainly non-literal, relationship to the films. However, Hard Werken's inventions, though subjective and informed by ironic humour, did not represent any stated ideology or theoretical position and the group's rule-defying experimental designs coexisted from the outset with more conventional approaches to design, which eventually predominated as Hard Werken mutated into a commercial design group before finally, in the mid-1990s, changing its name. The deviations were not, for its founders, a 'precondition of progress', though their early experiments would continue to attract younger designers for some years. Nor was punk, for the most part, a clearly formulated attack on the professional limits of design. Punk treated visual form with the same freedom as punk music, as part of the same milieu, but the audience for these gestures was society in the broadest sense, rather than designers, though young designers were often members of the audience.

With the tendency termed 'deconstructionist' (and sometimes, confusingly, 'deconstructivist') design, the conventions of professional graphic design, both modernist and eclectic, were subjected to deliberate interrogation, destabilized and repudiated. Deconstructionist designers were fully aware of what design had been, in a historical sense, and of the prescribed forms that conventional opinion believed it should take in the present. However, for reasons that will become clear, the term 'deconstructionist' is problematic in a number of ways when it comes to graphic design. Deconstruction was never a full-blown movement or a coherent, clearly defined 'ism' – like Constructivism or Surrealism – in the sense of having adherents who described themselves as deconstructionists, held meetings, organized exhibitions and issued statements announcing their convictions

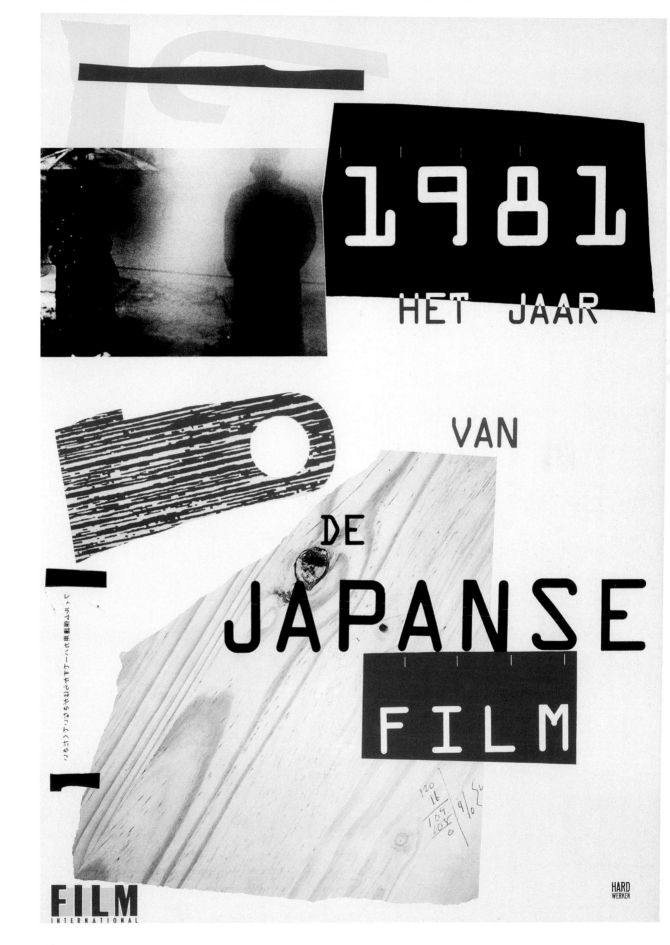

Tom van den Haspel, Hard Werken.
The Year of Japanese Film, film
festival poster, The Netherlands, 1981

and plans. Few of the designers who worked in a 'deconstructionist' way made any direct reference to deconstruction in its theoretical sense, or displayed any close knowledge of key deconstructionist thinkers and texts. If deconstruction was seen as anything at all by most designers, it was as a transiently fashionable, lamentably misguided style, and the small number of designers and critics who did understand deconstruction, or believed in its possibilities for graphic communication, were quick to point out the inadequacy of this view.

Even within philosophical and theoretical circles, deconstruction remains a concept every bit as controversial as postmodernism and the relationship between the two is also open to question. A consideration of such matters falls outside the scope of this book, but it should be borne in mind that deconstruction is an enterprise in which it would be unwise to claim any fixed or final definitions, since the method sets out, with the utmost scepticism and rigour, to interrogate such certainties. The term 'deconstruction' was introduced by the French philosopher Jacques Derrida in his book *On Grammatology*, published in 1967 and translated into English in 1976, and in the following decade, Derrida's ideas had an enormous impact in the universities on the teaching of humanities – to the dismay of those who contested them.[6] *On Grammatology*'s discussion of writing as a distinctive form of representation makes it probably Derrida's single most significant text for graphic designers, since typography and design, as material processes, fall within its concerns.[7] The literary critic Jonathan Culler suggests that we understand deconstruction's essential project as a critique of the hierarchical oppositions that have traditionally structured Western thought. Among these are inside|outside, mind|body, speech|writing, presence|absence, nature|culture and form|meaning. These oppositions are not natural and inevitable, as we tend to assume, but cultural constructions produced by discourses that depend on our taking them for granted. Deconstruction's purpose is not to destroy these categories but to dismantle and 'reinscribe' them – to change their structure and make them function differently.[8] As literary critic Christopher Norris puts it, the deconstructive method 'seeks to undo both

Barnbrook Design. Heathen by David Bowie, CD booklet page, ISO Records, UK, 2002. Photograph by Markus Klinko

a given order of priorities *and* the very system of conceptual opposition that makes that order possible'.[9] Some basic assumptions of deconstructionist thought are that linguistic meaning is unstable and indeterminate; that, for this reason, no method of analysis, not even philosophy (always seen as privileged category), can lay claim to ultimate authority when it comes to textual interpretation; and that interpretation is consequently closer to game-playing than to analysis, as we have traditionally understood the term.[10] In a much-quoted phrase, Derrida went so far as to say, 'There is nothing outside the text.' He coined the word *différance*, combining the French verbs for 'to differ' and 'to defer', to suggest the way that language depends on the play of differences between one word and another, while meaning itself is always deferred (*différance*'s elusive meaning graphically illustrates the point). The purpose of such devices was to prevent conceptual closure, or the reduction of his texts to an ultimate meaning. All of these ideas can be seen at work in postmodern graphic design and Derridean concepts such as *sous rature* – the tactic of putting an idea 'under erasure' by crossing it out, in order to alert the reader not to accept it at face value – have found their way into graphic practice.

It was the 'Deconstructivist Architecture' exhibition held from June to August 1988 at the Museum of Modern Art (MoMA), New York, and its catalogue, that probably did most to introduce deconstruction to graphic designers. Curated by Philip Johnson, with the assistance of Mark Wigley, the exhibition featured architectural projects by Frank Gehry, Daniel Libeskind, Rem Koolhaas, Peter Eisenman, Zaha Hadid, Coop Himmelblau and Bernard Tschumi. What distinguished and linked their work, argued Wigley, was a sensibility in which 'the dream of pure form has been disturbed. Form has become contaminated.'[11] Deconstructive architecture, he explained, does not dismantle buildings, rather it locates the inherent dilemmas within them, exposing the 'symptoms of a repressed impurity'. Deconstructivists pick up where an earlier generation, the Russian Constructivists, left off. In the 1910s and 1920s, avant-garde artists such as Tatlin and Rodchenko proposed radical structures, based on unstable geometric forms, but they never realized them as buildings.

Neville Brody. Magazine advertisement for Torchsong, UK, 1984

Deconstructivism does not want to demolish, decompose or destroy a building's structure by attacking it from the outside. Such a strategy produces a decorative 'æsthetic of danger', but no sense of genuine, concrete threat. Instead, deconstructivism seeks to disrupt, dislocate and deviate by incorporating a disturbance into the building's internal structure. Wigley pointed out that these projects did not share a single style or æsthetic direction, but he also stated that, in his view, they did not derive from the mode of philosophy known as deconstruction and should not be seen as applications of deconstructive theory. Yet, just a few months earlier, the first International Symposium on Deconstruction, at the Tate Gallery, London, had opened with a specially recorded video interview with Derrida by Christopher Norris that made the connections between theory and architecture an explicit point of departure. Eisenman and Tschumi, the two most theoretically aware architects among Johnson and Wigley's seven at MoMA, both disagreed with Wigley's idea of deconstruction in architecture as non-Derridean.[12]

It was hardly surprising, given these differences of interpretation in the architecture camp, that graphic design's borrowing of the label 'deconstruction' lacked focus and rigour. In 1990, in the article 'De-constructing Typography', one of the first published discussions, design historian Philip Meggs uses the term 'deconstructivist' in relation to design and typography, even though the developments he describes do not relate to Constructivism in the way that architectural examples had been shown to do by Johnson and Wigley. This misleading usage would persist for several years and still sometimes occurs. Taking the word 'deconstruction' at face value, Meggs defines it as 'taking the integrated whole apart, or destroying the underlying order that holds a graphic design together'.[13] This reduces visual deconstruction to dismantling, the interpretation that Wigley had been at pains to avoid, and neglects the sense of a disruption or deviation arising from within an architectural (or typographic) structure. Nor does it really explain all the examples that Meggs discusses. In Neville Brody's ad for Torchsong, the letters of 'Torchsong' have been scrambled to form a typographic personage.

Neville Brody. The Face, nos. 50–55, progressive breakdown of magazine contents page logo, UK, 1984

This may not be traditional, linear typography, but it is still a form of æsthetic order and results in 'a vigorous structure', as Meggs notes, not chaos. The 'underlying order' has not been destroyed by this process so much as dynamically rearranged. However, in 1984, in a series of six designs, Brody subjected the word 'contents', on *The Face* magazine's contents page, to a process of progressive degeneration, month by month, until the letters became an illegible collection of abstract marks. By the early 1990s, the issue of legibility would be one of the main points of concern in discussion about deconstructionist tendencies in design.

In another early article, also published in 1990 in the United States, the designers Chuck Byrne and Martha Witte base their definition of deconstruction in design on a more critically aware sense of deconstruction's origins in theory. For them, the word refers to 'the breaking down of something (an idea, a precept, a word, a value) in order to "decode" its parts in such a way that these act as "informers" on the thing, or on any assumptions or convictions we have regarding it'.[14] Their emphasis on meaning is a significant step on from the notion that deconstruction is simply taking things apart in the hope of 'reinventing' form and 'revitalizing print media'.[15] They suggest that typographic design, with its basis in words and text, is probably the most logical visual extension of deconstruction and they go on to argue that 'when the deconstructionist approach is applied to design, each layer, through the use of language and image, is an intentional performer in a deliberately playful game wherein the viewer can discover

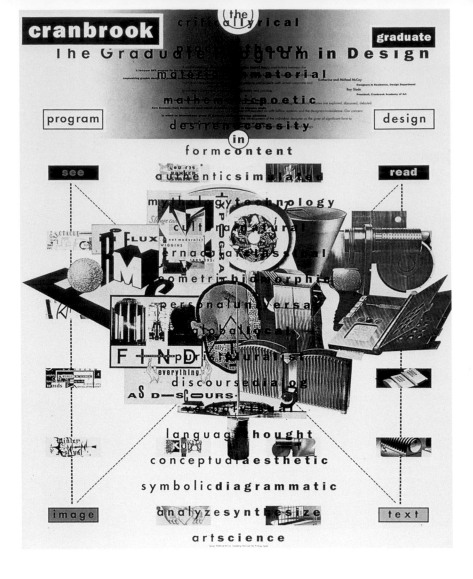

Katherine McCoy. **The Graduate Program in Design,** poster, Cranbrook Academy of Art, USA, 1989

and experience the hidden complexities of language.'[16] Where early critics of deconstructionist design tended to reject its devices as little more than the application of superfluous complexity and extraneous style, Byrne and Witte advance the view that, on the contrary, these devices potentially act to clarify or develop aspects of a communication that uniform, modernist treatments sometimes obscure.

From the late 1980s, such approaches were most strongly identified with the design department at Cranbrook Academy of Art, where Katherine McCoy and her husband Michael McCoy had been co-chairs since 1971. In 1990, the book *Cranbrook Design: The New Discourse* was published to accompany an exhibition of the same name shown first at Cranbrook Academy of Art Museum (November 1990), then at Steelcase Design Partnership in New York (January 1991). Its design by Katherine McCoy, P. Scott Makela and Mary Lou Kroh offered a striking and then highly unusual example of deconstructive tactics in action. A vertical fault line runs through each of the essays, splitting the text into two columns separated by a narrow gully. The right-hand column is set a millimetre below the left so that the reader's eye, as it travels along the line, must not only jump the text

KATHERINE mcCoy
MICHAEL mcCoy
mcCoy

Art science
Nothing pulls you into the territory between art and science quite so quickly as design. It is the borderline where contradictions and tensions exist between the quantifiable and the poetic. It is the field between desire and necessity. Designers thrive in those conditions, moving between land and water. A typical critique at Cranbrook can easily move in a matter of minutes between Mathematic poetic a discussion of the object as a validation of being to the precise mechanical proposal for actuating the object. The discussion moves from Heidegger to the "strange material of the week" or from Lyotard to printing technologies without missing a beat. The free flow of ideas, and the leaps from the technical to the mythical, stem from the attempt to maintain a studio plat- Desire necessity form that supports each student's search to find his or her own voice as a designer. The studio is a hothouse that enables students **the** and faculty to encounter their own visions of the world and act on them — a **new** process that is at times chaotic, conflicting, and occasionally inspiring.

Watching the process of students absorbing new ideas and influences, and the incredible range of in- terpretations of those ideas into design, is Mythology technology an annual experience that is always amaz- ing. In recent years, for example, the de- **discourse** partment has had the experience of watching wood craftsmen metamorphose into high technologists, and graphic designers into software humanists. Yet it all seems consistent. They are bringing a very personal vision to an area that desperately needs it. The messiness of human experi- Purist pluralist ence is warming up the cold precision of technology to make it livable, and lived in.

Unlike the Bauhaus, Cranbrook never embraced a singular teaching method or philosophy, other than Saarinen's exhortation to each student to find his or her own way, in the company of other artists and designers who were en- gaged in the same search. The energy at Cranbrook seems to come from the fact of Individual communal the mutual search, although not the mutual conclusion. If design is about life, why shouldn't it have all the complexity, vari- ety, contradiction, and sublimity of life?

Much of the work done at Cranbrook has been dedicated to changing the status quo. It is polemical, calculated to ruffle designers' feathers. And Dangerous rigorous

Katherine McCoy, P. Scott Makela and Mary Lou Kroh. Cranbrook Design: The New Discourse, book page, Rizzoli, USA, 1990

gap, but step down to the lower level. In a poster for the Cranbrook graduate programme, created in 1989, Katherine McCoy had used a series of Derridean oppositions – 'art|science', 'mythology|technology', 'purist|pluralist', 'vernacular|classical' – to structure the composition around a central spine. In the McCoys' essay exploring aspects of the 'new discourse' at Cranbrook, the designers insert these paired concepts into the text between the widely spaced lines, forming both an unexpected interference and an alternative reading path. The McCoys describe the uses of theory at the academy:

'The emerging ideas emphasized the construction of meaning between the audience and the graphic design piece, a visual transaction that parallels verbal communication. Building on the linguistic theories of semiotics but rejecting the faith in the scientifically predictable transmission of meaning, these ideas began to have an impact on the students' graphic design work. New experiments explored the relationships of text and image and processes of reading and seeing, with texts and images meant to be read in detail, their meanings decoded. Students began to deconstruct the dynamics of visual language and understand it as a filter that inescapably manipulates the audience's response.'[17]

Cranbrook Academy of Art students. Visible **Language,** spreads from 'French Currents of the Letter' issue, USA, 1978

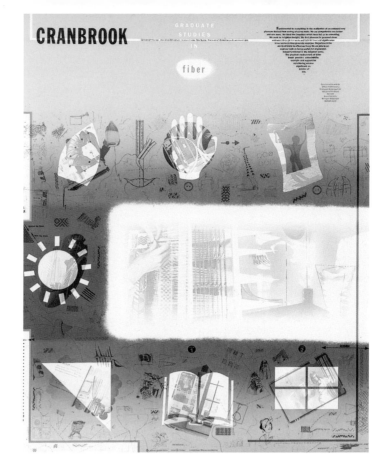

Jeffery Keedy. Graduate Studies in Fiber,
poster, Cranbrook Academy of Art, USA, 1984

These experiments were already under way by 1978,
when several students, under the direction of Katherine McCoy
and Daniel Libeskind (head of architecture at Cranbrook), designed
'French Currents of the Letter', an issue of the journal *Visible
Language* devoted to poststructuralist literary theory. As the reader
proceeds through the eight essays, standard book conventions
are progressively undermined. The text column expands to fill
the inner margins, interlinear space increases, word spaces inflate
until the text explodes into particles, and footnotes, usually
confined to a subsidiary role, slide across into the body of the text.
The intention was to highlight the physicality of the printed word's
presentation and to establish new non-linear connections between
words, opening the possibility of alternative ways of reading.

By the mid-1980s, the students were actively involved
in determining the direction of these investigations and critical
theory was assuming increasing significance. Jeffery Keedy,
a Master of Fine Arts student at the academy from 1983 to 1985,
occupied a significant position in these developments. Under
the influence of Hal Foster's *The Anti-Æsthetic* (1983) and the writings
of Roland Barthes, Keedy began to seek ways of exploring design
as a cultural practice closely connected to the themes of popular
culture so skilfully deconstructed by Barthes, rather than
as a focused, professional, problem-solving tool. A 1984 poster
for Cranbrook's fibre studies programme was a calculated exercise
in, as Keedy put it, 'doing everything wrong'. There is no strict

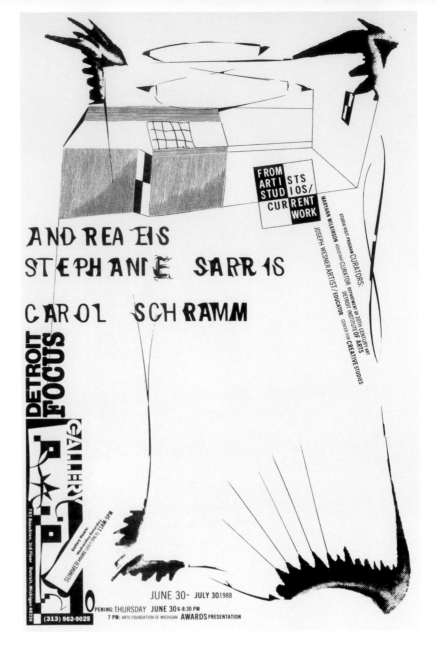

Edward Fella. Exhibition poster,
Detroit Focus Gallery, USA, 1988

hierarchy of information or unified message. Instead, quirky
details from student sketchbooks are distributed haphazardly
across its surface to convey the pulse and flux of the creative
process and this intricately layered visual field cannot be absorbed
at a single glance. The pursuit of theory continued through the
1980s, as designers such as Andrew Blauvelt, David Frej, Allen Hori
and Edward Fella joined the school. While McCoy did much to
distil her students' concerns and to act as their public face in her
conference appearances and writings, it was not without a certain
amount of resistance on her own part and a reluctance to succumb
entirely to poststructuralism's assault on established values.

For Keedy and Fella, the pressing task was to challenge
the rigid thinking, worn-out visual schemas and sterile corporate
applications of modernism in America. Keedy rejected modernism's
utopian vision as bankrupt and resisted what he saw as an obsession
with regularity and clarity in design. He stressed the personal

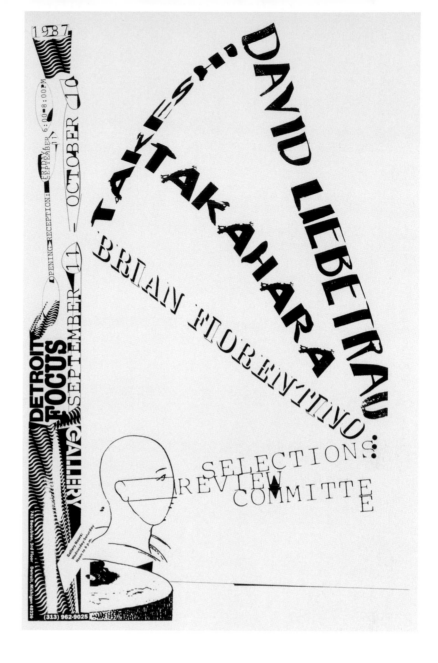

Edward Fella. Exhibition poster,
Detroit Focus Gallery, USA, 1987

nature of his approach and, like McCoy, insisted on the human value
of ambiguity for audiences who were fully capable of negotiating
these complexities. Where graphic design is concerned, he
remarked, 'You don't really need a lot of rules to protect the general
public.'[18] In a conversation published in *Emigre* magazine – virtually
a house journal for deconstructionist design in the early 1990s –
Keedy and Fella discussed the impulses that informed the practice
that Fella termed 'anti-mastery'. Fella complained that design
was becoming smarter and slicker and expressed the view that the
moment had arrived when this 'conceit' must be punctured. His
own response was to base his designs on principles of inconsistency
and irregularity, as seen in late 1980s projects for clients such as the
Detroit Focus Gallery. 'In fact, the irregularity is rigorously thought
out, based loosely on deconstruction,' he said. 'If deconstruction
is a way of exposing the glue that holds together western culture,
I thought, "What is it that holds together typography? It's space."'[19]

Template Gothic

ABCDEFGHIJKLM
NOPQRSTUVWXYZ
abcdefghijklmnop
qrstuvwxyz ^ampers-AND &Nº
ÆæfiO123456789

Barry Deck. Typeface for Emigre,
USA, c.1990

The goal in typography has always been to control and regularize the use of space – between individual letters, words and lines, between kinds of typographic material (title, main text, subheading, caption), between the text and the page's edge. Fella treated these spaces in a totally elastic way. In a poster for Andrea Eis and other artists (1988), there is no consistency in the spacing within and between the names and the irregularity is pushed further by Fella's distortion of a sanserif typeface with his own hand-drawn thickenings, curves and tails, so that each character is different. Even in the smaller, purely functional typographic elements, there are continuous size changes and a constant flouting of the typographic baseline. At first sight, to many designers coming across Fella's work at the time, his designs could appear random and incompetent, as though their creator were ignorant of every rule governing 'good' typography. His effects were, however, knowing and self-reflexive. He had worked for 30 years as a commercial artist before deciding to become a student at Cranbrook and, as intellectual inspiration, he cited Barthes, the novelist Vladimir Nabokov, semiotics, structuralism, literary criticism and poetics. (Talking to Keedy, Fella quoted Hard Werken: 'A lot can be used.') His well-practised hand-skills meant that he was in no hurry to take up the computer and he bypassed the early bitmap phase, while recognizing – as soon proved to be the case – that his fluidly transformative æsthetic was entirely compatible with the open realm of digital space.

Fella had a marked influence on a generation of designers, both in the United States and elsewhere. This began at Cranbrook, which he often visited before becoming a student, and continued after he graduated when he joined the design faculty at California Institute of the Arts (CalArts) in 1987. By 1990, his experiments were beginning to be publicized more widely and this work continued throughout the decade, in the form of posters to announce lectures by visiting artists – often produced after the event – as well as his own lectures at other institutions. Keedy, who was also teaching at CalArts, acknowledged this influence and a series of programmes created for Los Angeles Contemporary Exhibitions (LACE) from 1988 to 1990 explore the ideas of pastiche, cultural gluttony and the 'anti-

Jeffery Keedy. Event programme, Los Angeles Contemporary Exhibitions, USA, 1988

æsthetic' with an aggressive, though intellectually systematic, disregard for conventional graphic decorum reminiscent of the rule-breaking mutations in Fella's work. Keedy's typeface Keedy Sans, launched in 1990 by *Emigre Graphics*, flaunts Fella-esque inconsistencies in its spacing, while the terminals of the characters are rounded in some cases and sliced at an angle in others, making it feel simultaneously soft and sharp – it was advertised in *Emigre* with the slogan 'Wilfully contradict expectation'. 'It was a typically postmodern strategy for a work to call attention to the flaws and artifice on its own construction,' Keedy explained.[20] A similar strategy can be observed in CalArts graduate Barry Deck's Template Gothic – another typeface project with an acknowledged debt to Fella – which, as Deck noted, was intentionally imperfect to reflect the 'imperfect language of an imperfect world'.[21] It became one of the defining typefaces of the new decade.

If deconstructionist design in the 1980s was a semi-underground, seemingly rather subversive activity, carried out

Allen Hori. Typography as Discourse,
event poster, American Institute of
Graphic Arts, USA, 1989

in the insulated 'hothouses' of the academy and viewed by
professionals with deep suspicion, in the early 1990s deconstruction
was primed for popular assimilation. In Europe, one of the channels
by which this would occur had been opened in 1985 when Katherine
McCoy asked Gert Dumbar, Dutch founder of Studio Dumbar, to
lecture at Cranbrook. Dumbar did not share the students' theoretical
agenda, but he was interested in their inventive and expressive
approach to form and, from the mid-1980s onwards, a stream of
Cranbrook students – among them Jan Jancourt, Edward McDonald,
David Frej, Robert Nakata, Allen Hori and Martin Venezky –
became interns at Dumbar's base in The Hague, where their work
helped to redirect the studio's output, especially for cultural clients.

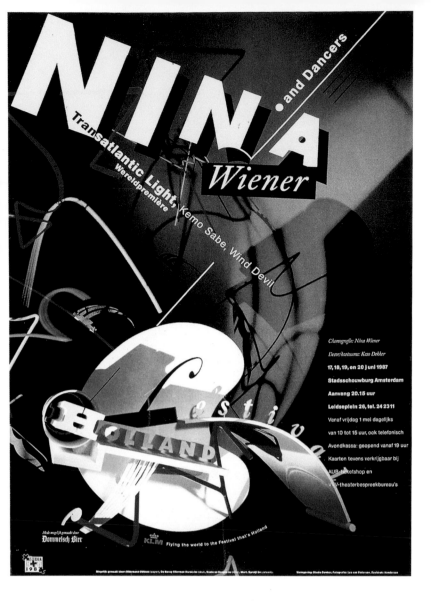

Studio Dumbar. Performance poster, Holland Festival, The Netherlands, 1987. Photograph by Lex van Pieterson

[Right] **Why Not Associates. Next Directory,** catalogue cover, front and back, Next, UK, 1991. Photography by Why Not Associates and Rocco Redondo

From 1985 to 1987, Dumbar was professor of graphic design at the Royal College of Art in London, where he had a marked impact on a number of students, most notably David Ellis and Andrew Altmann, who, on graduation in 1987, formed Why Not Associates. Where Cranbrook design had been steeped in theory and sometimes made these ideas the subject matter of the design – as in Allen Hori's 'Typography as Discourse' poster (1989) – Why Not's commercial projects of the late 1980s and early 1990s employed superficially similar visual devices for largely æsthetic effect. In a directory cover for the Next clothing company, the typographic elements float at random in an indeterminate, partly photographic, pictorial space. The second half of the date, 1991, is flipped to form a

Rick Valicenti and Michael Pappas, Thirst.
Brochure for Esse paper range, spread,
Gilbert Paper, USA, 1990

mirror image (this happens three times) and the catalogue number, 7, is rendered as a word, a number and a roman numeral on the front alone and is then repeated many times on the back. Some kind of 'deconstruction' of these few simple components has been performed, but the effect is decorative rather than revelatory in its spinning of visual seduction from such slender textual threads.

In Chicago, as the 1990s began, Rick Valicenti and his company Thirst, were among the most prominent early American disseminators of the deconstructionist 'style' as it was rapidly coming to be perceived. Until 1988, when he decided to change direction, Valicenti produced slick corporate design for Chicago's financial institutions, which rarely departed from formula. His aim with Thirst was to offer 'art with a function' that fully acknowledged the design process and pushed his own self-expression to the fore. In a 1990 brochure for the paper company Gilbert, a regular Thirst client, the organization of information is bitty, agitated and non-linear, with many focal points. Lateral devices such as arrowed rules and blocks of colour encourage horizontal scanning across the entire spread and information must be extracted piecemeal, in no particular order. On another spread, devoted to Elvis Presley, news about posthumous sightings of the 'king' is presented in irregular text boxes filled with a jumble of type styles and sizes. As with Why Not, the aim was to use 'excessive' design as a way of engaging and entertaining the viewer. When a colleague, Paula Scher, suggested to Valicenti that all his work was about Dada, Valicenti responded self-referentially

There...
Another Nail In The Coffin—Get It?!

JUST A LITTLE HUMOR: to make ya feel comfortable.

Boy, I love this job. 'Cuz what I do is

an art form...it's a gift! I'm not kidding, I'm serious!! Take my best friend Rose.

S·T·E·R·E O T·Y·P·E·S

She went to that school, you know? That place on the East Side? She wanted to be a nailer too — a nailer — that's what they call us in the business.

But she didn't have the gift! No touch. Poor Rose.

...Now She Answers Phones

HEY, RELAX HONEY...you're soooooo tense.

For Some Hotshot Fancypants Accountant Ten Years Younger Than She Is.

How Do You Like That???

You Do Got Nice Hands Though. Whaddya Do? Not Construction. —That's For Sure

My cousin Ernie does that. His hands I wouldn't touch a baby with — Godawful, really. Like a cat's tongue. You know how their tongues are??

Anyway, Me?

I just do what my mother always told me...a little moisturizer — the good kind — and a pair of white gloves to bed.

'You wake up like Cinderella ready for the ball. None of that dishwashing soap stuff — you don't believe that, do you?? —For my money

Soap Is Soap oooooooh,

Did that hurt? That's some nasty cuticle. You wanna stick a gum?

Rick Valicenti, Thirst. Stereotypes, insert
for **Step-by-Step** magazine, USA, 1990.
Photography by Tony Klassen

by designing a four-page magazine insert, aimed at fellow designers, specified in a way that encouraged the typesetter, a non-designer, to make all the critical decisions about type.

It was David Carson, however, more than any other designer, who, in the early 1990s, was most active and effective in popularizing these approaches. For many young designers, his work as art director of *Ray Gun* magazine from 1992 to 1995, supported by lectures and workshops around the world, provided an introduction to experimental design – one so overwhelming for some viewers that it tended to obscure his work's relationship to earlier experiments. *Ray Gun* also delivered the first experience of this type of design to many non-designers, especially outside the US, and it was often assumed, in media coverage, that Carson's approach was entirely without precedent. Certainly, the success of *Ray Gun*'s design as a hip signifier of 'Generation X' youth culture encouraged the deconstructed style's rapid take-up up by corporate advertising and Carson himself created ads for Pepsi-Cola, Nike and, later, Microsoft.[22] By 1997, a British newspaper was hailing him, in a headline, as 'A Hero of Deconstruction'.[23]

In Carson's body of work, the rule-breaking impulse seen in punk and deconstruction became the central idea. No convention was too unassuming to challenge and any structural principle could be disregarded in the cause of expressive design. In his first book, *The End of Print* (1995), he describes his way of working as a 'loose, intuitive, no-formal-training kind of approach'. He goes on to explain: 'Maybe at some subconscious level things are done to upset somebody – part of me continues to see no valid reason for many of the accepted rules of design. Perhaps that is why I have not bought into many of the accepted rules … I'm not anti-school, but when I became interested in design I really didn't know what those rules were and so I just became fascinated by exploring the look and feel of the subject.'[24] Echoing designers from Cranbrook and CalArts, Carson argues that the rationalism of grid systems and other kinds of typographic formatting is 'horribly irrational' as a response to the complexity of the contemporary world.

Carson's repudiation of design and editorial conventions began in earnest at *Beach Culture* magazine, where, in 1991, he first abandoned page numbers. On the fifth issue's contents page, the now role-less numerals become ingredients in a thick stew of typographic matter, with no definite top or bottom, which also attempts to generate interest from the 'worst typeface at hand'.[25] At *Ray Gun*, typographic material was treated with an even more painterly and emotive degree of freedom. In a feature on a band called Deconstruction, published in 1994, the columns are carved into irregular shapes, angled fracture lines run through the text, forced justification is used to space out the last line of each paragraph and one of the columns is pushed out to the edge of the page, so that the page trim (never totally predictable) cuts off some of the letters. The second half of the final paragraph, beginning mid-sentence, is placed at the start of the article. Carson's word pictures were often evocative. On the opening spread of an interview with the reclusive British rock star Morrissey, titled 'The Loneliest Monk', a pull-quote from the piece – 'I have no interest in any aspect of whordom [sic]' – is broken into three irregular type-clusters which revolve around a photo of the singer, who is about to move out of shot, returning the viewer to the image. At other times, in a challenge to fixed editorial hierarchies still unthinkable in most publications, though never far from the surface in 1990s postmodern design, Carson interposed himself unavoidably between reader and story. In one famous case, he replaced a feature about the singer Bryan Ferry with two columns of unreadable dingbats (the text was printed in full, for those who cared, at the back of the magazine). The assumption with all these devices was that readers would readily enter into the process of disentangling, deciphering or dismissing the text. At a time when young people were reading less, Carson suggested (as did many others at the time) that such devices were necessary to compete with other media attractions and that material designed to this degree might be better absorbed and remembered, if the reader had to work at it. Many letters from readers did seem to bear this out, at least in the case of *Ray Gun*, though the argument is at odds with the suggestion by Carson and others that much of the writing in the magazine was not worth reading in the first place, and its application in more general reading contexts was disputed by critics (see chapter 6).

While *Ray Gun*'s art director and cast of young designers employed graphic devices that bore a resemblance to earlier deconstructionist work, the magazine's success signalled the emergence of a new graphic style – grunge – that in some ways looked back even further, to punk's torn edges and dirty graphics, just as the grunge rock of the early 1990s partly rekindled the spirit of punk rock. Grunge, like punk, was energetic, disrespectful, angry (or perhaps just angry-seeming) and subcultural in origin, though this could not last. 'The "Clean Grid of Modernity" has been formally rejected by the nihilism of Industrial Youth Culture,' wrote Joshua Berger, art director of *Plazm*, published in Portland, Oregon, and second only to *Ray Gun* as a product of the grunge sensibility.[26] Typefaces by American companies such as Plazm Fonts (an offshoot of the magazine) and House Industries display ravaged outlines and decayed, crumbling edges, where chunks appear to be missing. Elliott Earls' dysfunctional trio of typefaces – Dysphasia, Dysplasia and Dyslexia – sprout strange, unseemly excrescences. Luc(as) de Groot's font, Jesus Loves Your Sister, spurts liquid trails from every available surface. The essential difference between 1970s punk and 1990s grunge was one of technology. Punk graphics were made cheaply by hand, with biros, photocopies, found type, scissors and

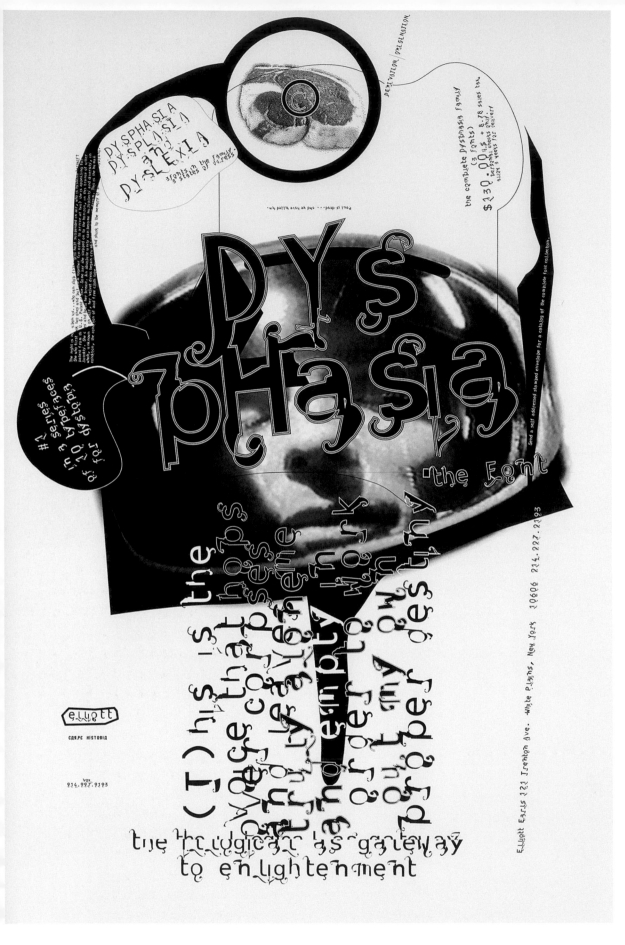

Elliott Earls. **Dysphasia,** typeface
family poster, USA, 1995

EROSIVE

ABCDEFGHIJKLM
NOPQRSTUVWXYZ
0123456789 PLAZM FONTS ?/
@ © ® & !?/• /•§%!()

Condemd House

ABCDEFCHIJKLMNOPQR
STUVWXYZabcdefghijklmn
opqrstuvwxyz0123456789

Jesus Loves
Your Sister

ABCDEFGHIJKL
MNOPQRSTUV
WXYZabcdefg
hijklmnopqrst
uvwxyz012345
6789 @

[Top] **Pete McCracken.**
Typeface for Plazm Fonts, USA, 1993

[Above] **House Industries.** Typeface for
Bad Neighborhood series, USA, 1995

[Right] **Luc(as) de Groot.** Typeface,
Germany, 1995

paste. Grunge, despite its degraded, broken, untechnological appearance, was a product of powerful digital tools that potentially allowed anyone with the talent and inclination to knock up a typeface in a day. Yet, as type designer Tobias Frere-Jones observed, one reason for the development of this style at the moment when the computer could render everything with seamless perfection was that it allowed designers to offer something that ordinary computer users, working with predetermined templates, could not achieve: aggressively artistic individuality. 'For designers who want a non-Modernist and individual portfolio, grunge becomes a seductive method of self-identity.'[27]

By the late 1990s, grunge had long since shed its initial transgressive charge. As the American critic Jon Wiener observed in 1997, deconstruction had 'gone pop'. A database search revealed that the word or a variant had appeared in almost 7,000 articles over the previous two years, from *Entertainment Weekly* to *The New York Times*, from *Playboy* to *Sports Illustrated*.[28] In everyday journalistic parlance, deconstruction had become a trendy synonym for 'analysis' or 'explanation' and sometimes for 'taking things apart' or even 'destruction'. In design, by the mid-1990s, deconstruction was understood – if it was understood at all – in much the same way, to the consternation of those who had, a decade earlier, attached high hopes to its critical possibilities for design. As Katherine McCoy noted: 'One of the regrettable things about the term is that people who haven't read about it very deeply conclude that it is just about form and, more than that, that it is about the disassembling of visual language. That is part of the process, but I am interested in the idea of deconstructing the relationship of written and visual language to understand the dynamics and intentions of communication.'[29] The aim was never to develop a new graphic style – the style that became grunge. It was to discover from the process of analysis new ways of encouraging the audience's participation and to 'open up' meaning so that audiences could be involved in its construction and interpretation.

Yet it could be argued that something like this is exactly what occurred. Open-endedness and freedom of personal interpretation were often used as rationales to explain how *Ray Gun* and similar projects engaged their audiences. As Ellen Lupton and Abbott Miller remark: 'Post-structuralism's emphasis on the openness of meaning has been incorporated by many designers into a romantic theory of self-expression: as the argument goes, because signification is not fixed in material forms, designers and readers share in the spontaneous creation of meaning. Interpretations are private and personal, generated by the unique sensibilities of makers and readers.'[30] Such a view can be used to justify almost anything and, in practice, often effaces rather than facilitates critical thinking. In their book *Design Writing Research* (1996), Lupton and Miller suggest that we see the production of meaning not as a private matter but as structured by external codes in language, education, media and custom within which an individual must operate. From this basis, they argue for a much more focused application of deconstruction and a return to the ideas set out by Derrida in *On Grammatology*, *The Truth in Painting* and other texts. Instead of consigning deconstruction to a brief moment in the late 1980s and early 1990s, they see it as part of the continuing development of design and typography as modes of representation. They suggest that a study of typography and writing informed by deconstruction would examine graphic structures that 'dramatize the intrusion of visual form into verbal content, the invasion of "ideas" by graphic marks, gaps, and differences'.[31] By 'reshuffling and reinhabiting' the normative structures of mass media, design could be used as a critical tool to 'expose and revise' the mechanics of representation.

At such moments, Lupton and Miller appear to hint at a more politically engaged form of design – what, otherwise, is the purpose of this reinhabiting and revision? – but the abstractions of their terminology leave questions of personal commitment and politics unclear for even the sympathetic reader. Who will undertake these revisions, in what circumstances, with what motivations and to what end? In the postmodern period, many designers have struggled critically and productively with issues of engagement and resistance, without any need for direct reference to deconstruction (chapter 6 will return to this theme). It must be clear that, while some designers with a theoretical cast of mind will continue to find uses for deconstruction's difficult source texts, a wider application of these theories in design seems unlikely, even now that deconstruction has run its course as a style. The number of significant design projects that can be related in a direct way to deconstruction as a philosophical enterprise remains small and the few notable examples, such as Derrida's *Glas* (English edition, 1986) or Mark C. Taylor's *Hiding* (1997), tend to feature the close involvement of the theorist|writer and have a complexity in their relationship of content and form that highlights the superficiality of projects that treat deconstruction as nothing more than a fashionably distressed style. More than a decade after its publication, Avital Ronell's *The Telephone Book* (1989), a deconstruction of 'phonocentrism' – a pun on Derrida's term for the privileging of speech over writing – remains a bizarre landmark, the *Ulysses* of deconstructive typography. Designed by Richard Eckersley (designer of *Glas*), the book reconsiders the telephone in historical, literary and psychoanalytical terms. It opens with a joint statement from its 'textual operators':

'Your mission, should you choose to accept it, is to learn how to read with your ears. In addition to listening for the telephone, you are being asked to tune your ears to noise frequencies, to anticoding, to the inflated reserves of random indeterminateness.... At first you may find the way the book runs to be disturbing, but we have had to

The Nervous Breakdown

We have to cut the shit.

Or perhaps you have not understood. It is no longer a question of adducing causes to the telephone, assigning its place, and recognizing in it a mere double and phantom of an organ (like Woman, reduced to the phantom of a missing organ). This would be much, and much that is engaging: the phone as a missing mouth, displaced genital, a mother's deaf ear or any number of M.I.A.–organs such as the partial object-ear transmitting and suturing the themes of *Blue Velvet*. Put through the body-slicing machine, the telephone will have become an organ without body. But "without body"—what is this? The ear, eye, even skin, have been divested of authority as they acquire technical extension and amplification in media. [69] All this belongs to our subject. But the radicality of the transaction takes place to the extent that technology has broken into the body (every body): this includes the body politic and its internal organs, i.e., the security organs of state). The somaticizations that a neurotic might chart are little compared with the electric currents running through the schizonoiac body. Hitting the lights on Reich's contention, we read: "With respect to their experiencing of life, the neurotic patient and the perverted individual are to the schizophrenics as the petty thief is to the daring safecracker."[70] The schizophrenic gives us exemplary access to the fundamental shifts in affectivity and corporeal organization produced and commanded by technology, in part because the schizophrenic inhabits these other territorialities, "more artificial still and more lunar than that of Oedipus."[71] In the

O mouth!

at the moment" (*W*, 120). At this point, Heidegger appears to rely on a communality of sense, a *sensus communis*, or an essential consensus, into which the unpresent tense of schizophrenic discourse could not, admittedly, be happily entered. However, even in this convocation of something like a contractual agreement of sense, a common contextuality and steadiness of address, Heidegger amends the speaking to include, as an address, the human and the thingly: "That includes fellow men and things, namely, everything that conditions things and determines men. All this is addressed in word, each in its own way, and therefore spoken about and discussed in such a way that the speakers speak to and with one another and to themselves. All the while, what is spoken remains many-sided. Often it is no more than what has been spoken explicitly, and either fades quickly away or else is somehow preserved. What is spoken can have passed by, but it also can have arrived long ago as that which is granted, by which somebody is addressed" (*W*, 120). **The Laingian** reading of Heidegger establishes a dimension which appears to set objections to schizophrenogenic modes of address, to the distortions of the place of sender and recipient toward which Heidegger's thinking may appear to harbor intolerance. Nonetheless even in these passages, the temporal rendering of that which is spoken in addition to the incomparable inclusion of thingly speakers already complicate any itinerary that would seek reliably to reroute schizophrenic Saying from a more normative grasp of language. But the material with which to seek presence of person in the speaking cannot be securely retrieved from any Heideggerian path of language. In "The Way to Language," Heidegger continues in this way, averting the dangers of the straight and narrow:

Everything spoken stems in a variety of ways from a spoken, whether this be something not yet spoken, or whether it be what must remain unspoken in the sense that it is beyond the reach of speaking. Thus, that which is spoken in various ways begins to appear as if it were cut off from speaking and the speakers; and did not belong to them; while in fact it alone offers to speaking and to the speakers whatever it is they attend to, no matter in what way they stay within what is spoken of the unspoken. (*W*, 120; italics added)

Not long after this reading, which in part corresponds to the descriptive analysis of schizophrenic utterance in Lainguage, Heidegger offers to accentuate the cutting. Analyzing the sign in terms of *secare*, "to cut," he returns to the decisive disconnectedness in all language tracings. The speaking which appears as if disconnected from speaking and the speakers cannot therefore be used to explicate an essential dimension, gleaned from Heidegger, of schizophrenia in its most advanced stages of psychosis—unless, of course, Heidegger were himself to be implicated in the unfolding of a schizophrenogenic understanding of language. This would be going very far, on the other way to language, whose essential signpost reads "Wrong Way, Do Not Enter." **In another** essay, "The Nature of Language," Heidegger has the following to say on the question, raised so often by the doctors, of not being there:

All is way. . . . The way allows us to reach what concerns us, in that domain where we are already staying, why think, one may ask, still find a way to it? Answer: because where we already are, we are in such a way that at the same time we are not there, not yet properly reached because we ourselves have what concerns our being, not even approached it. The way that lets us reach where we already are differing from all other ways, calls for an escort that runs for ahead. (*W*, 92–93)

That which has been with us, the companion, stretches itself apart from us in answer to a call. The escort does not cease to be an escort when a long-distance runner is called for. It is one that reaches the place where we are not but toward which we point. We are where we are in such a way that, at the same time, we are not there. This is where we stay. Heidegger places some words after one that is simple, single, and armed with the antennae of a colon, *Answer:* Why do we care to mention this total response unit?

[Opposite] **Richard Eckersley. The Telephone Book** by Avital Ronell, book spreads, University of Nebraska Press, USA, 1989

break up its logic typographically. Like the electronic impulse, it is flooded with signals. To crack open the closural sovereignty of the Book, we have feigned silence and disconnection, suspending the tranquil cadencing of paragraphs and conventional divisions.'[32]

Agitated by moments of noise and silence, *The Telephone Book*'s text is unstable, reforming itself from page to page. Letters collide, blur and ripple as size changes pulse along the line length. Letter spaces increase, word spaces enlarge, gaps open between the lines, then close until the letters touch. Columns expand and contract, assuming temporary new shapes. Undulating fissures form and the text splits apart schizophrenically, doubling itself, before fusing back together a page later. The point of these typographic modulations is not that they offer the reader a set of competing visual amusements, or encouragements to read, or doubtful graphic mnemonics, but that they arise from the text, in a close cooperation between writer, designer and compositor, and serve textual meaning.[33] *The Telephone Book*'s lasting impact derives from the playful intelligence and systematic critical purpose with which it puts 'under erasure' every rule in the book.

3

Appropriation

In 1978, the German electronic music group Kraftwerk released the
latest in a series of highly original albums whose austere synthetic
melodies and pulsing robotic rhythms would have a lasting influence
on the development of dance music. The 12-inch record was titled *Die
Mensch-Maschine* ('The Man-Machine') and its front cover announced
at first glance that its musical and æsthetic concerns were radically
different from most popular music of the time, whether rock, disco
or punk. The four band members, wearing identical red shirts and
black ties, were framed by diagonal rules and panels of block-like
type reminiscent of Russian Constructivist typography of the 1920s,
a historical reference confirmed by the use of red, black and white
as the main colours. The same slanted composition and typographic
manner was used on the back cover, which also featured various
geometrical shapes. A credit confirmed that the design by Karl
Klefisch had been inspired by the work of El Lissitzky, avant-garde
'constructor' of such works as *About 2* (1922); the back cover was, in
fact, a quotation from one of the book's pages. *Die Mensch-Maschine* was
not a parody in any direct sense, but two ideas were communicated
clearly: that the music, too, was to be understood as 'avant-garde',
infused by a spirit of bold artistic exploration; and that it was
'futuristic', anticipating a new world that would be different from
everything we know, but in some sense still positive. Nevertheless,
the designer and musicians chose to construct an image that was
backward-looking, if not quite nostalgic, and whether they intended
it or not, the cover could also be read as tongue-in-cheek and
humorously camp in its straightfaced seriousness. If Kraftwerk's
music was so progressive and new, one might ask, why did it need to
be represented by imagery that referred ambiguously to a moment
of political failure in the past?

El Lissitzky. About 2, detail of book page, Germany, 1922

The Kraftwerk cover was an early sign of a postmodern phenomenon that rapidly became a trend. In graphic design, it was particularly apparent on record sleeves, a small boom industry at the time and a field that had always allowed a high degree of experimentation, though the trend was by no means confined to this area. Before the 1980s were very far advanced, these years had been dubbed 'the age of plunder' and by the decade's end it was common to see newspaper and magazine articles lamenting it as 'the age of parody'. The literary critic Fredric Jameson, writing in 1983, summarized the prevailing cultural obsession with the past. All the styles and worlds that can be invented by writers and artists have already been invented, he argued, and after 70 or 80 years of classical modernism, the result is exhaustion. 'In a world in which stylistic innovation is no longer possible, all that is left is to imitate dead styles, to speak through the masks and with the voices of the styles in the imaginary museum. But this means that contemporary or postmodernist art is going to be about art itself in a new kind of way; even more, it means that one of its essential messages will involve the necessary failure of art and the æsthetic, the failure of the new, the imprisonment in the past.'[1]

Jameson draws a critical distinction between pastiche and the related phenomenon of parody. Both involve the imitation or mimicry of the mannerisms and tics of other styles. In the case of parody, the aim is to emphasize the peculiarities of the original in a way that mocks them and this applies whether the parody is sympathetic or malicious. The effect depends on a shared sense in the audience that the original is excessive in some way and departs from an accepted norm. However, if as Jameson contends, the idea of the normal has broken down as society has fragmented and if postmodern society is now composed of a multitude of separate groups each speaking a private language or idiolect of its own, then there can be no shared linguistic norm against which a parody can register its comic effect. This is the moment, he argues, at which pastiche appears. Pastiche resembles parody in the way that it puts on the mask of a pre-existing style and in the accuracy of its imitation, but, unlike parody, it has no underlying satirical impulse, or intention to ridicule and deflate its subject. On the contrary, it is a neutral practice. 'Pastiche is blank parody, parody that has lost its sense of humor,' Jameson notes.[2]

Jameson's distinction between parody and pastiche hovers over any attempt to examine the ways in which postmodern graphic design has made use of the histories of design and art. The issue is further complicated by the fact that the designers themselves would, in most cases, certainly not have viewed their own practice in the negative light that Jameson's use of the word 'pastiche' suggests. Nor would their audiences necessarily have agreed that their consumption of these images was as dead-eyed and directionless as terms such as 'neutral' and 'blank' make it sound. Graphic design has always borrowed images and approaches from other fields, especially from fine art and popular culture; visual references of all kinds are an essential feature of the way that it communicates. Are the countless 'appropriations' of the last two decades any different in essence? As we shall see, the issue of appropriation has been the source of considerable debate within design, just as it has within art.

In Britain, in the late 1970s, Barney Bubbles was a crucial figure in the development of postmodern graphic design. He was already an influence on an emerging, younger generation of designers because of his work for the hippie rock group Hawkwind, when in 1976, at the height of punk, he became full-time designer for Stiff Records, set up by Jake Riviera. Bubbles' exceptional facility as a 'new wave' image-maker of the post-punk period was soon evident in his cover for the album *Music for Pleasure* by the Damned (1977), a Kandinsky-like semi-abstract built out of lines, zig-zags, semi-circles, symbols and planes of colour mashed together in a composition that throbs with kinetic energy. The band's name and portraits of the band members are hidden in the thicket. As with Kraftwerk, the cover is not exactly a parody – more a tribute that gleefully embraces its source material – though its humour is the antithesis of Jameson's blank pastiches. Willing to use anything that seemed to work, Bubbles was just as likely to base a design on suburban tastes in interior decoration, as he did with *Do It Yourself* by Ian Dury and the Blockheads (1979), which came clad in a choice of 52 different wallpapers. His most ambitious sleeve, *Armed Forces* (1979), for Elvis Costello and the Attractions, is a riotous *mélange* of art historical allusions to Mondrian, Abstract Expressionism, Op Art and Pop, fronted by a painting of a herd of elephants in a kitsch popular style. Five cover flaps can be opened and closed to form alternative compositions, according to the viewer's whim. Clothing his own identity in the borrowed garments of fine art, Bubbles, whose real name was Colin Fulcher, concealed what appears to be a joky self-portrait, with large red nose, behind the splattered yellow band details at the heart of the fragmented image.

Younger British designers such as Malcolm Garrett and Neville Brody were quick to acknowledge Bubbles' influence on their work. However, for these designers and for Peter Saville, with whom they are often grouped, historical inspiration came, even more than it did for Bubbles, not only from postwar art, but – as with *Die Mensch-Maschine* – from early twentieth-century modernism in art and design. Herbert Spencer's book *Pioneers of Modern Typography*, first published in 1969, was a key influence on this generation, providing short introductions to the work of

Barney Bubbles. Armed Forces by Elvis Costello and the Attractions, album cover with folding flaps (two views), Radar Records, UK, 1979

[Above] **Neville Brody.** The Face,
no. 23, magazine spread, UK, 1982

[Right] **Malcolm Garrett. A Different
Kind of Tension** by the Buzzcocks,
album cover, EMI Records, UK, 1979.
Photograph by Jill Furmanovsky

El Lissitzky, Theo van Doesburg, Kurt Schwitters, H.N. Werkman,
Piet Zwart, Paul Schuitema, Alexander Rodchenko, Laszlo Moholy-
Nagy, Herbert Bayer and Jan Tschichold. Malcolm Garrett's cover
for *A Different Kind of Tension* by the Buzzcocks (1979) interprets
the album title in a cheerful, day-glo graphic with a clear debt
to Lissitzky's 1919 poster *Beat the Whites with the Red Wedge* (shown
in Spencer's book), in which a red triangle breaks through the
perimeter of a circle. In 1982, when Neville Brody was designer
of *The Face*, he fashioned the opening spread of a feature about
Kraftwerk in a style that referenced both *Die Mensch-Maschine* and
its graphic origins in Lissitzky's work. (The same issue also profiled

Garrett, who namechecked the Futurists, the Dadaists, Lissitzky and Tschichold.[3]) This was a period in which ambitious young designers constantly invoked the achievements of modernism's leading lights half a century earlier. Brody was careful, however, to draw a distinction between merely copying the work of the Dadaists or the Constructivists, which he deplored, and deriving more general lessons from their example. 'I looked at it and tried to evaluate the core of what was being done, and why. What I took from it was a sense of dynamism, a sense of humanism and a non-acceptance of traditional rules and values. Once you looked at that, you could then pursue your own response. I have always felt that the last fifty years of design have been recycling these already explored areas.'[4]

In 1990, declaring that 'All art is theft', Garrett coined the term 'Retrievalism' to describe his method. 'We live in a Retrievalist world where the past is a bottomless pit that can be infinitely ransacked. Invention is a myth. We create only from using what already exists. There are no new colours. Retrievalism acknowledges the past, yet detests nostalgia. We must by necessity retrieve from the past to re-invent the future. This is a new Futurist age.'[5] Garrett seems to agree with Jameson's argument that stylistic innovation is no longer possible and that everything has already been invented, yet he insists that postmodern recombinations of the old can still become the building blocks of an authentic cultural moment. What gets overlooked, when the past is treated as a quarry from which useful visual material can be extracted at will, are the changes of meaning – the drainage of meaning – that occurs when visual ideas with specific purposes are applied in new contexts. In Lissitzky's *Red Wedge* poster, the triangle and circle stand for political factions and progressive visual form underscores a progressive political message. The Buzzcocks' sleeve treats similar motifs as super-stylish product packaging that benefits from a historical association with a radical moment, without representing anything of comparable significance, if it represents anything at all.

In a well-illustrated article in *The Face* titled 'The Age of Plunder', published in 1983, the cultural critic Jon Savage launched one of the earliest broadsides (certainly in Britain) against the use and abuse of historical form. Among other examples, Savage showed

Peter Saville. Movement by New Order, album cover, Factory Records, UK, 1981

Bubbles' *Music for Pleasure* sleeve; a design for *Mechanix* by UFO (1982) based on a Jean Carlu poster for the US Office of War Information (1941); and a cover for the single *Ziggy Stardust* by the rock group Bauhaus (1982) that modified the hugely influential German art school's famous stylized 'face' logo. Savage took the view that this visual plunder was a symptom – one of many – of a Thatcherite political culture in which everything is turned into a disposable consumer commodity. 'The Past then, is being plundered in Pop as elsewhere in order to construct a totality that is seamless, that cannot be broken. It is a characteristic of our age that there is little sense of community, of any *real* sense of history, as THE PRESENT is all that matters.'[6] Refashioned in our own image and reduced to triviality, history's lessons can be ignored.

Two of Savage's most provocative examples were drawn from Peter Saville's work for the Manchester rock band New Order, which grew out of the earlier group, Joy Division. In his opening spread for the article, Neville Brody chose to highlight one of these cases, the sleeve of *Movement* (1981), by placing it next to its historical source and alongside the admonitory headline, 'The Age of Plunder'. To those who had assumed, until this point, that Saville, as Factory Records' regular designer, had single-handedly devised this strikingly austere and powerful design, it must have come as a surprise to learn how closely it was based on a Futurist poster created in 1932 by Fortunato Depero (the original sleeve did not credit Depero, although a credit line was later added to the CD release). A few details had been changed – a vertical rule had been moved to the left, four lines of type had become three, a second colour had been introduced – but in its most salient features, it was the same. The second sleeve, for New Order's *Procession* (1981),

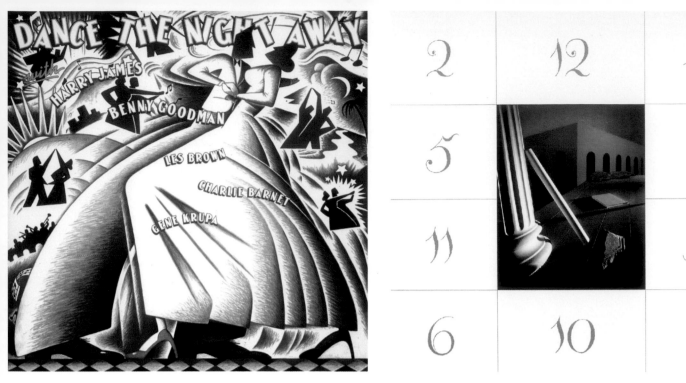

Paula Scher. **Dance the Night Away**, album
cover, CBS Records, USA, 1980. Illustration
by John O'Leary

[Right] **Peter Saville. Thieves Like Us** by New
Order, 12-inch single cover, Factory Records,
UK, 1984. Photograph by Trevor Key

was even closer to its source, also a Depero design, this time for
a Futurist publication of 1933; the only substantial difference
was the removal of the title, 'Dinamo Futurista'. Saville's
wholesale quotation of his sources was quite different from
American designer Paula Scher's use of Futurism. For the cover
of *Dance the Night Away* (1980), a compilation of big band recordings
by the likes of Benny Goodman and Gene Krupa, released by CBS
Records (where Scher was an in-house art director), she
commissioned an original illustration in a Futurist style. Scher's
design, incorporating her own typography, was a lively pastiche.
If Saville's designs weren't outright plagiarism, then they had to
be understood as graphic examples of the kind of postmodernist
'appropriation' seen in the art world in the early 1980s, where
works by earlier artists were absorbed and 'recontextualized'
by contemporary artists as new artworks. In one of the more
controversial examples, American artist Sherrie Levine presented
photographs by Edward Weston and Walker Evans as her own,
insisting that by claiming them in this way they became new pieces.
As Saville later explained: 'To me, it was better to quote Futurism
verbatim, for example, than to parody it ineptly – it was a more
honest, more intellectual and in a way more artistic approach.
It was so literal and so obvious that it never crossed my mind
that people would think that I had invented this work.'[7] In
another New Order sleeve for *Thieves Like Us* (1984), Saville created
a convincing-looking facsimile of a Giorgio de Chirico painting.
There was a forensic precision in his appropriations that gave
them a lasting allure as graphic objects, but his work's power
also came from the way that his selections functioned as *ideas* in
relation to the musicians and music they expressed, and the way

THE METAMORPHOSIS 1919

1

As Gregor Samsa awoke one morning from **uneasy** dreams he found himself transformed in his bed into a **gigantic** insect.

He was lying on his hard, as it were **armor-plated**, back and when he lifted his head a little he could see his **dome-like** brown belly divided into stiff arched **segments** on top of which the bed **quilt**, could hardly keep in position and was about to slide off completely. His numerous **legs**, which were pitifully thin compared to the rest of his bulk, waved **helplessly** before his **eyes**.

FRANZ KAFKA

Paula Scher and Terry Koppel. Great **Beginnings,** self-promotional book spread, USA, 1984

that the designs contributed as a series to Factory's identity and mystique as a record label.

In the course of the 1980s, especially in the United States, 'retro' became one of the defining styles of the decade. Paula Scher's understanding of historical form – Futurist, Constructivist, De Stijl, Bauhaus, Art Deco, Pictorial Modernism – and her eclectic ability to reinvent it in the service of her clients made her an influential figure. In 1984, after leaving CBS, Scher started a new firm, Koppel & Scher, with partner Terry Koppel. One of the duo's first projects, a self-promotional brochure that was almost a manifesto, titled *Great Beginnings,* presented the opening lines of literary classics such as Goethe's *Faust,* Kafka's *Metamorphosis* and Thomas Mann's *Magic Mountain* in period styles appropriate to the texts. Other designers such as Louise Fili, art director of Pantheon Books, and Carin Goldberg, also a book jacket designer, produced work that borrowed from historical sources, ranging from the typography of the Vienna Secession to Bauhaus designer Paul Renner. Any historical style was deemed fair game and though the results were often accomplished and commercially astute, the recycling trend looked increasingly problematic to some observers as the decade wore on. In 1990, at a conference on the theme of 'Modernism & Eclecticism' in New York, Tibor Kalman gave a keynote lecture in which he addressed the uses of history in graphic design, good and bad, and a revised version of the text, co-written with J. Abbott Miller and Karrie Jacobs, was subsequently published in *Print* magazine. 'Designers abuse history,' they argue, 'when they use it as a shortcut, a way of giving instant legitimacy to their work and making it commercially successful ... historical reference and down and outright copying have been cheap

Paula Scher and Terry Koppel. Great **Beginnings,** self-promotional book spread, USA, 1984

that the designs contributed as a series to Factory's identity and mystique as a record label.

In the course of the 1980s, especially in the United States, 'retro' became one of the defining styles of the decade. Paula Scher's understanding of historical form – Futurist, Constructivist, De Stijl, Bauhaus, Art Deco, Pictorial Modernism – and her eclectic ability to reinvent it in the service of her clients made her an influential figure. In 1984, after leaving CBS, Scher started a new firm, Koppel & Scher, with partner Terry Koppel. One of the duo's first projects, a self-promotional brochure that was almost a manifesto, titled *Great Beginnings,* presented the opening lines of literary classics such as Goethe's *Faust,* Kafka's *Metamorphosis* and Thomas Mann's *Magic Mountain* in period styles appropriate to the texts. Other designers such as Louise Fili, art director of Pantheon Books, and Carin Goldberg, also a book jacket designer, produced work that borrowed from historical sources, ranging from the typography of the Vienna Secession to Bauhaus designer Paul Renner. Any historical style was deemed fair game and though the results were often accomplished and commercially astute, the recycling trend looked increasingly problematic to some observers as the decade wore on. In 1990, at a conference on the theme of 'Modernism & Eclecticism' in New York, Tibor Kalman gave a keynote lecture in which he addressed the uses of history in graphic design, good and bad, and a revised version of the text, co-written with J. Abbott Miller and Karrie Jacobs, was subsequently published in *Print* magazine. 'Designers abuse history,' they argue, 'when they use it as a shortcut, a way of giving instant legitimacy to their work and making it commercially successful ... historical reference and down and outright copying have been cheap

Herbert Matter. Travel poster,
Switzerland, 1934

[Right] **Paula Scher.** Poster for
Swatch watches, USA, 1986

and dependable substitutes for a lack of ideas.'[8] For the writers,
this kind of design was 'jive modernism', feeding off modernism
like a parasite for gains in prestige, style, clients and awards, while
ignoring its underlying politics and philosophy. Like Savage, who
had drawn close links between historicist design and conservative
politics, they argued that jive modernism contributes to a
'prevailing Reaganesque conservatism'.

As one of their principal examples, Kalman, Miller and
Jacobs showed a poster by Paula Scher advertising Swatch watches
(1986) based on a Swiss travel poster designed in 1934 by Herbert
Matter. Scher's poster is neither parody (it has no obvious satirical
intention) nor is it quite pastiche (it isn't a wholly new image in
the general style of Matter). It is closer in visual approach to
Saville's appropriations, but without the attempt to create a third
idea in the imaginative space between image and subject matter.
Where Saville's use of Futurism is metaphorical, encouraging us
to ask what it has to do with New Order's electronic rock, Scher's
selection of source image is literal and descriptive. It shows
something typically Swiss, skiing in the mountains, thereby
identifying the product with exhilarating outdoor pursuits. Scher
takes the main elements of Matter's original image, which had a
broadly economic purpose – to encourage tourism – and re-creates
them, without Saville's fetishistic fidelity to detail, for the simple
purpose of selling Swiss timepieces. The angle of the model's head

TALKING HEADS

PRO-A-903

CROSSEYED AND PAINLESS

12

STEREO   INCH SINGLE   45 R.P.M.

Tibor Kalman, M&Co. Crosseyed and Painless
by Talking Heads, 12-inch single cover, Sire
Records, USA, 1980

is adjusted so that she looks towards the viewer, emphasizing the watches on her wrist, which replace the Swiss flag, and the word 'Swatch' is twice the size of 'Suisse' (Switzerland) in the original poster. While there is nothing particularly heinous about the appropriation – the original hardly embodied any deep revolutionary intention – Scher's poster continues to provoke discussion because it so tellingly embodies the assumption, expressed by Garrett, that the past is a 'bottomless pit' available for postmodern ransacking by designers.[9]

Kalman's position as critic was in any case complicated by the use made in his own work of existing source material. In the 1980s, Kalman and his New York design company M&Co became strongly identified as champions of the 'vernacular' – design produced by ordinary people rather than professional designers, such as roadside sign painting, shopfront lettering and posters announcing social events or items for sale. Vernacular design's appeal lay in its authenticity, the sense that it was a natural, unfiltered expression of the way people felt, of their local concerns, untainted by strategy, marketing imperatives and the slickness and calculation typical of design's elite professional class. Kalman admired the 'invisible' quality of vernacular design, the fact that it is just there, part of the landscape, a form of visual slang, and the way that it seems to be from another time (often because it is). 'We're interested in vernacular graphics,' he explained, 'because it's the purest and most honest and most direct form of communication. We will unabashedly steal from vernacular work.'[10]

An early M&Co design for the 12-inch single *Crosseyed and Painless* by Talking Heads (1980) was modelled on the flat colours and deadpan presentational style of a scientific equipment

A.I.G.A.N.Y.

PRESENTS

FRESH DIALOGUE 1986 :

Design without Designers:

OR

HOW I LEARNED TO
STOP LETTERSPACING
AND LOVE THE NON.

TIBOR KALMAN OF M&Co.
LEADS THIS YEAR'S ROMP THROUGH
THE GOOD, THE BAD AND THE ADEQUATE.
FEATURING TEN
YOUNG AND RESTLESS DESIGNERS.

ICONS WILL CRUMBLE.
OPINIONS WILL FLY.
CONVENTIONS WILL BE FLOUTED.
LATECOMERS WILL BE SEATED.
BE THERE OR BE SQUARE.

Who?	*Who?*	*What?*
CBS Records Art Director. Insisted that speakers be listed alphabetically.	CHRIS AUSTOPCHUK	Out of the mouths of babes; The teacher learns, the students teach.
Hails from the Buckeye State, and has seen Massimo Vignelli in his underwear.	MICHAEL BIERUT	The client as designer.
Important person at Bonnell Design Associates. Wears glasses.	BILL BONNELL	Will think of something important.
Famous downtown graphic design denizen ('70-73), presence ('73-82), personage ('82-)	JO BONNEY	Designing artists.
Couple of white designers sittin' around bitchin'.	DOUBLESPACE	Letterheads: When they're good, they're very, very good. When they're bad, they're fabulous.
Creative Director (not allowed to sign checks) at Drenttel Doyle Partners.	STEPHEN DOYLE	Stealing from the blind.
Wears many hats. Teacher, writer, graphic designer, furniture designer, artist, bon-vivant.	DAN FRIEDMAN	Modernism gone wild.
Reputed Underboss of the M&Co. Family. Also wears glasses, but just for effect.	ALEXANDER ISLEY	Unseen design.
WJMD seeks fun-loving & well-endowed clients for creative afts, in well-appt'd conf. rm. (rw. vu) Photo a must. No deadlines, please. Box 9.	TIBOR KALMAN	Will attempt to show portfolio and pass out business cards.
Of Strong Cohen, New Haven. This is Tom's first trip to New York, so let's all be on our best behavior. Thank you.	TOM STRONG	Buildings that talk. (Yes, they really do.)

Tibor Kalman with Alexander Isley, M&Co.
Design without Designers, event invitation,
American Institute of Graphic Arts, USA, 1986

catalogue. In 1986, for an American Institute of Graphic Arts (AIGA) symposium titled 'Design without Designers', M&Co created a set of publicity materials flaunting the kind of clumsily spaced, mismatched typography more likely to issue from a back-street printshop than a national design organization committed to professional standards. The graphics devised by M&Co from 1985 to 1993 for Restaurant Florent, a 24-hour 'diner for the debonair and the dispossessed' in the meatpacking district on Manhattan's West Side, were the studio's most elaborate essay in vernacular style. None of these designs was a wholesale quotation, appropriation or parody of vernacular sources, but each made constant, surprising references to everyday (non)design. For a promotional postcard, M&Co designer Alexander Isley matched icons from the Yellow Pages – of a chair, a truck, a gun, the Bell telephone company logo, a globe and a coffee cup – against location and service details. Other promotional materials showed cut-out photos of a steak or underwear or a comb that brought to mind the artlessly direct publicity shots of an earlier era. In 1985, for an issue of *Print* devoted to graphic parodies, Paula Scher had written and illustrated a feature purporting to reveal how two émigrés, Lubevitch and Moscowitz, were the overlooked originators of delicatessen design. As an example of their innovative 'corporate signing', she showed a sandwich menu board with cheap plastic movable type.[11] Taking the idea a step further, Kalman used movable type in typographically dyslexic print ads for Florent that gloried in wonky alignment, characters upside down and optimistic substitutions – an inverted 'V' for a circumflex accent, a '$' sign for an 'S'.

Tibor Kalman, M&Co. Print advertisement for
Restaurant Florent, USA, c. 1987

[Right] **Alexander Isley and Tibor Kalman,
M&Co.** Promotional postcard for Restaurant
Florent, USA, 1986

M&Co's work was extremely witty, but its relationship to the vernacular was not without its contradictions. If it was unacceptable to steal ideas from design history, why was it acceptable, even desirable, to 'unabashedly steal' from vernacular sources? Surely a sophisticated metropolitan design firm that made clever use of naïve examples of 'un-design' or 'non-design' came perilously close to the kind of knowingness and calculation that Kalman railed against in other areas of the design profession? Was there not also an unspoken assumption in such borrowings, as visual ideas were transported from low culture (everyday designing) to high culture (professional design), that high was inherently superior? A professional designer receiving the 'Design without Designers' leaflet understood immediately that its typography was 'wrong' and, since it came from the AIGA, that it had been purposely designed to look like it was produced by someone ignorant of the 'rules' of good design. To get the joke was to collude in its mockery of naïve popular sources.[12]

In 1990, some of these issues surfaced in a debate between Kalman and Joe Duffy, head of the Duffy Design Group in Minneapolis, which was published in *Print* magazine.[13] Duffy's work had become famous, in the late 1980s, for a decorative retro style that drew on Pictorial Modernism, Expressionism and Art Deco, as well as the vernacular, to create a warm, nostalgic, reassuring blend that could be applied to food labels (Classico pasta sauce), paper samples (French Paper's Speckletone), product packaging and annual reports. In 1989, Duffy's company joined the Michael Peters Group, then the largest design firm in the world, and this union was announced by a full-page ad in the *Wall Street Journal* aimed at corporate CEOs – 'How two guys with art degrees can do more for your business than a conference room full of MBAs.' Kalman and others took exception to this move, seeing it as the latest step in the inexorable transformation of design into an activity that was primarily about business. Yet their impassioned discussion about historical sources was ultimately inconclusive. In each of the cases raised by Kalman, Duffy argued that there was a logical business reason why the product required nostalgic forms of design to communicate its essential qualities. For instance,

French Paper, founded in 1871, family-owned and based in Niles, Michigan, was one of the smallest paper mills in the US – about as 'down-home and nostalgic', said Duffy, as it was possible to be in the paper industry. Kalman countered by arguing that the essential difference was that M&Co used elements from the past in a new way, while Duffy did nothing new with them. Duffy replied that they were used for exactly the same purpose that M&Co used them for – to communicate – and that the contexts in which they did this were certainly new.

Perhaps the difference, if there was one, came down to the spirit in which the vernacular was appropriated and revived. In its purest forms, vernacular-inspired design was another way of reacting – like punk and deconstruction – against the cloying, impersonal slickness of so much professional design. It was bound to look most suspect when it was recuperated as the latest gimmick by these same commercial forces and to look freshest and most convincing when it was applied in the more open cultural contexts that Kalman cited with approval during his debate with Duffy.

In the work of Art Chantry, based in Seattle from 1978 to 2000, the American vernacular found one of its most enthusiastic and attentive archaeologists – a designer-archivist able to reanimate his sometimes trashy sources without beautifying or sanitizing them to suit a bland, middle-class, supermarket taste. Chantry fashioned hundreds of street posters and album covers infused by the throwaway, unselfconscious visual language of the old newspaper ads, magazines, parts catalogues and clip art that he hoarded in his studio. In one of the most accomplished examples, from 1991, he used spanners, screwdrivers, a toolbox and a drill taken from 1950s tool catalogues and industrial ads to advertise 'The Night Gallery', a performance art series at Seattle's Center on Contemporary Art. Details of the individual performers are scattered across the hardware, like explanatory panels, and a tear-off coupon gives ticket information. In form, the poster mimics a cheap-looking ad, yet its luxurious scale and quality of printing encourage viewers to peer at the details and savour the rhythmic energy and communicative impact of a kind of commercial design that would usually be dismissed by designers

Art Chantry. The Night Gallery, performance art poster, Center on Contemporary Art, USA, 1991

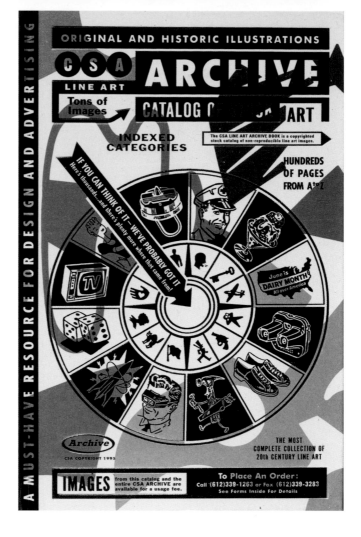

Charles S. Anderson. CSA Line Art Archive
Catalog, vol. 1, book cover, USA, 1995

Art Chantry. Logos for Estrus Records,
USA, 1990s

as conceptually and æsthetically worthless. Nor is there anything
patronizing or cute about Chantry's assimilation of his sources.
He used similar material from old advertising for a series of related
'Night Gallery' promotions and, in 1992, designed a CD cover for the
band Liquor Giants in the style of a store ad, offering paper towels,
baby lotion and grass seeds (marijuana) at bargain prices. His many
humorous logos for Estrus Records – a Seattle grunge label that, he
notes, 'prides itself on its lack of subtlety' – add up to an alternative
history of trademarks.[14]

Equally committed to the evocative power of early
Americana is Charles S. Anderson, a designer at Duffy Design Group,
before setting up his own Minneapolis studio in 1989. Anderson
continued to work for French Paper, producing many promotions
in a much-imitated style recalling the commercial art of the 1920s to
1960s that he dubbed 'bonehead'. Anderson's interest in 'un-designed'
vernacular imagery began at high school when he met a retired
commercial artist, Clyde Lewis, who left him hundreds of hand-
drawn cuts, which became the starting point for Anderson's own
collection. In 1995, he published *CSA Line Art Archive Catalog* vol. 1,
containing 7,777 examples from an archive that now numbered
hundreds of thousands of images taken from old books, magazines,
catalogues, matchbook designs, cocktail napkins and vintage

Charles S. Anderson. Seinfeld poster for
Entertainment Weekly, USA, 1998

packaging. Nearly all of these line art images had been cleaned
up and redrawn to simplify them or make them bolder and more
graphic, and to unify the collection. They were organized by
alphabetical category – magic, mail, military, money, monsters –
and, as copyrighted items, could be ordered for a usage fee
from the archive, which functioned much like a library of stock
photography. The archive's clients included Nike, Levi's, *Ray Gun*
magazine, Nissan, Lee Jeans and MTV, and advertising agencies such
as Weiden & Kennedy and Chiat|Day|Mojo, indicating the enduring
popular appeal, however ironic in spirit, of instant, ready-made
signifiers of supposedly simpler, more innocent times. A poster
by Anderson, commissioned by *Entertainment Weekly* to commemorate

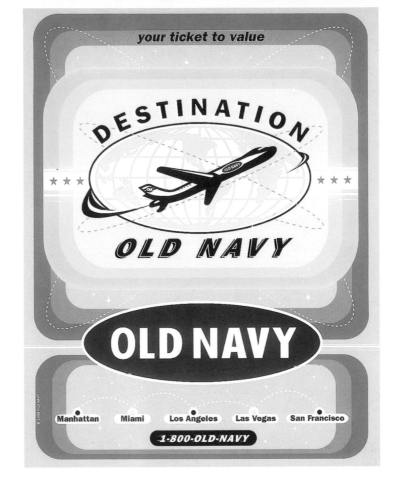

Alan Disparte. Seasonal advertising campaign for Old Navy, USA, 1998

the 169th and final episode of the situation comedy *Seinfeld*, is an intricate collage of such images, mixed with product logos, packaging and other types of graphic ephemera. This dense textural backdrop flows through the line art image of a television to suggest the way that TV itself contributes to a mental landscape saturated with an easily summoned nostalgia for product experiences we have loved.

In the 1990s, many commercial ventures deployed postmodern nostalgia to trigger reassuring emotions in consumers. In 1994, Gap launched a new division, Old Navy, which would design, manufacture and sell casual clothing and accessories for adults and children. The new stores were committed to a concept of retailing that Old Navy's creative director, Dennis Leggett, labelled as 'shopper-tainment'. To communicate a sense that Old Navy offered fun for all the family, the in-house team devised a graphic identity that was comfortingly old-fashioned, apparently issuing from any point between the 1930s and the 1960s, while simultaneously contriving to look invitingly new – a balancing act characterized by one writer as 'nouveau-retro'.[15] This bright, colourful, vaguely familiar pastiche was splashed across hang-tags, pocket stickers, packaging, advertising and in-store promotions. The personnel who worked on Old Navy's graphics shared a love of popular culture, including music, film and television from the 1950s and 1960s, and senior art director Alan Disparte described how he had 'learned to appreciate the kind of distressed and degenerated

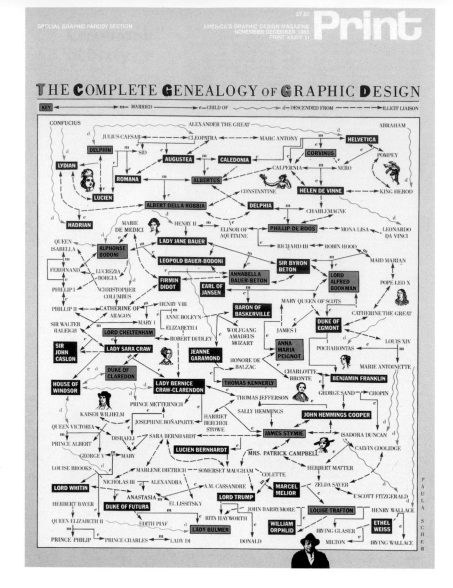

Paula Scher. The Complete Genealogy of
Graphic Design, cover for **Print** magazine,
USA, 1985

beauty of things that are retro. If the packaging worked way back
then, why wouldn't it work now?'[16] Disconnected from any specific
point of origin, a vernacular that was largely commercial in the
first place could be recycled ad infinitum to stimulate further sales.

Yet postmodern forms of reference could also, on occasion,
be put to more pointed, nuanced and even critical uses. Paula Scher's
cover for *Print*'s parody issue, in 1985, inaugurated a trend in which
diagrams, maps, charts and types of information design usually
found in worthy encyclopædias and text books were appropriated
for alternative, often satirical purposes. Scher's 'Complete Genealogy
of Graphic Design' purports to show how an impossibly convoluted
genealogical tree that records every illicit liaison descends from
Confucious, Alexander the Great and Abraham, via the likes of
Caledonia and Helvetica, to arrive eventually, centuries later, at Milton
Glaser. With *Spy* magazine, launched in 1986, the hyperactive info-
graphics look – at once studious and sarcastic – became one of the most
distinctive calling cards of postmodern graphic design. Initially art
directed by Drenttel Doyle Partners, then by Alexander Isley and
B.W. Honeycutt, *Spy* was in all senses a postmodern product, entirely

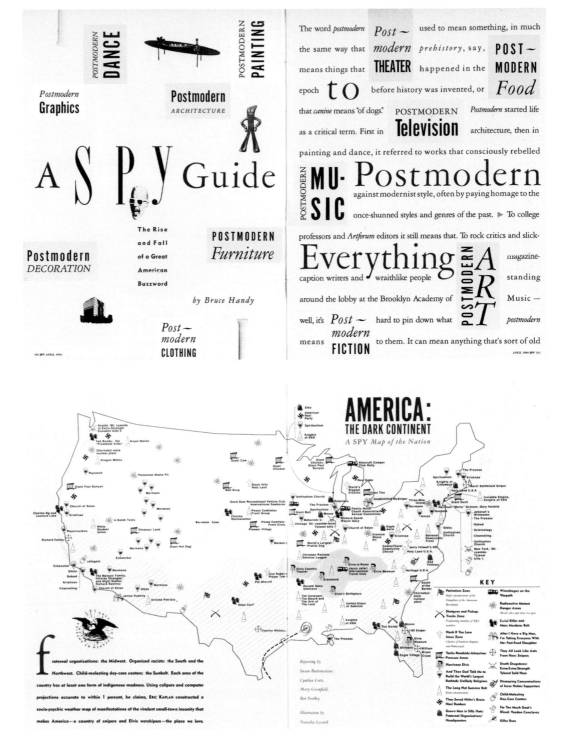

[Top] **Alexander Isley.** Spy, magazine spread, April 1988

[Above] **Alexander Isley.** Spy, magazine spread, June 1988. Illustration by Natasha Lessnik

self-conscious about every detail of its own mechanics. In 1988, it even published 'A Spy Guide to Postmodern Everything', which presented readers baffled by this ubiquitous buzzword with handy hints for recognizing postmodern artefacts in architecture, painting, television, literature, cuisine and graphic design: 'Is it like MTV? Do the layouts look like this one?'[17] The feature's pastel-hued opening spread, art directed by Isley, was a quintessential *Spy* layout: it was fussy, overloaded with words (all of them cutting), an interlocking puzzle that had to be tackled piece by piece. In another issue, *Spy* conducted a graphic analysis of 'America: The Dark Continent', using a stylized map and specially drawn icons explained in a key, to chart the

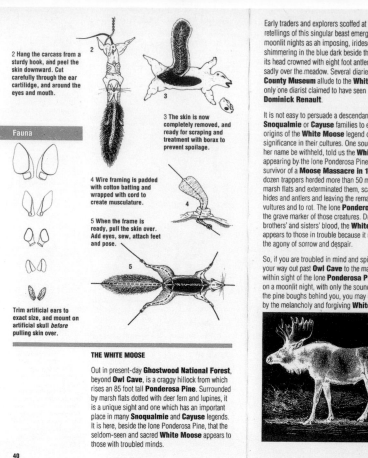

Annie Kook and Stuart L. Silberman.
Welcome to Twin Peaks by Richard Saul
Wurman, David Lynch and Mark Frost, book
cover and spread, Penguin Books, USA, 1991

distribution across the nation of Nazi sympathizers, Ku Klux Klan members, snipers, serial killers, voodoo conclaves, child-molesting day-care centres, and 'dismaying concentrations' of supporters of Republican senator Jesse Helms. A story published after Honeycutt became art director offered a surefire guide to making Hollywood hit movies the 'Buddy-o-Matic' way. Readers had to choose between multiple alternative readings, each one supported by a footnote giving film references and other information – a mind-bogglingly elaborate concept for a monthly magazine. Here and elsewhere in *Spy*, writing and design fused in visual reports that caught the spirit of the postmodern moment because they were both authoritative and absurd.

A genuine curio, in this regard, was a spin-off from one of the defining cult television series of the early 1990s, *Twin Peaks*, created by film-maker David Lynch, a show that came to be seen as the epitome of postmodern TV. The architect turned publisher Richard Saul Wurman had become well known in the course of the 1980s for his informative, cleanly designed 'Access' guides to cities around the world. *Welcome to Twin Peaks* (1991) by Wurman, Lynch and series producer Mark Frost treats the fictional northwestern town and its peculiar inhabitants as though they actually exist. TV tie-ins are commonplace, but the guide's strangeness makes it an intriguing one-off. Its deadpan layouts and routine illustrative style, detailing Twin Peaks' flora, fauna, sawmill production and styles of doughnut, flatten out the fantastical dimension, rendering it almost dull, and

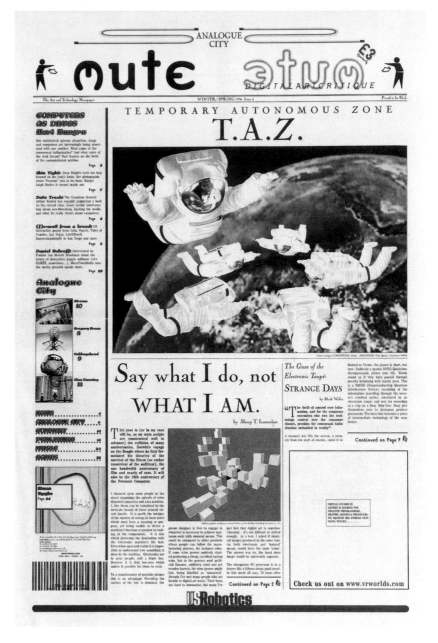

in consequence only serve to heighten its surreality. By pouring fictional content into a format recognized for its authority, the book becomes a parody of the 'Access' series and of the very idea of reliable guides to the world 'out there'.

This strategy of appropriating not merely the graphic form but the entire generic container can prove highly fruitful. It potentially allows a more complex, multifaceted and suggestive interrelationship between the new content and the graphic medium it inhabits. Instead of merely pastiching stylistic fragments, often for no more than superficial æsthetic or nostalgic effect, it opens up the possibility of deeper kinds of parodic resonance. Early issues of the British digital culture publication *Mute*, edited and designed by Simon Worthington and Pauline van Mourik Broekman, were printed on broadsheet-sized newsprint. Features were laid out like news stories and the paper was pale pink, making an instant visual connection with financial publications such as the *Financial Times*. *Mute* was

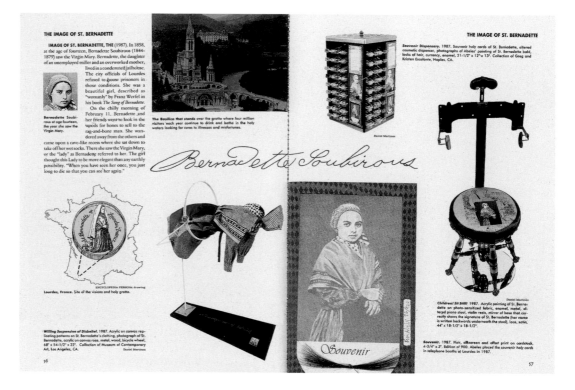

Susan Silton. *Encyclopedia Persona* by Kim Abeles, catalogue spreads, Santa Monica Museum of Art, USA, 1993

struggling to establish its critical voice and the borrowed format gave it a veneer of seriousness and authority, though one that was playful and ironic for regular readers who were in on the joke. Ironic parody was implemented with even more exacting attention to generic convention and detail in the case of American artist Kim Abeles' 1993 catalogue, *Encyclopedia Persona*, a 15-year survey of her work. Conceived by Abeles, curator Karen Moss and designer Susan Silton, the book mimics the alphabetical structure, matter-of-fact page layout, and typographic and pictorial conventions of an early 1960s encyclopædia; even the textured binding has a hushed, reading-room air about it.

The book's aim is to make a wealth of art and non-art information accessible to the reader and it reflects the artist's research process and methods of presentation. As Moss notes, Abeles 'plays with the pre-conceived idea of an encyclopedia's absolute authority by creating entries that function as meta-histories of her subjects. [She] freely embellishes each entry and compares this process to the art of storytelling. While she sincerely wants people to understand her ideas and her work, parts of the book mimic and mock the didacticism of an encyclopedia.'[18] At the same time, the catalogue's makers readily acknowledge that it is a 'nostalgic tribute' to the simple pleasure – perhaps no longer so popular in a screen-based era – of browsing through reference books in search of knowledge.

Do graphic works such as these represent, in Fredric Jameson's words, 'the failure of the new, the imprisonment in the past'? Certainly, a project such as *Encyclopedia Persona* depends on our familiarity with the conventions being parodied, and this is bound to reaffirm and legitimate them to a degree. Even so, these conventions are interrogated rather than merely parroted and, in the process, they are rendered more problematic than they might otherwise have been. Postmodernist graphic design is often 'about design' just as postmodernist art is often about art, though this is not a wholly new development in applied visual communication: a great deal of graphic design has always worked in this way. Nevertheless, it is significant that design's obsessive preoccupation with the past emerged at a point in the late 1970s when the once fast-flowing waters of innovation had grown stagnant. Designers of all kinds, both the commercially minded and those with the avant-garde aspiration to 'make it new', looked back with a mixture of envy and nostalgia to a time (modernism) when novel inventions seemed to pour from the drawing board. Paradoxically, the arrival of the Apple Macintosh in 1984 only confirmed this strain of retro-futurism among some designers, as the profession struggled to discover whether the computer was simply a handy production tool – as some continued to insist well into the 1990s – or the liberating medium of a new graphic sensibility. It was both of these things, but it was also a boundless, ecstatic, rule-free space, in which cultural tendencies already identified by postmodernist thinkers would find even fuller and more elastic styles of expression.

4

Techno

As some critics were quick to point out, the fragmented and intricately layered designs made possible by the computer often resembled a kind of neo-Futurism or neo-Dada and this was true even when no conscious parody was intended. Yet there were a few attempts, even in the 1980s, when the technology was comparatively new and limited in terms of memory size and processing power, to explore the possibilities for a new æsthetic. American West Coast designers such as April Greiman and the Emigre team, Rudy VanderLans and Zuzana Licko, acquired Apple Macintosh computers as soon as they were introduced in 1984 and set about experimenting enthusiastically with the tools. For Greiman, the computer was 'a new paradigm, a conceptual "magic slate" opening up a new era of opportunity for graphic artists'.[1] Greiman understood immediately that, however much those trained in traditional methods might protest, the computer did change the design process in fundamental ways. In that sense, it was not, as she herself expressed it, 'just another pencil'.[2] A pencil makes physical marks and even if these marks are erased some trace often remains, while other kinds of mark-making – crayon, paint, ink, things cut up and stuck down – leave even more indelible impressions. By contrast, the computer's 'undo' function, as Greiman herself noted, allows something to be removed instantly, without any trace. Ease of deletion gives every aspect of the design a provisional, less certain quality. It no longer exists in such a definite, physical way, so there is much less need to be sure that a particular decision is 'correct', since it can be instantly retracted and changed. This condition of uncertainty and instability extends to the entire design. In digital space, nothing is ever finished; as long as the computer file survives, any element can be rethought – 'The paint never dries in the Mac universe.'[3] Ease of generation allows even more options and variations to be considered.

The fact that accidents need not have lasting or negative consequences means that these chance occurrences and 'mistakes' can potentially be used to provoke unexpected directions in the design process.

To many at the time, low-resolution bitmapped graphics looked like a step backwards, but the earliest exponents of Macintosh design made a virtue of the computer's limitations. In an article titled 'The New Primitives', VanderLans and Licko quoted Piet Zwart with approval – 'We are the primitives of the new technical era' – and argued that coarse bitmaps could be the basis of a new computer æsthetic.[4] Set in bitmapped typefaces designed for use on the Macintosh by Licko and distributed by Emigre, the article showed the æsthetic in action. 'Much of the scepticism and disfavor currently attached to digital images will disappear as a new generation of designers enters the profession,' they prophesy (they were soon proved correct). 'Having grown up with computers at home and school, these designers will assimilate computer technology into the visual communication process as it penetrates everyday practices.'[5] They showed an example by San Francisco illustrator John Hersey, a catalogue cover created in 1987 for 'Pacific Wave', an exhibition of Californian graphic design. Hersey's vibrant image exploits the computer screen's potential as generator of jagged, patterned backgrounds, using its 'primitive' rawness for optical animation. Issues of *Emigre* produced at the time also demonstrated that bitmapped typefaces and images, used sensitively, could convey an unexpected degree of vitality and warmth.

It was Greiman, though, who was responsible for perhaps the most ambitious early attempt to put desktop technology through its paces. Her 2 x 6 foot (0.6 x 1.8 metre), double-sided poster collage, designed for *Design Quarterly* magazine in 1986, is a landmark not only in technical terms, but as a self-authored, cosmological statement that depended on electronic tools for its conception and realization and reflected an exuberant, uncompromised digital sensibility. On the poster itself, Greiman describes her design process: six months spent gathering materials; three months of sketching with MacPaint and digitizing images with MacVision; then three months composing, layering and stretching the image with MacDraw before printing it out on a LaserWriter – a task

Rudy VanderLans. Emigre, no. 5,
magazine spread, USA, 1986

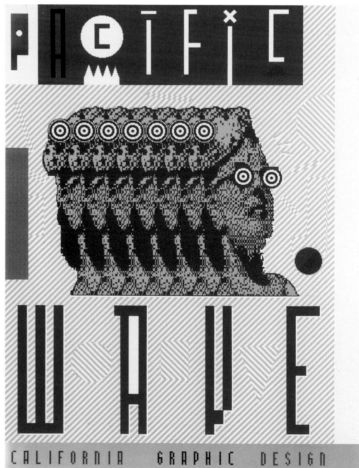

John Hersey. Pacific Wave, catalogue
cover, Magnus Edizione, Italy, 1987

which came close to defeating the technology. The poster shows a life-sized image of Greiman naked and, at her feet, also materializing from a vapour of pixels, her 'spiritual double'. She is surrounded and overlapped by smaller images: a dinosaur, a brain, a spraycan, an astronaut, hands making gestures. A timeline marks various inventions and developments, including her own birth, which culminate in the Mac. It looks a bit like one of those schematic images of humankind despatched across space to extend the hand of friendship to passing extraterrestrials. The cover poses the question 'Does it make sense?' and Greiman answers with a quotation from Wittgenstein: 'If you give it a sense, it makes sense.' On the poster, another Wittgenstein quotation suggests 'the sense lies far in the background'. While some questioned whether the poster made any sense at all, this well-publicized project was significant as a sign of how the designer was becoming increasingly central, as a creative personality, to the presentation, perception and consumption of postmodern graphic design. It was also, as one American critic noted at the time, an important early step in the search to 'determine the computer's unique characteristics and the impact of those characteristics on the future "look" of visual communications'.[6]

The key point about Greiman's poster was that it was *excessive*: in conception, in size, in detail, in the sheer quantity of information with which it deluged the viewer. For many designers, the point of design was still to eliminate extraneous information (noise), to thwart the possibility of ambiguity by reducing a design to its essentials. In the early 1990s, as computer processing power burgeoned, designs created on the screen became increasingly overloaded and complex, overwhelming the viewer with a wild network of pathways to penetrate and decipher, plunging the spectator into the vertiginous reaches and turbulent coordinates of a new kind of digital space. Ten years earlier, thinking about television, advertising and radio rather than the impact of personal computers, Jean Baudrillard described how, in contemporary culture, we inhabit an incessant, instantaneous surfeit of information and solicitation, which invades our private spaces, forcing the 'extroversion of all interiority', obliterating our sense of a separate, inner life. 'We live in the ecstasy of

April Greiman. Design Quarterly, no.133,
poster for a magazine, USA, 1986

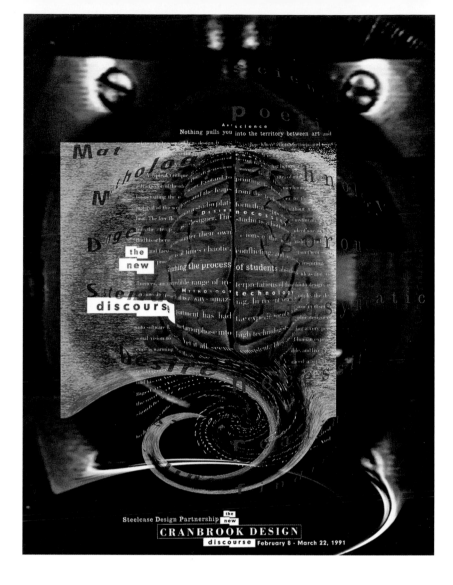

P. Scott Makela. Cranbrook Design:
The New Discourse, exhibition
announcement, USA, 1990

communication,' writes Baudrillard. 'And this ecstasy is obscene.'[7]
This is not, he says, the obscenity of the forbidden or the repressed;
it is 'the obscenity of the visible, of the all-too-visible, of the more-
visible-than-the-visible. It is the obscenity of what no longer
has any secret, of what dissolves completely in information and
communication.'[8] He ends this tirade with a vision of the spectator
as 'a pure screen, a switching center for all the networks of
influence' – an image that possesses even greater resonance in
the era of the Web.[9]

In P. Scott Makela's image of a melting orange brain,
created in 1990 to advertise the 'Cranbrook Design: The New
Discourse' exhibition, the brain itself becomes a 'pure screen'
framed by a pulsing field of video texture, across which lines
of type flow and scroll. At the brain's stem, language dissolves
into a vortex of illegible marks sucked towards a vanishing point
in the darkness, an image both 'ecstatic' and threatening, which
suggests a Baudrillardian surrender to the omnipresent demands
of electronic networks. Inspired by cyberpunk fiction and
'wirehead|hacker technologies', Makela was one of the most
cranked-up, excessive designers of the period; in his own words,

P. Scott Makela. On Doing Nothing
by Tucker Viemeister, spread from
Rethinking Design, Mohawk Paper
Mills, USA, 1992. Digital photography
by P. Scott Makela and Benoit Barbier

Dead History

ABCDEFGHIJK LMNOPQRSTU VWXYZabcdef ghijklmnopqr stuvwxyz012 3456789&@¶

P. Scott Makela.
Typeface for Emigre,
USA, c.1990

'100% digital'.[10] In 'Redefining Display', a project and text published in *Design Quarterly* in 1993, he evokes the unprecedented multitasking possibilities, density of inputs and layering of experience delivered by electronic work environments. 'Awareness of my own working methods has helped me to visualize others' data-processing needs. Every day I make multiple phone calls while my Macintosh runs up to six software programs at once. I send faxes and e-mail, and I am productively addicted to good electronic bulletin boards. I watch obscure TV stations for interesting images or textures, and I enjoy CDs played at high volume.'[11] Makela designed a hybrid font called Dead History and recorded an album of pounding techno music for Emigre with titles like 'Telepresence' and 'Waiting with Baudrillard'. His designs for print, such as a 1992 visual essay for Mohawk Paper's *Rethinking Design* journal, bulge against the edge of the page, straining to burst through its boundaries. Everything communicates at a thunderous volume, as though the controls have been turned up as high as they will go, then jammed on maximum. 'I know all the rules of space and balance and contrast and all the things that make a formal construction work,' he explained, 'but I am after something else. I am after a certain effect. And there might be a hierarchy there, too, but it's very subtle.'[12]

Makela's designs have the hyperreal, super-bright aspect of a dream or hallucination. Like Baudrillard's vision of the individual reduced to a 'switching center', they are a kind of science fiction, but where Baudrillard's cold analysis suggests intellectual disgust, Makela was excited and energized by the prospect of information overload. These were speculations about future technology at a moment in the early 1990s when, despite the media's infatuation with the revolutionary promise of virtual reality, the World Wide Web had yet to arrive, the computer was far from being a household item (especially outside the US) and most people had yet to discover the convenience of e-mail. In his 'Redefining Display' project,

P. Scott Makela with Alex Tylevich.
Design Quarterly, no. 158, magazine
cover, USA, 1993

**The Designers Republic. 3MB Featuring
Magic Juan Atkins,** album cover, Tresor,
Germany, 1993

Makela presented 'subjective forecasts' of how digital 'work walls'
might be used by a plumber, a parish priest, a multimedia artist
and a motorcycle mechanic. Images flow and collide in temporary
formations meant to mirror the concerns, experiences and dramas
of the user's everyday life. The priest answers videophone calls,
pages through religious texts, keeps an eye on CNN, and hears an
on-line confession from behind the red curtain on the left of his
screen. Here, as elsewhere, Makela unleashes a torrent of signals
in which the separate units of data seem to matter less than the
sensation of ecstatic immersion in the information stream.

A similar sense of immersion can be seen in the work of
The Designers Republic (DR), founded in Sheffield, England, in 1986
by Ian Anderson. Where Makela favoured photographic or televisual
images set in realistic, representational spaces, DR's work is
far more graphic, unfolding with kinetic abandon across the two-
dimensional flatness of the printed sheet. DR, like Makela, seem
fully adapted to postmodern reality, treating it as an invitation
to surf opportunistically through the floating world of corporate
signs, yet perhaps without Makela's sense of optimism. 'The core
of remix culture is the product of sampling both in attitude and
experience, and is the inevitable result of the desire for progress
in the absence of anywhere to go ... In the context of remixism the
original is purely a seed,' writes Anderson.[13] As with postmodern
design's use of retro and vernacular imagery, there is a feeling that
culture has stalled, that there is nothing left to invent and that
'newness' can only lie in sampling and remixing what already exists
into novel constructions with new subjective uses. Nevertheless,
in DR's work, a computer-driven æsthetic emerged that would prove
highly influential as the 1990s progressed, particularly in Europe.
The style's essence is replication. Shapes and symbols – dots, circles,
arrows, hearts, parallel lines and graph paper grids – multiply
to form sheets of graphic texture that modulate and merge like
scientific charts and diagrams in the process of mutation. Embedded
in these graphic fields are logos, cartoon characters, fragments
of Japanese (DR are obsessed with an imaginary Japan), panels
full of fake technical information and cryptic statements from the
designers in miniscule type. In a 1993 record sleeve for Magic Juan

The Designers Republic. Sissy, poster, UK, 1995

[Right] **The Designers Republic. Pho-Ku Corporation**, poster, UK, 2000

Atkins, the banded structure breaks apart as a rogue cloud of dots swarms down over the titlepiece, which is shattered into horizontal slices as though it were shooting past in a blur of speed. The design vibrates with released electric energy.

DR's inspirations were electronic gadgets, 'magic' technology, UFOs, films such as *Blade Runner* and science fiction in general, and 'computers as big as planets and as small as teardrops'.[14] A self-taught designer who originally studied philosophy, Anderson was an articulate observer who viewed the postmodern context for design with a mixture of resignation and subversive wit: 'People may view modern society as being shallow, riddled with capitalist failure or as being consumed by senseless consumerism like a dog chasing its own tail – and they are right. But until I'm in a position to improve its condition, I'm going to enjoy the game I find intriguing.'[15] DR undertook projects for Warp Records, Sony, MTV, Warner Brothers and the Ministry of Sound. While they refrained from overtly critical statements, a more ambivalent view of the electronic consumer culture they mostly appear to celebrate surfaced in self-initiated banners and posters for exhibitions, which featured ad-like incantations

[Top] **Me Company. Army of Me**
by Björk, CD single cover, One Little
Indian, UK, 1995. Astro Boy
modelling by Martin Gardiner

[Middle] **Me Company. Bachelorette**
by Björk, CD single cover, One Little
Indian, UK, 1997. Photography by
Toby McFarlan Pond

[Bottom] **Me Company. Alarm Call**
by Björk, CD single cover. One Little
Indian, UK, 1998

declaring 'Department stores are our new cathedrals', 'Let's hear it for consumer fascism' and 'Design will eat itself'. To sell their own products, DR established the Pho-Ku ('fuck you') Corporation, with the irresistible slogan 'Buy nothing. Pay now'.

The most suggestive expression of this ambivalence is a fictitious toy called Sissy produced by Dr Deth Toys, a registered trademark of The Designers Republic. Sissy™ has blue eyes, blond bunches, a frilly dress and looks about three years old; behind her back she carries a heavy baseball bat with the slogan 'I love my DR'. Product advertising informs the viewer that the doll is suitable for age 16+, that 'she is cute she will kill you' is a protected slogan of DR (the barcode reads '5 155Y. K1LL.' – Sissy kill), and that batteries are not included. Sissy is sponsored by DR Cola. The figure was originally rendered in outline, but later versions are three-dimensionally modelled, giving Sissy the simplified, textureless look of a character in a computer game or a Japanese anime. Her face, hair, limbs and clothes have an unreal, plastic sheen.

In the work of Me Company, based in London, three-dimensional modelling had, by the mid-1990s, become almost a house style. Science fiction and Japanese popular culture were once again the inspiration for digital worlds that are entirely artificial yet obscenely vivid and real, impossible techno-spaces built up from dazzling reflections and shimmering, glutinous matter. A recurrent image, in much of this design output, is the cyborg – an artificial fusion of man and machine. In 'A Cyborg Manifesto', published in 1991, American theorist of science Donna Haraway proposes that 'cyborg politics insist on noise and advocate pollution, rejoicing in the illegitimate fusions of animal and machine'.[16] Machines, she goes on to suggest, can be 'prosthetic devices, intimate components, friendly selves'.[17] In a series of projects for the Icelandic singer Björk, Me Company subjected the idiosyncratic star to a series of intimate cybernetic couplings and transformations in which her literal image is sometimes completely effaced. For the single *Army of Me* (1995), the designers used a battery of software programs – Elastic Reality, 3D Studio, Form-Z, Infini-D, Photoshop and Freehand – to gene-splice her with Astro Boy, the Japanese cartoon character, and so create Astro Björk.

On Friday, June 13, the Buzz Crew continues the Sting party series with a diverse selection of international techno, jungle/drum 'n' bass and trip-hop/acid jazz talent.

Me Company. Print advertisement for Nike, The Netherlands, 1995

[Right] **Airline Industries. Sting 9,** rave flyer, USA, 1997

On *Bachelorette* (1997), Björk's otherworldly likeness, caught in the reflections and shadows cast by spores of shining pollen, merges with a cyborgian garden in which the 'plants' themselves appear to be organic-robot hybrids. Finally, with *Alarm Call* (1998), her features are reduced to a series of pulsing, cyberscan contours, composed of luminescent dots, as the singer becomes a ghost in the digital machine.

Digital representations of this kind were second nature to a generation that had come to adulthood using computers and spent much of its leisure time in front of the screen, playing *Tomb Raider* and *Myst*. Me Company were soon applying their cyborg style to a series of print ads for Nike, commissioned by Wieden & Kennedy in Amsterdam, in which four Dutch football stars become screaming manga warriors rocketing towards the viewer out of throbbing digital space. Even more than with Makela's work, the viewer is sucked into a maelstrom that borders on delirium. By the mid-1990s, the techno graphic style was recognized everywhere as a lingua franca for techno music events. In the thousands of flyers produced to publicize raves in Britain, the United States, Germany and

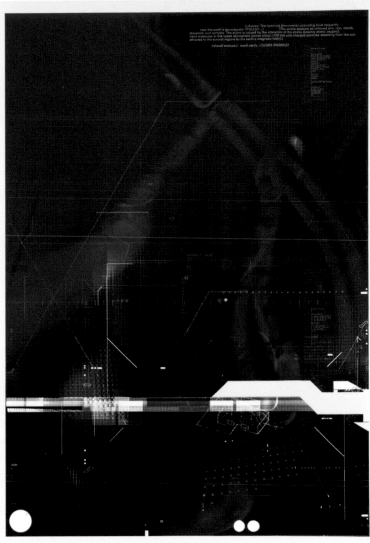

Attik. Noise 3.5: Analytical Experiments
in Graphic Science, book spread, UK, 1998

elsewhere, the preferred graphic mode could involve any or
all of the following: cute little robots, cartoons, insects, UFOs,
spacecraft, futuristic cities, wave forms, scientific diagrams,
neo-psychedelic swirls of colour, Japanese 'transformer' toys,
drifting clouds of plasma, and chunks of three-dimensional
type whizzing through space. Attik was one of the most relentless
exponents and exporters of commercial techno, with offices in
Huddersfield, London, New York, San Francisco and Sydney, and
clients such as Sony, Kodak, Levi's, Coca-Cola and Virgin. In a series
of self-promotional books, Attik's designers presented a mixture
of studio experimentation and client work. *Noise* 3.5: 'Analytical
Experiments in Graphic Science' – includes a spectacularly detailed
computer-generated image of a cyborg's head encrusted with
technological implants and layered with diagrams and information
read-outs. 'Humanic and orgobionic RESYNTHESIS is inevitable
and completely inescapable,' declares a caption, apparently
without irony. 'We have a biological hunger to join with our
machines.' This brings to mind McLuhan's observation: 'We are
all robots when uncritically involved with our technologies.'[18]

Only occasionally did techno's feel-good calls to join the warehouse party and its thrusting commercial offshoots give way to the more detached and ironic style of commentary seen in The Designers Republic's work. Barry Deck's speed-slanted typeface Cyberotica (1994), released by Thirst, captured the genre's rush of libidinal energy with a shrewdly anthropological eye. In Prague, the cultural magazine Zivel illustrated a special issue about pornography with a cover showing a computer graphic of a tumescent porno pig – an ambiguous icon for the complexities of 'posthuman' sexuality. In a report published in 1996, J. Abbott Miller of Design|Writing| Research in New York showed examples of 'dimensional typography' in which the normally flat and static realm of the letter was subjected to spatial and temporal extrapolation. In 'Polymorphous', based on Zuzana Licko's Modular Ribbed typeface (1995) – a design seemingly inspired by textured prophylactics – Miller developed the letter 'f' into a rubbery, three-dimensional avatar, bristling with nipple-like protuberances, 'designed for heightened reading pleasure in intimate settings'.[19] Another project, 'Rhizome', takes as its starting point Luc(as) de Groot's typeface Jesus Loves You. In the 1990s, the image of the 'rhizome' – introduced into theoretical discourse by the French philosophers Gilles Deleuze and Félix Guattari – was often invoked in postmodern cyberculture.[20] Where trees have roots, linking them to a single point of origin, plants such as grasses and bamboos have an underground network of stems, a rhizome, which can sprout new plants at any point. As Erik Davies notes in TechGnosis, these botanical structures without beginning and potentially without end resemble the myriad networks that make up the Internet, 'that wild digital weed whose very name underscores the interruptions and inbreeding that give postmodernists such interminable delight'.[21] Miller's 'Rhizome', based on the letter 'j', can be seen as a node in this promiscuous network, with dozens of thick and spiky shoots erupting from its tuberous length.

For graphic designers concerned with the relationship between image and text, the computer seemed to promise an end to all the old hierarchies, barriers and restrictions. 'Perhaps the most profound implication for the future is that digital technology

Cyberotica

ABCDEFGHIJKLMNOPQRSTUVWXYZabcdefg
hijklmnopqrstuvwxyz0123456789№?ÆfiÆ

[Top] **Barry Deck.** Typeface
for Thirst, USA, 1994

[Above] **Klára Kvízová and
Petr Krejzek.** Zivel, no. 10,
magazine cover, Czech
Republic, 1998

[Right] **J. Abbott Miller.**
Rhizome typeface, USA, 1996

[Far right] **J. Abbott Miller.**
Polymorphous typeface,
USA, 1996

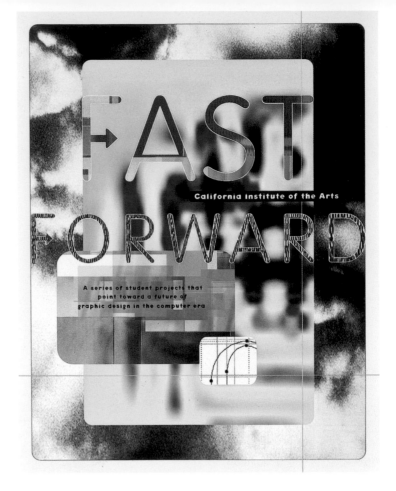

James Stoecker. Fast Forward, book cover, California Institute of the Arts, USA, 1993

collapses all media into a single desktop tool speaking one digital language. It is really a *metamedium*,' writes Eric Martin.[22] In *Fast Forward* (1993), a catalogue for a series of student projects at California Institute of the Arts, Jeffery Keedy cites science fiction writer William Gibson's portrayal – in books such as *Neuromancer* (1984) – of a future in which cybernetics, genetics, neurochemistry, ecology, designer drugs and technology are on a collision course with pop culture and there is a 'hallucinogenic melding of mind and information structures'. 'If this is the construct of our future world,' notes Keedy, 'then it's the graphic designers that will be creating our total "human environment".'[23] There is a strain of wild utopianism in such statements – not to mention an overestimation of the designer's role – that is typical of a moment when everything seemed open and it was possible to imagine that technology itself could be the gateway to a different ordering of reality. Keedy's text is arranged on the page in a series of floating blocks that can be read in any order. Lines ripple, cast shadows and overlap as though they are already part of the 'electronic flow' into which Keedy expects words, sounds and images to dissolve. In accordance with deconstructionist theory, the text has been 'decentred'; it no longer feels like the most important thing happening on the page, but in that case what is? The design itself, perhaps? Keedy, writing in the least inflected passage on the spread, explains that the most important aspect of the computer's impact on

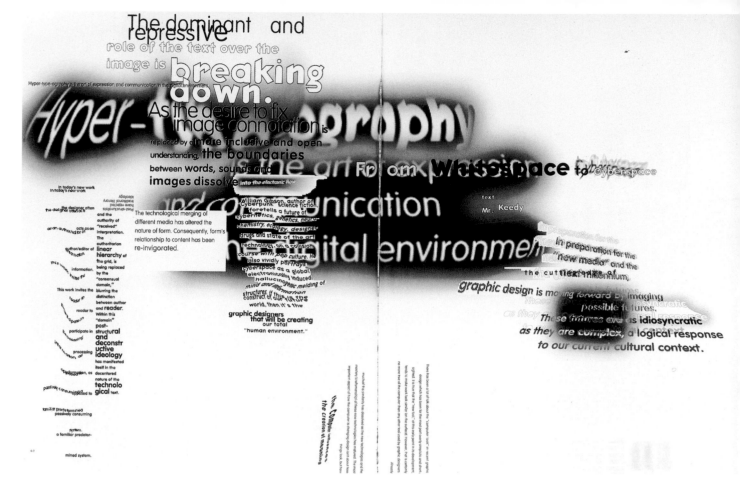

The dominant and repressive role of the text over the image is **breaking down.** As the desire to fix image connotation is replaced by a more inclusive and open understanding, **the boundaries** between words, sounds and **images dissolve** into the electronic flow.

Hyper-type-ography is a form of expression and communication in the digital environment.

Hyper- art of expression **-ography**

From whitespace to cyberspace

and communication digital environment

text
Mr. Keedy

The technological merging of different media has altered the nature of form. Consequently, form's relationship to content has been re-invigorated.

William Gibson, author of cyberpunk science fiction, foretells a future of cybernetics, genetics, neurochemistry, ecology, designer drugs and state of the art technology, on a collision course with pop culture. He also vividly portrays cyberspace as a global, electronically induced hallucinogenic melding of mind and information structures. If this is the construct of our future world, then it's the graphic designers that will be creating our total "human environment."

In today's new work the designer often acts as an author/editor of information. This work invites the reader to participate in processing

In preparation for the "new media" and the the cutting edge of the new millennium, graphic design is moving forward by imaging possible futures. These futures are as idiosyncratic as they are complex, a logical response to our current cultural context.

Jeffery Keedy. Fast Forward, book spread, California Institute of the Arts, USA, 1993

design is not the way that things look, but how 'the computer influences the creation of meaning'.[24]

The spirit of sweeping digital change was most fully and persuasively expressed in *Wired* magazine, launched in 1993 by editor and publisher Louis Rossetto. Under creative director John Plunkett, *Wired*'s use of design was instantly striking. In the first issue, the opening words of Marshall McLuhan's *The Medium is the Massage* float across the surface of three digital collages created by illustrator|designer Erik Adigard. 'The medium, or process, of our time – electric technology – is reshaping and restructuring patterns of social interdependence and every aspect of our personal life. It is forcing us to reconsider and re-evaluate practically every thought, every action, and every institution formerly taken for granted.'[25] Behind McLuhan's words drift melting images of a hand, a keyboard, a brain and people watching television translated into hallucinogenic shades of orange, green and pink. This set a pattern that would be repeated in every issue: *Wired*'s first two or three editorial spreads were devoted to a visual interpretation of a central idea extracted from one of the articles (although the second issue had another McLuhan quote against a background inspired by the first line of Gibson's *Neuromancer*: 'The sky ... was the color of television, tuned to a dead channel'). While almost every page of *Wired*, lavishly printed in pulsating fluorescent inks on a six-colour press, was a high-impact visual event, it was the magazine's pre-

"Immersive technology represents, on the **one** hand, the grail at the end of the history of cinema, and on the **other** hand, the beacon that draws creative energies toward the culmination of computing…

THE ROCK STAR, UP ON STAGE, BATHED IN LIGHT, INACCESSIBLE, IS AN OUTDATED IMAGE FROM A DEFUNCT SOCIETY.

DEFUNCT SOCIETY

IN A WORLD WHERE INFORMATION PLUS TECHNOLOGY EQUALS POWER, THOSE WHO CONTROL THE EDITING ROOMS RUN THE SHOW. DJs ARE EDITORS OF THE STREET. HUGH GALLAGHER

[Top] **Fred Davis. Wired,** no. 1.06, magazine spread, USA, 1993. Creative director: John Plunkett

[Above] **Erik Adigard, M.A.D. Wired,** no. 2.08, magazine spread, USA, 1994. Creative director: John Plunkett

contents page experiments that most vividly transmitted the impression that, as Keedy had claimed, digital design would be central to 'immersive technology'. 'In the world of immersion,' writes Brenda Laurel, a researcher into human-computer interaction, 'authorship is no longer the transmission of experience, but rather the construction of utterly personal experiences.' [26] *Wired*'s pages offered avid readers among the self-styled 'digerati' an intoxicating metaphor for what such immersion in the electronic flow might be like. In 1996, *Wired* published the first three years' worth of spreads as a book, *Mind Grenades: Manifestos from the Future*, a title that suggests – like much of P. Scott Makela's work – a nostalgia for a future that has yet to happen and that seems, on present evidence, unlikely to arrive soon. The Internet, rapidly colonized by commerce, is no longer a wild frontier. The dotcom bubble has burst and virtual reality, once touted as the answer to

SATYRS
+
CYBORGS

>>>Post-Edenic Garden of Technology

Erik Adigard, M.A.D. Architecture
Must Burn by Aaron Betsky and Erik
Adigard, visual essay spread, Thames
& Hudson, UK, 2000

everything, is the least of our concerns. *Wired* itself, now owned by Condé Nast, has become a business magazine like any other, and people find they are more attached to physical reality (not least paper) than the digital visionaries of the early 1990s liked to think.

The temperature of digital rhetoric may have cooled, but design is still produced, for the most part, on computers and this has irrevocably changed the way that many designers and design theorists think about design. In 2000, Adigard applied his experience with *Wired* to a series of visual essays for the book *Architecture Must Burn* by Aaron Betsky, then curator of architecture, design and digital projects at the San Francisco Museum of Modern Art.[27] Functioning much like *Wired*'s opening pages, Adigard's densely layered compositions are based on key ideas and phrases in the text, and image-led spreads are allowed to alternate on equal terms with text-led spreads. His digital interpretations have a rawness and an awkwardness that often seems deliberate – a textural embodiment of the book's claim that architecture is a form of 'unbuilding, collage and folding' that is ultimately about constructing the self. The text, too, is treated as an image; decentred within the book form's conventional hierarchies – in both the literal and postmodern senses – it flows outwards to the pages' boundaries, changing size and width from column to column and often within the same column. It is an effort to read it in a linear way and there is more text than seems necessary in a book that purports to be a 'manifesto', but ideas still jump out of the page, making their impact sensually as much as sequentially. For Betsky (and, it would seem, for Adigard) the 'electrosphere' composed of advertising, television, film and cyberspace is a postmodern 'floating world' with no material reality, nowhere yet everywhere:

'The floating world is the realm of the graphic designer. Ever more powerful computer technologies have expanded the scope of the floating world, giving them a great deal more freedom. Instead of cutting and pasting, they now assemble; rather than working with images they have prepared for the page, they can scan and manipulate whatever they want.... Information sprawls within the confines of the graphic designer's frame, but it does so in a way that the designer can control with absolute power.... Now that information is free to flow everywhere, graphic designers must invent compositions that no longer depend on physical structure.'[28]

To make sense of the floating world, argues Betsky, 'We must accept that what makes sense is not the law, syntax, rules or structure.'[29] Instead, he finds meaning in the way that information is delivered by the screen, announcing itself, then fading away in a blur, before it disappears behind new layers of information that, in turn, draw us towards other imagery (exactly the quality seen in Adigard's image-fields). In this quintessentially postmodern view, there is no moment of arrival, no meaning to form itself, just a perpetual journey in which signs that no longer refer to a pre- or post-existing reality offer their own mainly sensory forms of satisfaction and solace.

This might sound like an implausibly thin and inward-looking rationale for graphic communication. It takes as its starting point observable facts about the postmodern world, but in the process of formulation and expression it seems to become intoxicated with its own rhetoric and starts to float ecstatically free from the realm of everyday encounters with graphic messages of all kinds. In the enormous and ever-increasing volume of graphic production (which is, in itself, a postmodern phenomenon) most projects do, however, still have to concern themselves with communicating relatively defined and prosaic forms of message, even if the graphic languages they employ no longer conform to out-moded rules, syntax or structure. It may be true, as a generalization, that the viewer, like the designer at his screen, is floating through a boundless media-world with few fixed bearings. Many of the examples shown in this chapter express this sensation. But in a practical sense, people still make continuous choices about what to engage with or ignore and design still tries to seize attention for an instant, sometimes longer, in the hope of conveying an intelligible message. The danger with the simulated world of the screen is that its introverted excitements are so deliriously intense and absorbing that they begin to eclipse all other considerations. From this unreal perspective, scanning, manipulating and assembling at will, everything else also starts to look unreal. The 'process' – a word much used by designers in recent years – becomes an end in itself. [30]

Driven by changes in technology, graphic design is in a process of transition, which, at the time of writing, is still under way. In the last decade, the *look* of graphic design has changed enormously. It is now possible to cram a design with a quantity of imagery and detail that would have been unthinkable in most cases in earlier decades, when mechanical artworks were constructed at the drawing board layer by layer. A glistening perfection of finish that would once have exceeded even the finest draftsman is possible now as a matter of routine. Periodic reassertions of the communicational value of minimalism make no difference; if anything, they simply confirm that easily attainable complexity and spectacular graphic excess have become the new norms.

While the United States was at the forefront of technological design change from the mid-1980s to the mid-1990s, in the late 1990s other graphic cultures, which had been slower to embrace the computer's possibilities, began to pull design in new experimental directions. In Switzerland, birthplace of the International Style, younger designers such as Büro Destruct (founded in Berne in 1994), Martin Woodtli and Norm (both based in Zurich) moved into the professional spotlight. [31] Woodtli combines old and new versions of programs to produce deliberate errors that provoke the unexpected. He invents strange technological icons and pictograms that can be moved around, according to the temporary grammar of a given project, within his autonomous graphic worlds. 'Every work has its own materiality which arises from the tool – the computer.' [32] Norm, too, devise 'laws' for each assignment, discarding them for new rules when the project is completed. Their book, *Introduction*, is a studio manifesto that seeks to return

Norm. Introduction, spreads
from a self-published book,
Switzerland, 1999

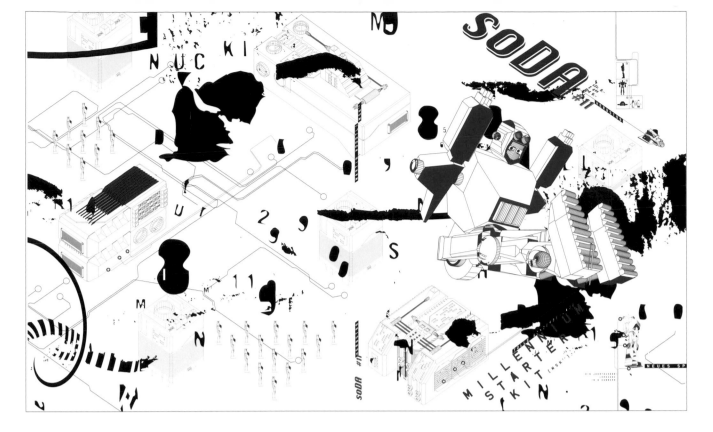

Martin Woodtli. Soda, no. 11,
magazine cover, front and back,
Switzerland, 1999

graphic design to zero. 'We want to talk about graphics via our own
medium – to articulate our reflections graphically. Not as cultural
theoreticians who don't have a clue about fonts,' explains team
member Manuel Krebs.[33] *Introduction* divides graphic representation
into four categories: things that occur in two-dimensional space,
but refer to something that exists in three dimensions; things
with no reference to three-dimensional space; things that refer
to nothing or to themselves; things that are unforeseeable, not
yet known. The diagrams and flow charts that result from this
investigation are fabulously intricate and impenetrable graphic
labyrinths that seem to negate the very clarity they seek. As self-
initiated experiments, they embody the continuing paradox
about contemporary graphic design. On one hand, design is our
omnipresent, everyday reality: 'Everyone lives within it, [yet] no
one discusses it.'[34] On the other, and perhaps for this very reason,
postmodern digital design culture has spawned an inventive and
energetic global subculture that often appears to exist mainly
to talk to itself about itself.

5

AUTHORSHIP

The emergence of the 'designer as author' is one of the key ideas in graphic design of the postmodern period. It is also one of the more problematic ideas, since, as some strands of critical theory would have it, the very notion of an 'author' as a validating source of authority for a cultural work is outdated, backward-looking and reactionary. This idea was most memorably expressed in Roland Barthes' essay 'The Death of the Author', first published in 1968, and the Author's demise has been regularly proclaimed as a desirable goal ever since, even though in every practical sense the author – not least the postmodernist cultural critic – continues to flourish. Barthes makes an argument which is in some ways perfectly logical and reasonable. He notes that, while we continue to search for the explanation of a literary work in the life and experiences of the man or woman who produced it, in reality a piece of writing is a 'tissue of quotations' that owes everything to the mass of writing that preceded it. A text is 'not a line of words releasing a single "theological" meaning (the "message" of the Author-God) but a multidimensional space in which a variety of writings, none of them original, blend and clash'.[1] Take away the author, argues Barthes, and all claims to decipher a text and attribute to it a final, definitive meaning become futile. He proposes instead a process of disentangling the multiplicity of texts: 'the structure can be followed, "run" (like the thread of a stocking) at every point and at every level, but there is nothing beneath: the space of the writing is to be ranged over, not pierced'.[2] With the author pushed into the wings, the reader – usually overlooked by criticism – can take centre stage. It is the reader, not the writer, who decides the meaning of the multiple quotations that compose a text, the reader who gives a text its unity, and it is consequently the reader on whom the future of writing depends. Barthes famously concludes: 'the birth

"Rol and
Bar
the author is
de ad!
Man!
Punctum!
Punctum?"
Punctum?

Bob Aufuldish. Selected Notes 2
ZeitGuys by Mark Bartlett, detail from
a feature in **Zed,** no. 2, USA, 1995

of the reader must be at the cost of the death of the Author.'[3]

As we saw in chapter 2, designers attuned to postmodern theory and its popular expressions have often invoked the reader or viewer using similar ideas and terms. Their aim, they said, was not to impose a single closed and restrictive reading, but to provide open structures that encourage the audience's participation and interpretation. Yet there was usually not the smallest hint of self-effacement, let alone a deathwish, in this strategy. Experimental design drew attention to itself and the inevitable result was to throw the spotlight on its makers. Since the earliest days of commercial art, a handful of designers had always become 'stars' of the profession, their work lauded in trade magazines, exhibitions and sometimes in monographs. Nevertheless, professional rhetoric insisted, at least until the 1960s (and sometimes even today), that design was essentially an anonymous activity, and in many ways it was and still is: few members of the public would be able to name even one graphic designer. In the 1980s, as design's sense of its own importance grew, so did its fascination with itself. The number of informal 'show and tell' lectures by designers and well-attended conferences featuring the same travelling band of international design luminaries increased dramatically. The nature of design journalism also changed. Enthusiastic profiles became commonplace, paying as much attention to the designers' personalities as their designs, and many books appeared celebrating individual bodies of work. A few graphic designers – Neville Brody, David Carson, Tibor Kalman – even attracted attention in mainstream media, where they were presented as significant shapers of contemporary visual culture.

The tendency then, in the last 20 years, has been for graphic designers of all kinds to assert their presence and significance. Other people may view them as a group whose job is to take a client's message and express it as effectively as possible in a spirit of neutral professionalism, and design rhetoric has often endorsed this interpretation of design's role. However, the motives that lead someone to become a designer have always been more complicated than this suggests. The act of designing can never be an entirely neutral process, since the designer always brings something extra to the project.[4] A design cannot fail to be informed, in some measure, by personal taste, cultural understanding, social and political beliefs, and deeply held æsthetic preferences. Moreover, designers have always insisted that, to function effectively, they need to question and perhaps 'rewrite' the client's brief. They have argued that the client's understanding of the communication problem may be imperfect and that this is why the client needs their help in the first place. At the same time, designers are motivated by the need for creative satisfaction and peer approval, significant but sometimes unacknowledged factors that have a powerful determining effect on their work.

Aesthesipol, 1982
10" solid extruded aluminum rod,
TV, and pay phone

None of this is sufficient, though, to make a designer an
'author' and, before the late 1980s, few designers – not even the
most idiosyncratic – would have described their own design practice
in terms of 'graphic authorship'. The phrase 'designer as author'
did not achieve wider currency until the mid-1990s, although it is
still primarily a North American phenomenon, and remains
controversial and prone to misunderstanding. Canadian designer
Bruce Mau was one of the earliest, most self-aware and deliberate
exponents of the idea. Citing Walter Benjamin's essay 'The Author
as Producer' (1934), and neatly reversing the image, Mau said he
wanted to occupy the role of 'the producer as author'.[5] In the early
1980s, he worked as a designer at Pentagram in London before
returning, disenchanted, to Toronto, where he set up the firm Public
Good, specializing in social, cultural and educational design work.
Bruce Mau Design, his second venture, came to wider attention in
1986, with the publication of *Zone 1|2*, a collection of academic essays
about the contemporary city that was anything but dry or detached.
Mau interspersed the texts, floating elegantly in spacious margins,
with stills from disaster movies, fold-out images by video artists,
city maps on see-through paper, and splashes of colour as vivid as a
Warhol screenprint. *Zone* was a desirable object in which the graphic
designer had clearly played a significant shaping role, and in this
and many subsequent projects for Zone Books, Mau's designs
combined serious intellectual intent with unapologetic sensual
appeal in a way that was soon imitated by other academic
publishers. His aim, he explained in 1994, was to 'roll Bruce Mau
Design on to the field upon which content is developed'.[6] In his

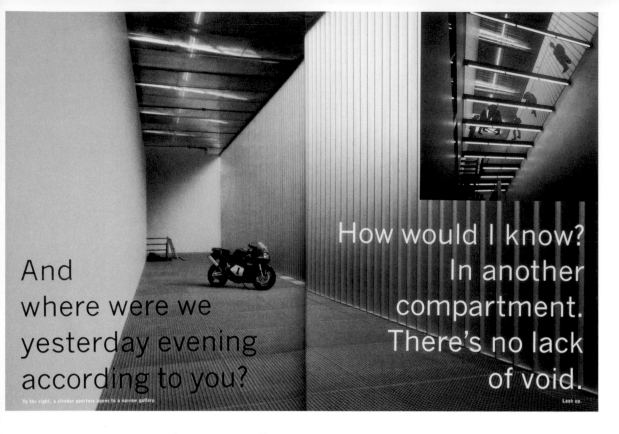

And where were we yesterday evening according to you?

To the right, a slender aperture opens to a narrow gallery.

How would I know? In another compartment. There's no lack of void.

Look up.

Bruce Mau. S,M,L,XL by O.M.A., Rem Koolhaas and Bruce Mau, book spread, 010/Monacelli Press, The Netherlands|USA, 1995

book *Life Style* (2000), Mau develops this idea by showing two diagrams that represent the typical trajectory of a book project and then the course he would prefer it to take. In the first, the designer arrives on the scene at the end of the research process, after all the key decisions about editorial content have been taken, and is allotted the task of giving form to the content. In Mau's preferred model, the designer undertakes research and the refinement of ideas from the project's inception, sometimes alongside the writer, sometimes exploring other possibilities independently. He writes:

'The new approach replaces division of labor with synthesis, clients and commissions with collaborators and partners, executing tasks with negotiating terrain, maximum output with maximum feedback, and form applied to content with form and content evolving and enriching each other simultaneously.... We are not sure whether this new way of working means the end of design, or whether it means designers become authors, or authors become designers, or all three.'[7]

Mau's collaboration with Dutch architect Rem Koolhaas on the book *S,M,L,XL* (1995) was the most exhaustive and overwhelming example of this approach.[8] The book took five years to complete, expanded from a planned 264 pages to an eventual 1,344 pages, and almost bankrupted Mau's studio in the process. Divided into four main sections corresponding to small, medium, large and extra-large projects, *S,M,L,XL* unfolds with a cinematic momentum and grasp of the relationship between images. Like the film director Chris Marker, whom he admires, Mau is prepared to 'hold a shot too long' to encourage the audience to look more closely.[9] It might be argued that the content is still essentially Koolhaas' – it is his career, his

PERIOD STYLES :
A HISTORY OF PUNCTUATION

The Herb Lubalin Study Center of Design and Typography ; The Cooper Union for the Advancement of Science and Art.

Ellen Lupton. Period Styles: A History of Punctuation, catalogue cover, The Cooper Union, USA, 1988

body of work, his writing – but Mau's visualization endows this daunting mass of material with a structural presence that far exceeds an ordinary monograph's. On the cover, Mau receives equal billing with Koolhaas as co-author, a degree of recognition achieved by few other designers.

As Mau argues, a close engagement with content is clearly essential before anything like authorship can be claimed. Mau's approach relied on finding clients who would respect and trust him sufficiently to invite him to become involved in their projects at an early stage. Other designers initiate their own projects and are unambiguously responsible for their content, which they generate entirely or largely themselves. In this respect, Ellen Lupton and J. Abbott Miller were two of the most significant designer|authors to emerge in the late 1980s. As with Mau, research was central to their conception of design practice and they made this commitment explicit in the three-word manifesto with which, in 1985, they titled their alliance: Design|Writing|Research. Steeped in the work of theorists such as Saussure, Derrida and Foucault, they wrote extensively as critics for design publications such as *Print*, *Emigre* and *Eye*. As curator of the Herb Lubalin Study Center at The Cooper Union art school in New York, from 1986 to 1990, Lupton created many exhibitions about design in which she combined a number of roles that would usually be separated: researcher, writer, editor, exhibition designer and catalogue designer. In an essay about the history of numbers for a 'Writing|Culture' monograph published by The Cooper Union, she illustrates her text by integrating images into the lines of type, allowing them to stand as numerical and pictorical representations of the words they replace. Miller, based at the Design|Writing|Reseach studio in Manhattan, founded in 1989, undertook editorial design and exhibition design projects in which he could achieve close editorial involvement and, from 1997, he was editor and art director of the visual culture magazine *2wice*. In one of their most ambitious collaborations as author|curators, *The ABCs of* ▲ ■ ●: *The Bauhaus and Design Theory* (1991), Lupton and Miller demonstrate how writing and design might be brought together in a new critical relationship: 'Modern art education often discourages graphic designers from actively engaging in the writing process … Instead, the graphic designer could be conceived of as a language-worker equipped to actively initiate projects – either by literally authoring texts or by elaborating, directing or disrupting their meaning. The graphic designer "writes" verbal|visual documents by arranging, sizing, framing, and editing images and texts.'[10]

Lupton's 'Visual Dictionary' applies this principle to the exploration of four techniques for organizing textual and pictorial material: graph, translation, grid and figure. Pages are conceived graphically, with equal attention to verbal and visual meaning and a commitment to design possibilities that is highly unusual in historical and critical documents about visual culture. On a spread dealing with the grid, Lupton presents a series of observations as short, separate notes, with their concluding words and phrases detached from the sentence and shifted by the page grid (here made visible) into an adjacent column to demonstrate its use for purposes of discontinuity, cutting and framing. Just as language is a grid which breaks down experience into repeatable signs – according to Lupton's reading of Saussure – so the grid itself is a form of language.

Lupton and Miller's positioning of themselves as writers and their fusion of writing and design gave credibility to any claim they might make to be 'graphic authors'. In 1996, the publication of *Design Writing Research*, a compilation of their critical writings on theory, design and media, confirmed their leading role.[11] With this book, they joined the ranks of designers who have formulated their ideas and principles in book form – figures such as Jan Tschichold, Emil Ruder, Josef Müller-Brockmann and Paul Rand. In the early 1990s, as discussion of authorship became more impassioned, it

The English word *score* means "a cut or indentation"; it also refers to the number twenty. The word gets its double meaning from an object called a *tally stick*, a length of wood or bone marked with a series of scratches ▦▦▦▦. The twentieth cut on a tally stick is sometimes called a *score*. Tally sticks have appeared in literate and non-literate cultures from prehistory to the present; they keep time, count objects, and record credits and debts.

The simplest form of tally is marked with one notch for each item recorded: to count five sheep 🐑🐑🐑🐑🐑, a shepherd might make five scratches on a stick ▌▌▌▌▌. This principle is called *ordering*: there is a one-to-one correspondence between the set of symbols and the set of objects counted. Ordering is also at work in modern dice, where ⚃ equals five, and in playing cards, where ⁙ is the five of diamonds.

The principle of *grouping* arranges an ordered collection of signs into smaller sets. Groups on a tally stick might be indicated with larger and smaller cuts ▦▦▦▦, or straight lines and diagonals ▦▦▦▦. In a tally convention familiar today, ||||̸ represents five single strokes grouped in a bundle.

The ancient principles of ordering and grouping have little relation to spoken numbers, arising not so much from the will to record speech as from the need to keep track or "keep score" of objects or events. Whereas the Hindu-Arabic symbol 3 corresponds with the spoken number "three," a particular tick on a score pad, such as the third mark in the series ||||, is a graphic substitute for an event (the winning of a point). Linguists call this kind of mark *indexical*: there is a relationship of cause and effect between the sign and its referent, as in foot prints 🐾 or a curve mapped on a graph ⩘. The figure X, for example, is not only a phonetic letter but a sign in its own right, serving as a record or "index" of events: X stands for a signature ✍, or X signals an act of ☒ selection or an act of deletion. X is also the Roman numeral for ten.

Roman numerals were the dominant written numbers in Europe from the period of the Roman empire until the rise of the Hindu-Arabic system. Employing the principles of ordering and grouping, Roman numerals consist of a graphic symbol for each power of ten (I, X, C, M), and for each subdivision of five (V, L, D). The numeral III represents three as one one one, and CCC represents three hundred as hundred hundred hundred.

The forms of the Roman numerals coincide with the Roman alphabet, but they may actually derive from tally markings. In tallies, the single vertical mark ❚ commonly represents one, while two diagonal cuts, such as ◪ or ◩, stand for five, and a crossed stroke such as ◙ or ◛ indicates ten. The Roman numeral D is half of the symbol ⊕, an ancient form of the sign for one thousand. The origins of the Roman numerals thus lie in a pre-alphabetic style of writing,

For material on early number systems, this essay relies on Georges Ifrah, *From One to Zero: A Universal History of Numbers* (New York: Viking Penguin, 1981, 1985), and Karl Menninger, *Number Words and Number Symbols: A Cultural History of Numbers* (Cambridge: MIT Press, 1958, 1969).

The English word *calculate* comes from the Latin *calculus*, meaning "small stone." Like tally sticks, stones are an ancient counting tool which, in their simplest application, require no verbal number sequence to operate: one stone is collected ⬤⬤⬤⬤⬤ for every object counted 🐑🐑🐑🐑🐑.

A counting technique used by the Sumerians beginning around 8000 B.C. involved small "tokens" manufactured out of clay ◖◗◐◑. Invented during the period when agriculture was supplanting an economy of hunting and gathering, tokens probably recorded business transactions between such parties as the temple government and a shepherd responsible for some 🐑🐑🐑.

Groups of tokens dating from around 3200 B.C. have been found enclosed in sealed clay envelopes. The shapes of tokens were impressed into the clay container, one sign for each token. Thus the envelope could be "read" without being cracked open, the three-dimensional tokens inside offering a hidden guarantee for the graphic signs on the outside.

Soon, however, the marks impressed into the envelopes replaced the tokens altogether, and records were kept on small clay tablets instead. The production of tokens appears to have ceased around 3100 B.C., when a system for graphically recording the spoken language was emerging in Sumeria. The new script retained some symbols from the older token system, but a basic conceptual change took place. Each token had represented a *quantity* of a *particular* product: a clay disc marked ✿, for example, stood for 🐑, and could not be used to count anything else. The collection ✿✿✿✿✿ signified 🐑🐑🐑🐑🐑: number and object were fused together. The new writing system, however, paired a separate number symbol with a sign for the object, so that [⚏] meant four 🐑. The number symbol 𒐉 might be paired with the sign for any other object. Number was now independent from physical things: with the rise of written language came a move away from concrete thought and towards abstraction.

Modern English contains a few words which signify a *plurality* of *particular* objects: a flock of 🐑🐑🐑🐑, a herd of 🐄🐄🐄🐄, or a school of 🐟🐟🐟🐟. The English word "pair" names objects or groups of objects to which *doubleness* is a natural state: a *pair* of 👟👟, a pair of ✄, a pair of ◗◖. Modern Japanese has separate "number classes" for different objects; words called "counters" are inserted between the number word and the name of the object counted: for example, *dai* for vehicles, *hai* for glassfuls, *ma* for rooms, *mai* for thin, flat objects, *hon* for long, cylindrical objects, *go o sya* for train car numbers, and so on. Linguists consider conventions such as these remnants of an older, less abstract stage of thought, which conceived of number as an integral characteristic of the objects counted.

For material on Sumerian tokens, see Denise Schmandt-Besserat, "Tokens: Facts and Interpretations," *Visible Language*, Vol. XX, No. 3 (Summer, 1986), 250-273.

---

grid

A **grid** organizes space according to an x and y axis.

The **grid**, a structural form pervading Bauhaus art and design, articulates space according to a pattern of oppositions: vertical and horizontal, top and bottom, orthogonal and diagonal, and left and right.

Another opposition engaged by the **grid** is the opposition of **continuity** and **discontinuity**.

On the one hand, the axes of the **grid** suggest the infinite, continuous extension of a plane in four directions; at the same time, the **grid** marks off that plane into distinct sections.

The **grid** is the underlying structure of the **chart** or **graph**, which organizes data according to an x and y axis. The data in a chart can be plotted as a continuous line, or it can be dispersed across the **grid** in columns and rows of discrete figures.

Figure 1 is an exercise from Johannes Itten's Basic Course, in which students were asked to assemble patches of materials in a loose **grid**; many of the materials themselves are structured as **grids**, such as cloth, wire mesh, and basketry each fragment invokes the extended field of fabric from which it was cut.

Kandinsky called a four-square **grid** *"the prototype of linear expression,"* it is an elementary diagram of two-dimensional space. [Figure 2] Similarly, the Dutch de Stijl movement, headed by Theo van Doesburg, identified the **grid** as the fundamental origin of art. The de Stijl **grid** suggests both the infinite extension of an object beyond its boundaries, and the cutting of this vast continuum into distinctly framed fields.

Conventional Western writing and typography is organized on a **grid**: a generic page consists of horizontal rows of type arranged in a rectangular block. Van Doesburg foregrounded the **grid** of conventional typography by framing fields of type with heavy bars. He also applied the grid to the alphabet, translating its traditionally organic, continuous, individualized forms into discontinuous, repetitive elements.

Although van Doesburg was not invited to join the Bauhaus faculty, he influenced the school by holding informal seminars in Weimar. De Stijl principles are evident in the typography produced at the Bauhaus by Laszlo Moholy-Nagy, Josef Albers, Herbert Bayer, and Joost Schmidt.

As described by Saussure, language is also a kind of **grid**: language articulates the *"uncharted nebula"* of pre-linguistic thought into distinct elements, breaking down the infinitely gradated continuum of experience into repeatable signs. Language is a **grid**, and a **grid** is a language.

Figure 1 Texture exercise by W. Diekmann, 1922, a student of Itten. The exercise is described in a 1925-6 curriculum statement as "Collecting and systematically tabulating samples of materials" (Wingler 109). The exercise also appeared at the New Bauhaus in Chicago; Moholy-Nagy labelled one example "Tactile chart / A dictionary of the different qualities of touch sensations, such as pain, pricking, temperature, vibration, etc." (68).

Figure 2 Kandinsky described the four-square grid as the "prototype of linear expression... the most primitive form of the division of a schematic plane" (66).

Figure 3 Advertisements from the magazine De Stijl, 1921, published by Theo van Doesburg. The design foregrounds the grid structure of conventional typography; van Doesburg has inverted the last line, playing with established syntax.

Figure 4 Moholy-Nagy's 1927 prospectus for 8 Bauhaus Books shows the influence of de Stijl.

Figure 5 De Stijl Alphabet, van Doesburg, 1917

Figure 6 Stencil alphabet, Josef Albers, 1925

"Without language, thought is a vague, uncharted nebula... Thought, chaotic by nature, has to become ordered in the process of its decomposition. Language works out its units while taking shape between two shapeless masses."

Figure 7 Saussure writes that before the emergence of language, the realms of sound and thought are continuous, amorphous planes. Language functions like a grid, cutting up the "uncharted" continuum of experience into signs.

[Top] **Ellen Lupton. Numbers,** catalogue spread, The Cooper Union, USA, 1989

[Above] **Ellen Lupton, J. Abbott Miller and Mike Mills. The ABCs of ▲■●: The Bauhaus and Design Theory,** catalogue spread, The Cooper Union, USA, 1991

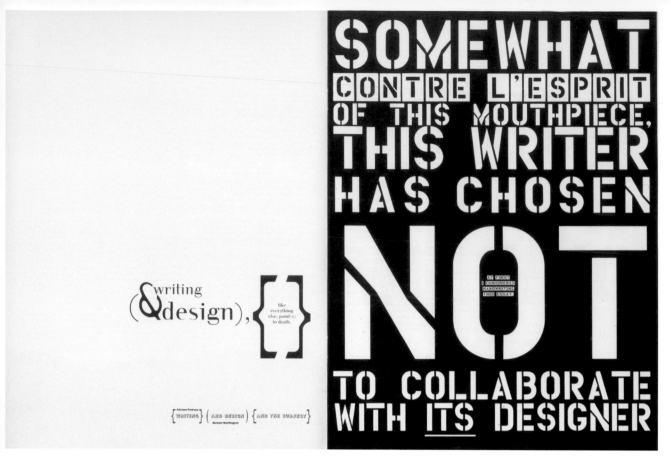

writing (&design), {} like everything else, point(s) to death.

{ Adrienne Pedrose
WRITING } (AND DESIGN) { AND THE SUBJECT }
Michael Worthington

SOMEWHAT CONTRE L'ESPRIT OF THIS MOUTHPIECE, THIS WRITER HAS CHOSEN NOT TO COLLABORATE WITH ITS DESIGNER

AT FIRST I CONSIDERED HANDWRITING THIS ESSAY.

Michael Worthington. Emigre, no. 35, 'Mouthpiece' issue, magazine spread, USA, 1995

seemed that writing would need to play a central role and that only those designers capable of total authorship – undertaking both writing and design – could hope to become fully fledged graphic authors. Following Lupton and Miller's example, this period was marked by an upsurge of interest in theoretical and critical writing among young designers, particularly in the United States, much of it published in the pages of *Emigre, Eye, Visible Language* and *Zed*.[12] In 1993, in an essay titled 'What has Writing got to do with Design?', American designer and design educator Anne Burdick challenged designers' ingrained reluctance to accept that graphic design is an inseparable marriage of the verbal and visual, and argued that design's written content should receive much closer attention. 'Writing can feed the profession in two ways: through the challenge of critical analysis and through the exploratory freedom of self-initiated work,' notes Burdick.[13] Her arguments are vigorous and convincing, yet her concluding words – 'Designers should write not in order to become better writers, but to become better designers' – suggest definite though somewhat arbitrary limits to authorial ambition.[14] In 1995, Burdick guest-edited two issues of *Emigre*, with the overall title 'Mouthpiece: Clamor over Writing and Design'.[15] Some writers undertook the design of their own writing. In other cases, Burdick brought writers and designers together in more or less sympathetic pairings intended to 'explore and exploit the privileged position of authorship'.[16] The essays are hugely disparate in form, giving rise to the 'clamor' of the title, but considered as

[Top] **Louise Sandhaus.** Emigre, no. 36, 'Mouthpiece' issue, magazine spread, USA, 1995

[Above] **Denise Gonzales Crisp.** Emigre, no. 35, 'Mouthpiece' issue, magazine spread, USA, 1995. Illustrations by Tom Tierney

individual pieces they involve design in a more active process than conventional publishing hierarchies and divisions of labour allow. They are often successful, too, in substantiating Burdick's claim, repeated by many designers at the time, that when words are made material in the form of typography, the meanings of 'writing' and 'design' cannot be separated. The designer, as initiator or working partner, shares responsibility with the writer for the production of meaning, though whether this is an equal responsibility remains a moot point.

Burdick, seemingly aware of the problems of authorship raised by Barthes and others, is careful to avoid suggesting that authorship is an attempt by designers to seize control of areas of the editorial process to which they have traditionally been denied access. Yet the central appeal of authorship for some graphic designers, irrespective of its inherent complexities, is precisely that it recognizes and elevates the position of the designer. The power struggle this is likely to involve was made explicit in the introduction to the exhibition 'Designer as Author: Voices and Visions' in 1996 at Northern Kentucky University. 'Author as authority manifests itself in print and electronic media across most disciplines, from serious scholarship to lowbrow tabloids,' writes co-curator Steven McCarthy. 'Designers as authors realize that despite some influence emanating from the domain of visual image and typographic form, a truly powerful weapon is to control the words themselves, and therefore more of the message.'[17]

In cases where the designer does not have control of the words – that is, in most cases – authorship remains, at best, a questionable concept. Designers have always determined or helped to determine the final form of a text, but this is a relatively minor aspect of its meaning compared to its factual content and the intricacies of argument it might contain. As one of Bruce Mau's former collaborators puts it: 'You can't claim authorship because you made the page pink.'[18] The centrality of form and surface in postmodern culture, often at the expense of content, and a McLuhan-esque belief that it is the overarching medium rather than the specific message that counts, contributes to designers' sense that design deserves greater attention and encourages the view that style itself is a sufficient form of content. Yet, as Burdick recognizes in her criticisms of designers' word-blindness, this argument is often based on a strategy of simply ignoring the communicative potential of words: the designer does not happen to read and concludes that reading must therefore be unimportant to everyone else.

In the most fully realized and persuasive examples of postmodern graphic authorship, the designer has full control over the text, as commissioner, editor or writer. Such work tends to take place in self-determined spaces and venues free from the constraints of client-given design and, for this reason, some see it as peripheral to design's core concerns as a service-providing activity. In the 1980s, some of the most significant and influential designer|authors emerged from the genre of the artist's book. These book artists were

CRIMES AGAINST LANGUAgE: MEAT WAS EXPECTED FROM THE MEAL. & FOLLOWING Sunset's sweet demise, a vanishing single point of reference, the phone jack was disconnected from the wall, hanging by a wire, signs of its past attachment still visible. If I

SELF and OTHER Late afternoon melodrama wide open TO THE AIR BLOWS THE HEADSTRONG CURTAIN BACK WITH The Breeze. CHASE'S FALL: in the way, the chair trips his backward retreat. Beyond circumstances,

Johanna Drucker. Against Fiction,
page from an artist's book, USA, 1983

not designers in the professional sense of the term, so they were not inhibited by the rules and codes of disciplinary practice, even if they used similar resources and forms. Their primary motivation was the expression of their own content and they taught themselves the techniques needed to articulate this effectively. In the United States, Johanna Drucker combined an academic career as teacher and author of *The Visible Word* (1994), *The Alphabetic Labyrinth* (1995) and *The Century of Artists' Books* (1995) with the production, starting in the early 1970s, of a series of experimental books, which she wrote, edited, designed and sometimes illustrated and printed by letterpress. Instead of feeling restricted by the physical limitations of letterpress, Drucker used its characteristics to structure her books and extend the investigation of language in printed form. In *Against Fiction* (1983), her intention was to deconstruct and subvert the formal conventions of traditional fiction by dismantling the linear mechanism by which it usually functions. Inspired by Peter Eisenman's architecture book *House X* (1982), each page is a transformation of the preceding page, retaining some of its formal elements and adding or rearranging others. Headlines, subtitles and short paragraphs help to make Drucker's demanding prose more accessible. In *The History of the/my Wor(l)d* (1990), an autobiographical work printed in letterpress in an edition of 70 copies, Drucker interweaves themes of official history and private memory, using linguistic play, visual puns and typographic experiment. She divides the page into a main text in large letters, interrupted by smaller

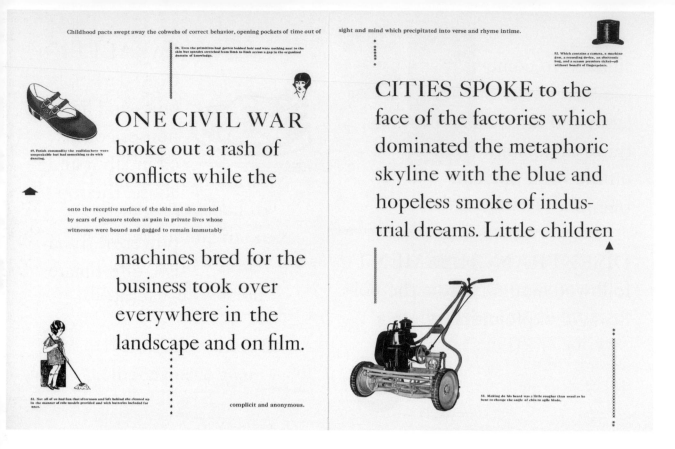

Johanna Drucker. The History of the|my
World, spread from an artist's book, USA, 1990

caption-like texts in red and found photo-engravings of glamorous women, majorettes, tools, machinery and articles of apparel. Drucker explains the book's theoretical premise:

'The main narrative line offers a feminist critique of history and memory. The smaller, more intimate red-printed line which constantly erupts through it is the force of personal memory taking issue with Lacanian-influenced feminist theory in its assignment of a masculine and exclusively patriarchal role to language. The premise of this work was that there was no world, only the knowing of it in and through language, and that the knowing of one's self was parallel to this, a construction of and in language through its acquisition.'[19]

Warren Lehrer, another important American book artist, studied painting at the City University of New York, where he first began to combine letterforms and words with hand-drawn marks and discovered concrete poetry, the collages of Kurt Schwitters and the books of Diter Rot. Believing that graphic design meant 'avant-garde research into visual literature', Lehrer enrolled at Yale University to study graphic design, though soon found himself at odds with the prevailing corporate ethos.[20] His first book, *Versations* (1980), is a typographically expressive, music score-like transcription in three languages – English, French and Chinese – of conversations he had tape-recorded. In *French Fries* (1984), written with Dennis Bernstein and published in an edition of 1,000 copies, Lehrer created a fiction of great visual complexity in which dozens of typefaces, images and shapes, and hundreds of screen tints build up

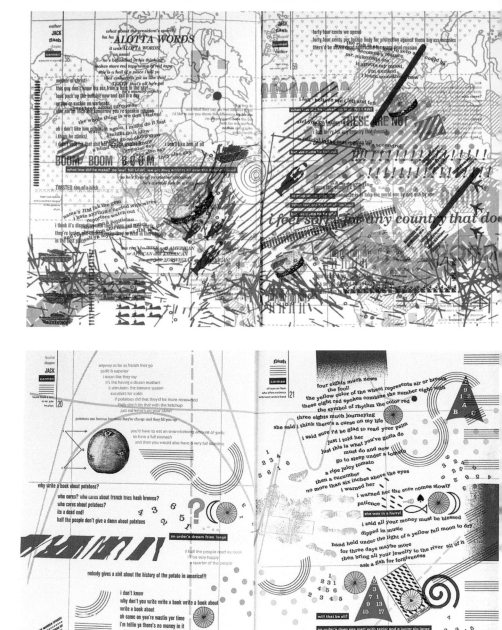

Warren Lehrer. French Fries, spreads
from an artist's book, USA, 1984

to form densely layered compositions of immense energy. The story,
originally performed as a play, is set in a Dream Queen fast-food
restaurant after a murder has taken place and the cast of characters
includes a manager, a cashier, four customers and many others, all
babbling away in their own voices represented by Univers, Bembo,
Helvetica, Kabel, Century Schoolbook, Clarendon, Bodoni, Cooper
Black, Futura, and other faces. Other kinds of sound such as a
blaring radio, a juke box and people talking on the phone are
also expressed graphically.

As one reviewer noted, books such as *French Fries* challenge
readers to explore the act of reading: to break with the usual linear
pattern, vary the pace, look back at earlier passages, or skip ahead.[21]
Lehrer's typographic experiments anticipated new directions in
1990s graphic design by several years. With his 'Portrait Series',

you just lie there on your mat in one position like a statue
with the horrible world buzzing around you
threatening to sting again at any moment

then after an hour or so you have to urinate
only you can't help but remember the times
you've gotten into trouble for having to urinate
asking to urinate or actually urinating in isolation rooms
but you have to do something
so you shove your face back up against
the tiny window in the large door and you look out
but there's no one there
no one to open the door and let you go to the bathroom
like any decent human being would do
for another human being
or even for a quarter of a human being
not to mention an animal

then you get to thinking that if you were a dog
and you had to pee
someone would in all likelihood take you for a walk
and you could breathe the fresh air
and they most likely would pet you and stroke you
and show some affection for you
cause that's a natural tendency
that humans have towards dogs
but nobody comes

you feel like you're gonna pee right then and there
you start knocking against the door
with the palm of your hand
but nobody comes

it gets to the point where
you can hardly hold it in any longer
so you knock some more
you knock and knock and knock
but nobody comes

your bladder feels like it's gonna finally explode
so you just pee right on the floor
the pee spills out beyond the door
the next morning one of the
two-hundred-pound attendants
wakes you up at six o'clock
sticks a broom in your gut and says
now clean it up
asshole!
through a haze of too much weird medication
you feel the broom against your gut

you don't even move
then you hear

**either you
clean the fuckin
floor with this
broom right
fuckin now
or you can use
your tongue to
do it later**

in terms of dignity that's got to be in your top five

you feel proud
fit as a fiddle
and ready to take on a new day

when dennis and connie and warren and biaja come to visit
we all squeeze into the ten-foot-square visiting room
and drum against the plastic lime green chairs
until the inevitable
keep it down in there
one time we were having so much fun
one of the two-hundred-pound attendants opened up
the visiting room door
looked dennis in the eyes
and said
**listen
if you don't keep it down
we got straightjackets
for all you people
especially you
mr. bernstein!**
unlike my parents and most of my relatives
these friends distrusted the mental health system

the things i come up with
nobody
nobody else could think of

at my age

i am looking at myself

i am looking at myself

i have screwed up a lot

i think i know... what the problem might be

i have an inability to belong

i have a resistance to belonging to anybody

to anyplace   to anything

i strive   to belong

not

to possess

Warren Lehrer. Charlie, book spread, Bay Press, USA, 1995

[Right] **Warren Lehrer. Claude,** book spread, Bay Press, USA, 1995

published in 1995 as a quartet of low-cost trade paperbacks rather than as limited edition artist's books, he showed how 'visual literature' could be used to engage broader audiences. Each of the volumes is a biographical monologue, recounting the life story and experiences of four of Lehrer's male acquaintances: Claude, Brother Blue, Charlie, and Nicky D. The books are unusually tall and narrow, reflecting the human proportions of their subjects, who are shown on their covers. Each character is assigned his own principal typeface, though more than 20 others are used in each book. In *Charlie*, a portrait of Charles Lang, a gifted musician with mental health problems, short lines of lower-case Gill Sans are ranged left like poetry; the text switches fluently into different typefaces and changes in size and layout, depending on the needs of the narrative, which is illustrated by Charlie's sketches. In *Claude*, a portrait of Claude Debs – painter, film-maker, entrepreneur, doctor, fashion photographer and undercover spy – the main type, Garamond, is centred in dense blocks, with individual phrases separated by slashes in an outpouring of reflection and sexual confession. Lehrer's books evoke the subjective experience of their subjects with great particularity and vividness, suggesting the possibility of a new literary genre that makes full use of design's rhetorical dimension. However, experiments of this kind remain a rarity in the bookshops.

In Britain, Jake Tilson's self-published magazines and books share the Pop Art exuberance of Lehrer's *French Fries*. Educated as a

painter, Tilson made the rapid, low-cost, readily available print
methods that designers usually shun – photocopying, instantprint,
even rubber stamping – central to his work. He did not set out to
flout the rules of publishing; he simply did not know what they were.
In the late 1970s and 1980s, Tilson made a stream of photocopy editions
in which his habitual themes – travel, geography, time – emerge from
compressed science fiction narratives inspired by his readings of
William Burroughs and J.G. Ballard. *The V Agents* (1981) is a collage tale
of global paranoia and possible apocalypse cast in the form of a spiral-
bound sketchpad; *The V Agents part 2* (1984) continues the story through
a series of alphabetical file cards and interleaved images supplied, like
snacks or toys, in a polythene bag. In the five-volume *Breakfast Special*
(1989), published in an edition of 100, Tilson presents five alternative
views of Mr Emerson, a character who reappears in different guises
throughout his *oeuvre*. Mr Emerson leaves an apartment and enters a

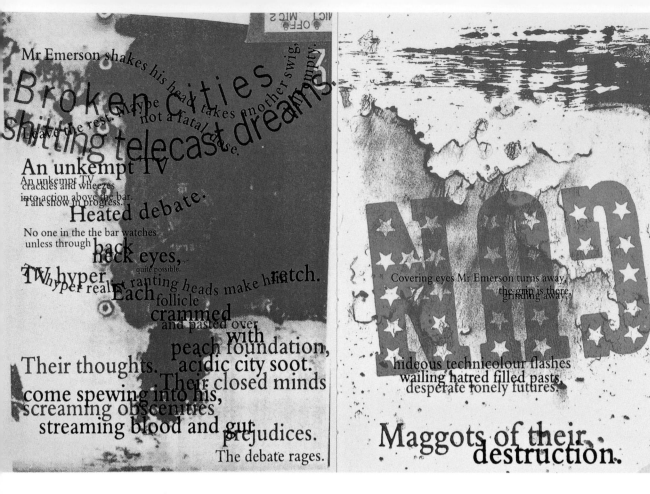

The following is text that appears within the artwork:

Mr Emerson shakes his head, takes another swig.
Maybe the rest of it? Maybe not a fatal dose.
Broken cities
shitting telecast dreams.

An unkempt TV
An unkempt TV
crackles and wheezes
into action above the bar.
Talk show in progress.

Heated debate.

No one in the the bar watches
unless through black
neck eyes,
quite possible.
TV hyper
Why hyper real? ranting heads make him retch.
Each follicle
crammed
and pasted over
with
peach foundation,
Their thoughts. acidic city soot.
Their closed minds
come spewing into his,
screaming obscenities,
streaming blood and gut prejudices.
The debate rages.

Covering eyes Mr Emerson turns away,
the grin is there,
grinding away.

GRIN

hideous technicolour flashes
wailing hatred filled pasts,
desperate lonely futures.

Maggots of their
destruction.

Jake Tilson. **The Terminator Line,**
spread from an artist's book,
Woolley Dale Press, UK, 1991

café for breakfast in Arezzo, Paris, New York, Barcelona and London, and these international scene changes give Tilson the opportunity to mount an exploration of local detail and atmosphere in which typography is as vital to the descriptive effect as the imagery with which it merges. The photocopied pages are sprinkled with tiny hand-glued Xeroxes, individually applied rubber stamp marks and hand-drawn lines, letters and numbers, fusing in informal but delicate compositions. Mr Emerson and the V Agents return in *The Terminator Line* (1991) where Tilson, continuing to avoid the by this time ubiquitous Macintosh computer, weaves lines of free-flowing, hand-positioned type into multilayered photocopy arabesques of considerable complexity.

Few professional designers operate, or seek to operate, at this level of authorship, working with self-initiated content that expresses a strong and consistent individual vision. However, in the course of the 1990s, two British creative teams, Tomato and Fuel, became identified with an authorial approach to design. Tomato, founded in 1991, was unusual in arguing that there was no essential distinction between its projects for clients and self-initiated projects by team members (Steve Baker, Michael Horsham, Karl Hyde, Jason Kedgley, Rick Smith, Simon Taylor, Dirk van Dooren, John Warwicker and Graham Wood). Hyde and Smith also belonged to the techno music group Underworld, and this performance side helped to establish the idea of Tomato as a team able to operate

convincingly beyond the borders of professional 'graphic design',
a term that they rejected, preferring to describe their creative
activities simply as 'work'. Tomato developed an elaborate,
passionately held studio philosophy in which 'process' – the act of
making their work – was prioritized: 'we are all on a journey; all
work is about experience and the mapping of that experience, and
for us at tomato [it] is where we go to compare these maps. in effect
we bring a map (or maps) from one territory and overlaying [sic]
one upon another to see what happens. this is how our individual
work evolves, and how we work together.'[22]

In their first book as a collective, *Process; A Tomato Project* (1996),
they presented a series of personal projects that flow from one to
the next without explanatory labelling in the form of titles or
introductory texts, or obvious divisions between each part. There are
no individual credits on the different contributions. While they may
be the work of particular people – and with inside knowledge of the
team, attributions can be made – authorship is effectively shared.
As a form of identity-building, this is similar to the approach taken
by a more conventionally configured design company such as
Pentagram. At Pentagram, projects are led by individual partners,
but in the first instance the work is presented to the world as being
'by Pentagram' as a collective entity, rather than by, say, Paula Scher
(who became a partner in 1991) or J. Abbott Miller (partner from 1999).
However, both of these designers had higher individual profiles
before joining Pentagram than most members of Tomato did before
joining Tomato. Shared authorship has some obvious advantages in
terms of giving Tomato strength through numbers and endowing
the collective's public image with a powerful mystique, but it also
confers the old-fashioned prestige of authorship on contributions
that might not stand up to such consideration if examined in their
own right. In Tomato's second book, *Bareback. A Tomato Project* (1999),
individual reticence is taken a step further and there is no mention
of the members' names anywhere in the book.[23] It could be argued
that this frames *Bareback* as an open, Barthesian verbal and visual
text, which readers can interpret any way they please, but the effect
is distancing. The book is not, in any case, anonymous; it is by one of
Britain's best-known experimental design groups and this knowledge

EVERYTHING IS MORE COMPLICATED THAN VISIBLE

実際、より複雑なものだ。
全てのことが、不可視的に。

空間で生活し、
脳は四次元を知覚する。
時間は脳に読み取られている。

どのように？

落葉を視覚でとらえる瞬間、
その連続性が画像になるのも、
聴覚は単音しかとらえないのに、
脳はメロディを意識するのも、

愛を亡くし、過ぎ去りし日を回想する時、
あなたは一体どの次元にいるのだろう。

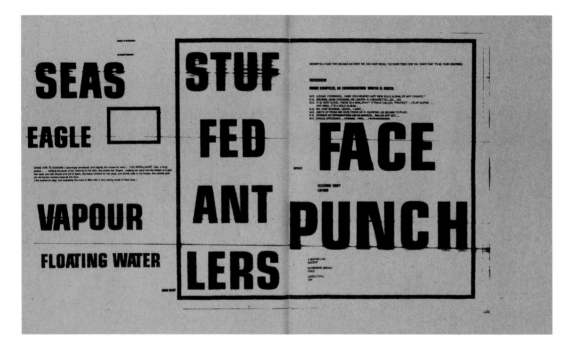

in my subsequent attempts to draw i could not disassociate myself from the obvious questions; 'what am i drawing?' and 'who am i?'. the symbiotic relationship between the drawing itself and the condition of drawing was, to me, a material fact. moreover it seemed to have a direct relationship to the issues of the self in the world.

it also placed the act of drawing within a conceptual and cultural complex. it was not only the most direct form of expression in order to quantify my experience but it also transformed looking into seeing, and seeing was process. the work that resulted from this process is the map of my journey.

the map is inconclusive
since neither the internal nor external are static.
the map is inconclusive
since neither the form nor content are static.
the map is inconclusive
since neither the search nor journey are static.
the map is inconclusive
since neither the individual spirit nor the world are static.

the fact that tycho proved that the universe
was not a fixed and unchanging place with his
observations of that supernova, in cassiopea.
until tycho brahe tracked the movement of that
far distant dead star in 1572, and showed that it
remained still in relationship to the stars
closer to the earth, we had no conception of the
universe beyond that of the celestial spheres.
the star had exploded around 18,000 b.c.: we were
still living in caves, just migrating north.
the star's light burned for 20000 years, passing
through the matter of the universe until it reached
on november 11, 1572; in his observatory.
26 years old, tycho brahe saw the light,
brighter than anything in the night sky.
it was visible during the day for weeks
after it appeared: it faded, and after eighteen
months, had disappeared. but tycho brahe
understood, a new star had appeared. the universe
was not fixed, forever unchanging.—

as the scientist speaks, notice the light sparkling and shifting
through their drinks. see the liquid images—it is as if the bubbles
have become stars, and the liquid is the universe, moving, oxygen
molecules in suspension. we are travelling through the liquid,
and the images become richer and more like galactic phenomena.
deep in the background of the starfield it seems there is an eye,
its pupil dilating, and the highlight in the eye starts to shift,
growing brighter as whiteness fills our sight. the brightness
suddenly clears away to reveal a spinning red and gold object
made of light, revolving, becoming whole from a multitude of
separately spinning atoms, everything then shifting away from us

as now we return, through the liquid,
to the scientist's hand holding his glass

Graham Wood. Tycho's Nova, spread
from a self-published book, UK, 2001

[Opposite, top & middle] **Tomato.**
Process; A Tomato Project, two book
spreads, Thames & Hudson, UK, 1996

[Opposite, bottom] **Tomato. Bareback.**
A Tomato Project, book spread,
Laurence King Publishing, UK, 1999

is bound to shape attempts at interpretation. One of the strongest
contributions returns to themes broached in a text in *Process* –
mapping, drawing, 'my grandfather' – and shows every sign of an
idiosyncratic voice, an author, struggling to articulate the subtleties
of private experience and memory. It is hard to see what is gained
by withholding the information that the piece is by Warwicker.
Subsequently, under his own name, Wood published *Tycho's Nova* (2001),
a work of fiction illustrated by his own atmospheric photographs.[24]

Fuel, founded in London in 1991, also pursued the path of
collective authorship, but with certain essential differences. First,
they were at pains to insist that they regarded themselves as
graphic designers rather than as artists or makers of non-specific
'work', and they wanted others to perceive them in this way, too.
It is a moot point which is the more challenging position: to reject
categorical distinctions, although these distinctions will probably
continue to obtain for the most part; or to argue for the tactical
expansion of an inherently limited category. Second, Fuel did not
suggest that there was an equivalence between client work and
personal work. They observed that work for clients usually involved
compromises over content that need not be made in self-initiated
projects. This may come down to the nature of the content itself.
Tomato's imagery was often gestural or abstract, embodying an
emotional mood that lent itself readily to inspirational promotional
uses. In their self-initiated projects, Fuel tended to work with hard-
hitting figurative and textual content that was less amenable to
commercial application. Third, in Fuel's case authorship was shared
equally. The three designers (Peter Miles, Damon Murray, Stephen

Peter Miles, Damon Murray and
Stephen Sorrell, Fuel. Fuel, spread from
a self-published magazine titled 'Dead',
UK, 1993. Photograph by David Spero

Sorrell) made indivisible contributions to all projects and
consequently 'Fuel' can be regarded as an author of a less ambiguous
kind than 'Tomato', where it was often unclear who had contributed
to a project.

Fuel's authorial method was grounded in the team's
practice as designers. Graphic designers often commission other
creative people – photographers, illustrators and copywriters – to
provide contributions to projects. Fuel applied the same approach
to their self-initiated work. Writing was fundamental to their aims
and they asked regular collaborators to produce copy on specified
subjects, which they then edited and crafted to work in concert
with their visual ideas. They began publishing their own irregular
magazine, *Fuel*, while they were students at the Royal College of Art.
In 1996, they authored their first book, *Pure Fuel*, which is divided
into ten chapters, Function, Leisure, Chaos, Spoilt, Aspire, Product,
Bred, Society, Truth and Space.[25] In both their commercial
commissions for Levi's and MTV and their self-initiated projects,
Fuel employed a graphic style of brutal simplicity and directness,
which, in the early to mid-1990s was completely at odds with the
prevailing taste for layered, expressive typography (exemplified
in Britain by Tomato) and looked more like advertising. In the large
pages of *Pure Fuel*, this is only intermittently effective and, despite
their occasional power, the pared-down, sloganistic spreads do not
cohere into a whole. *Fuel Three Thousand* (2000) is even sparer in its
combinations of type and image – many pages consist of a single
commissioned photograph – but its three sections, Anatomy,
Endings and Translation, unfold with greater fluency, although
the mood, as in their magazine and first book, is ambiguous and
enigmatic.[26] As with *Pure Fuel*, written by journalist Richard Preston,

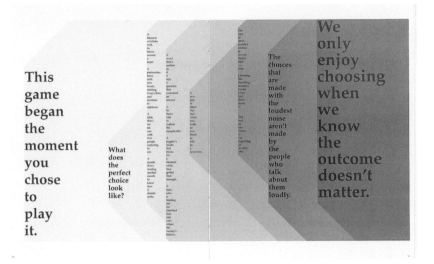

Peter Miles, Damon Murray and Stephen Sorrell, Fuel. Fuel Three Thousand, book spreads, Laurence King Publishing, UK, 2000. Photography by Matthew Donaldson

Fuel Three Thousand has a single writer, Shannan Peckham, an Oxford University academic, who specializes in cultural politics. Like Tomato's books, *Fuel Three Thousand* has an obvious kinship with the artist's book, and the two teams, like many artists, have also initiated their own moving-image projects. However, Fuel's book has a sophistication in its marriage of text and image that gives it a fundamentally different character from artists' often amateurish handling of typography, layout and print. Fuel's presentation of words on the page is highly structured: short passages of text are fashioned to fit boxes and shapes, and words are fitted three-dimensionally into photographic images; carved into surfaces; embroidered on a badge; printed on book covers, Post-it notes and a roll of sticky tape. Some designers professed themselves baffled by the book, but its sense of assurance and control did much to suggest the possibilities of a new graphic genre.

While the concept of 'designer as author' is increasingly familiar, and is also used in other non-graphic areas of design, it is still in some respects quite narrow.[27] Seeing the issue from the point of view of the (graphic) designer, the phrase suggests, as we have seen, that designers might assume a greater degree of influence in the shaping of content and perhaps seek to control it. If the cultural aim is to create new multidimensional forms of communication in which design, writing and content are more closely integrated, one might ask why the graphic designer is necessarily the most suitable person for the task. Why shouldn't content-makers coming from other areas and directions seek greater control of the graphic process? As far back as 1923, El Lissitzky declared that 'The new book demands the new writer.'[28] If the old categorical boundaries are really collapsing as postmodern rhetoric insists, and if the old rules of disciplinary craft no longer apply, then, in theory, the field of graphic authorship is open to anyone able to create 'work' that integrates a verbal and visual dimension. Given the overriding need for a content and for something to say or express in the first place, the specifically 'graphic' component is probably not the most significant part of such a venture. On the other hand, there are many examples of self-initiated design projects that have no discernible content or purpose other than the private satisfaction of making random graphic marks. Their audience, if they have one at all, is limited to other designers.

In the 1990s, intriguing examples of graphic authorship emerged from the fields of illustration, the graphic novel and writing. Where projects by artist|designers such as Drucker, Lehrer and Tilson arose within the genre of the artist's book, were usually produced in limited editions and only sometimes connected with broader audiences, graphic authors coming from outside the art world conceived and presented their work in more populist terms. Their creations could be found in ordinary bookshops, rather than specialist bookshops or galleries. What they shared with the book artists was an ability to take complete control of every aspect of their work, both writing and visual presentation, and a commitment to narrative, though usually of a fictional kind. While the centrality of narrative might seem conventional and even retrograde on one level – avant-garde art sought to banish figuration; avant-garde literature rejected the need for a story – these projects attempted to reach new audiences and to encourage fiction's existing readership to embrace reading experiences with an unfamiliar and sometimes controversial degree of visual content.

Graham Rawle. Diary of an Amateur
Photographer, book spread, Picador, UK, 1998

Like many postmodern cultural offerings, their creations provided
conventional pleasures in unconventional frameworks and forms.

In *Diary of an Amateur Photographer* (1998) by Graham Rawle,
the narrator's diary takes the form of a scrapbook.[29] Dated entries,
with plentiful crossings out, are typed on a manual typewriter and
stuck or stapled into its pages. Photographs, newspaper cuttings,
sections of text clipped from books, printed fragments and torn
edges give the collage-like pages considerable æsthetic richness.
The book's graphic form can be enjoyed in its own right, but Rawle
uses these textures to immerse the reader in the mental world of
his troubled protagonist, Michael Whittingham, member of a local
camera club. When Whittingham finds a strange photograph from
1959 that appears, in his eyes, to show an 'angel' floating against
the ceiling, he begins an investigation into the disreputable world
of 1950s glamour photography, a seedy milieu that turns out to have
unexpected connections with his own disturbed childhood. The
Diary's final revelation is concealed in an envelope, stuck in the
back of the book, which Whittingham, suspecting the worst,
declines to open, though the reader is free to look inside. The book
features a cast of models, who pose as the various characters shown
in the photographs, and it required the services of make-up artists,
hairstylists, and prop and costume suppliers, whose contributions
were directed by Rawle.

Rawle's book is not a graphic novel, but there is no doubt
that this small but persistent genre has helped to create the
conditions in which related forms of experimentation can occur.
Ordinary bookshops give shelf-space to graphic novels and in

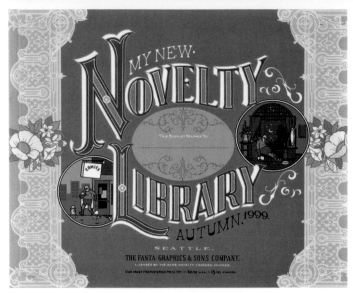

Chris Ware. Acme Novelty Library,
no. 5, comic book cover, Fantagraphics
Books, USA, 1995

[Right] **Chris Ware.** Acme Novelty
Library, no. 13, comic book cover,
Fantagraphics Books, USA, 1995

exceptional cases the books receive reviews alongside conventional
fiction. In December 2001, Chris Ware's *Jimmy Corrigan: The Smartest Kid
on Earth* (2000) won the Guardian First Book Award, a prize that
usually goes to a conventional piece of writing, though the judges
had trouble deciding whether it was art or literature.[30] Ware's strips
were published over a period of six years in a Chicago newspaper
and periodically gathered together in booklets, which he then
edited into the final form of the novel. The book has a complex
temporal structure, moving between three generations of father-son
relationships, and Ware orchestrates its melancholic mood with
great subtlety. As an artist, he draws with a designer's eye: forms
are simplified and boldly outlined; strong blocks of colour play
against each other graphically; pictorial repetition prolongs time
and creates atmospheres of painful languor and suspenseful ennui.
Much of *Jimmy Corrigan*'s graphic flavour comes from Ware's mastery
of period styles of lettering, a skill used to considerable effect on the
booklets' covers, which parody the look of old publications,
packaging and advertising, while fusing it with Ware's cartoon
imagery. The booklets are supposedly published by The Acme
Novelty Library and Ware fills their inside covers with diagrams of
houses, trees and miniature peep shows to cut out and construct,
surrounded by pedantically elaborate instructions in miniscule type.
The uncategorizable nature of Ware's brand of total authorship can
be seen in the folded poster which covers his graphic novel. This is
clearly 'design' of a complex and accomplished kind, even though
Ware is not a graphic designer. It unites writing, typography, hand-
lettering, information design, cartoon drawing and parodies of
historical graphic styles, and links these elements with
diagrammatic devices – rules, boxes, arrows – to form a
psychological portrait of the hapless Corrigan, placed at its centre.

Another unconventional fiction, Mark Z. Danielewski's
House of Leaves (2000), provides further evidence that new forms
of postmodern graphic authorship are emerging as more than just

Chris Ware. Jimmy Corrigan: The Smartest Kid on Earth, dust jacket|poster for a graphic novel, Pantheon, USA, 2000

theoretical possibilities.[31] Danielewski, an American first-time author, designed and typeset his entire novel himself in his publisher Random House's New York offices. The positive reaction to *House of Leaves* suggests the degree to which readers' tastes have already been transformed by exposure to the devices, texture and rhetoric of contemporary graphic culture. No one who managed to negotiate *Ray Gun*'s fractured page structures or even the electro-charged layouts of early *Wired* would have any difficulty dealing with *House of Leaves*' teasing pathways and tropes. These include alternating fonts, crazily proliferating footnotes, passages with crossed-out words and missing letters, backwards-reading type, text presented upside down and in strange shapes, and pages consisting of a single sentence. The issue is not so much what Danielewski has done to the text as the way he uses these effects to drive his narrative. For all the book's appearance of wilfulness and mystery, its lack of resolution, there is a carefully stage-managed relationship between typographic form and literary content: one expresses the other. This works especially well during the exploration of photographer Will Navidson's house, subject of the little seen film *The Navidson Record*, analyzed in *House of Leaves* by an army of scholars and critics, imaginary and real. The house is vastly bigger inside than out. A doorway appears where none had been previously, hallways lengthen, a staircase materializes and a deep growl reverberates from the cavernous dark. As a search party navigates these impossible spaces, the men's confusion and mounting panic is reflected in columns of type twisted on the page

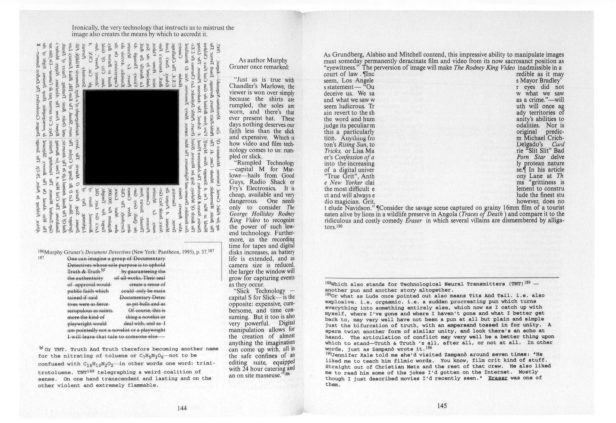

[Above & opposite] **Mark Z. Danielewski.**
House of Leaves, spreads from a novel,
Random House, USA, 2000

to form a maze of interlocking texts that can only be read by turning the book. In Navidson's final exploration, words shatter into tiny speech particles, centrally paced within the void of the page, as he crawls on his belly into the infinite recesses of a space he has come to think of as God.

In their different ways, Rawle, Ware and Danielewski answer Lissitzky's call for a new kind of writer able to conceive and author work both verbally and visually. Indeed, Ware found it hard to separate the two ways of thinking: 'I tend to think in all sorts of different ways. I guess more visually. I guess images flash into my mind [and] they might get transferred into words.'[32] Ware's work received considerable attention within the design world and designers often commissioned him for projects of their own. Danielewski's book, emanating from outside the design scene, was overlooked by the profession, although it made a considerable impact among literary reviewers. This oversight suggests the degree to which graphic authorship is still in the process of emergence. There is no generally held view of what it is or could be, or where it might be found, and no clear understanding of the conditions that would need to be met before work could be regarded as fully authored, especially in cases where the designer deals with a content and need supplied by someone else, as in the majority of commercial commissions. (Outside design, graphic authorship is not even an issue.) The cover blurb of Bruce Mau's *Life Style* refers to the designer's 'unique world view' and it seems reasonable to expect that authored design would aspire to offer a way of looking at the world that was personal to the designer and different from

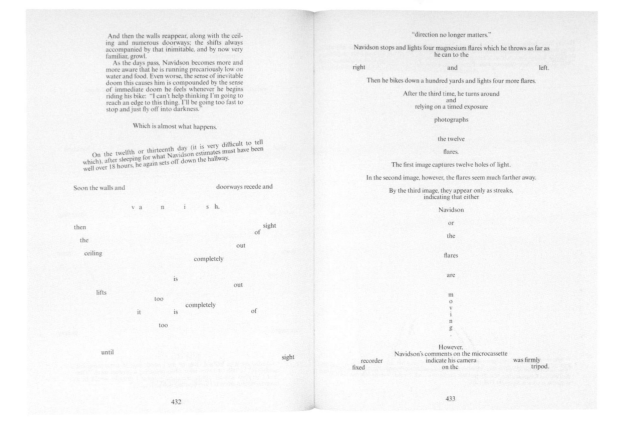

the norm. There is as yet barely any analysis of graphic design in these terms. For the most part, such claims are simply asserted as a way of gaining kudos rather than demonstrated by independent criticism to be a reality in the work itself.[33] Only in cases of total authorship such as Lupton, Lehrer, Tilson or Ware can one confidently address the work as the expression, unique or not, of an individual's 'world view'.

Nevertheless, despite these problems, the cause of authorship advances, particularly in the United States. In 1999, the School of Visual Arts in New York established the first Master of Fine Arts degree in design based on the idea of 'The Designer as Author'. Its founder, art director and design writer Steven Heller, stressed the non-theoretical, practical nature of the course. 'The concept of authorship is, first and foremost, rooted in the independent creation of ideas, which are turned into all manner of product – from books and magazines to toys and television programs, websites to *who knows what*. Our focus is on authorship in the broadest sense.'[34] The course posited the need for designers who wished to become authors to function as entrepreneurs and this made sense, since this is one of the few ways that designers can be sure of proceeding on their own terms. Emigre is an example of an entrepreneurially conceived design project that might be seen as a form of authorship 'in the broadest sense', although it also offered products – publications and typefaces – specifically authored by VanderLans and Licko. But is a designer who sets up a company to manufacture toys designed by other people an author? If so, the word starts to become so diffuse in its meaning that it is no longer helpful in determining what intrinsic qualities a designer might bring to a project as an author to make it different in essence from a non-authored piece of design. Authorship is only useful as a term to the degree that it opens up a space for thinking about design that transcends established and possibly limited definitions.

For some critics, though, it is the idea of the designer as author which imposes restrictions on design. Despite the persuasive example of her own practice as designer, critic, curator and author, Ellen Lupton questions the usefulness of authorship as a model for contemporary design practice, since it hinges 'on a nostalgic ideal of the writer or artist as a singular point of origin'.[35] As an alternative, Lupton proposes the idea of the 'designer as producer', returning to Benjamin's concept of 'The Author as Producer', which Mau inverted in the 1980s for his own purposes. In this model, the designer finds opportunities to seize control of the technological means of production and shares this control with the reading public, 'empowering them to become producers as well as consumers of meaning'.[36] It is not necessary for designers to become writers, notes Lupton, in order for them to take charge of the content and social function of their work. She compares the 'designer as producer' role to that of a film producer who brings together diverse skills in a work whose authorship is shared. This analogy sidesteps the argument that certain film directors (and less frequently film producers) can be regarded as the authors or *auteurs* of their films. According to the 'auteur theory', the director, through force of artistic personality, imposes a personal vision on the film, harnessing the talents of others (writer, cinematographer, costume designer, and so on) to this end.[37] The 'designer as producer' model could also be charged with its own form of romanticism. It accepts that there is a struggle for control of the means of production and trusts in designers' ability to emerge as victors. Yet it was precisely the realization that designers have limited power that gave rise to the ambitious claim that they might become authors. It is far from clear how making a lesser claim will succeed in challenging the balance of power.

The continuing problem for some critics is that designers' desire to become authors cannot be reconciled with criticisms of the author as authority figure by Barthes, Foucault and others.[38] As Michael Rock writes, 'if the proclivity of the contemporary designer is toward open reading and free textual interpretation – as a litany of contemporary theorists have convinced us – that desire is thwarted by oppositional theories of authorship.... By transferring the authority of the text back to the author, by focusing on voice, presence becomes a limiting factor, containing and categorizing the work. The author as origin, authority, and ultimate owner of the text guards against the free will of the reader.'[39] Rock points out, unarguably, that the few clear examples of design authorship are the exception rather than the rule, and concludes that the authorship model is not adequate as a way of thinking about most design. He proposes three alternatives – designer as translator, designer as performer, designer as director – as better models to describe the processes usually involved in design activity.

Yet the relative smallness at this stage of design authorship as a branch of design does not mean that it lacks potential or that it will not grow. The signs suggest otherwise. Problems of authorship have been exaggerated and it is paradoxical, to say the least, to vest so much authority in speculative critical texts that set out to challenge that authority. It is highly questionable, in any case, whether readers who choose voluntarily to engage with Drucker's *The History of the/my Wor(l)d* or Danielewski's *House of Leaves* are really in nostalgic thrall to oppressive authorities denying them the exercise of their own free will. One could make precisely the opposite argument. We live in a world where authority is increasingly dispersed within vast corporate entities that conceal their inner workings from the public gaze. By committing themselves to complex forms of literary and graphic invention, individual authors (those supposedly problematic 'singular points of origin') encourage readers to explore, experience and question the world in rich, open and ultimately empowering ways.

Opposition

The design approaches discussed so far were always controversial and, during the early to mid-1990s, at the height of these changes, they provoked a number of forceful critiques. In some of these responses, there is a strong sense of an old guard used to working in particular ways refusing to accept that anything about the new work might be valid. It was alarming to see rules of craft that had underpinned whole careers tossed aside so casually. At other times, postmodern design's critics framed arguments which have never received an adequate reply. The answer came, more prosaically, from tidal shifts of emphasis within graphic design practice. In the second half of the 1990s, designers' preoccupations moved on and 'deconstructive' complexity ceased to be a major issue, although visual communication still continued to display symptoms of the postmodern condition of which it was inescapably a part. Print might not have ended, as some had predicted, but there was a deep sense that *something* had changed.

The first critic to let fly, in 1991, was the New York modernist designer Massimo Vignelli. In his view, *Emigre* magazine was a 'national calamity', an 'aberration of culture' and a 'factory of garbage' that could in no way compare with the tradition of quality stretching from Roman times to the Renaissance and on to Malevich in the twentieth century.[1] The following year, Paul Rand, elder statesman of American design, weighed in with an essay titled 'Confusion and Chaos: The Seduction of Contemporary Graphic Design'.[2] For Rand, design's problem was twofold: its lack of humility and originality, and its obsession with matters of superficial style. On the latter point he is exhaustive, detailing a long list of stylistic errors and offences that begins with squiggles, pixels, doodles, dingbats and ziggurats, works its way through

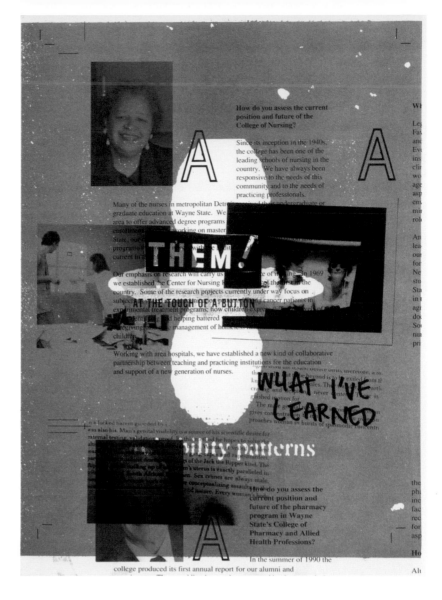

Students of Cranbrook Academy of Art.
Output, loose over-printed sheet, USA, 1992

'indecipherable, zany typography' and concludes with 'whatever "special effects" a computer makes possible'.[3] The most notorious and hotly contested of these attacks was Steven Heller's polemical essay 'Cult of the Ugly', probably because Heller, unlike Rand, singled out individuals for comment and showed examples, including student work from Cranbrook Academy of Art. 'How is ugly to be defined in the current postmodern design climate where existing systems are up for re-evaluation, order is under attack and the forced collision of disparate forms is the rule?' asks Heller. 'For the moment, let us say that ugly design … is the layering of unharmonious graphic forms in a way that results in confusing messages.'[4] Heller's principal concern was that rule-breaking experiments that might have some validity in design schools would be taken up and misapplied by impressionable young designers in the world outside, spreading the confusion and chaos that Rand also deplored. Yet setting out to create 'ugly design' was hardly the purpose of these experiments and their pejorative labelling as 'ugly' was subjective and questionable. In retrospect, it seems that the negative reaction among these designer|critics was largely an initial shock at visual forms that were new, unfamiliar and startling in the context of design. According to Heller, Edward Fella's work could be justified as personal research or art, but 'as a model for commercial practice, this kind of ugliness is a dead end'.[5] Evidently it wasn't, though, because just a few years later, in his capacity as art director of *The New York Times'* Book Review, Heller commissioned Fella to create a series of illustrations in his characteristic style for the paper's summer books review, while Vignelli had modified his views sufficiently to participate with Fella – a key contributor to *Emigre* at the time of his criticisms – in a good-natured public debate.[6]

There were, however, more fundamental criticisms of postmodern typography, which targeted its often repeated claims to be empowering readers by opening up the process of communication and treating them as active participants, rather than as passive receivers. Paul Stiff, a British academic specializing in information design, was one of the most trenchant in his questioning of this 'designer-centred ideology'.[7] Stiff points out that there are many sources of knowledge about reading and communication, including cognitive psychology, ethnology, ergonomics, discourse analysis and feminism, and asks why designers resort instead to sources that neither offer nor require evidence. Reading, he argues, is not the passive, mechanical process that postmodern designers like to imagine. It is an active, complex and purposeful pursuit, requiring strategic choices, inferences and hypotheses about intention, relevance and tone of voice. 'And all this,' he notes, 'is uncontroversially in line with postmodern theories of signifying practices which argue that each reading is a re-writing.'[8] Stiff points to a central omission within the generalizations of postmodern design rhetoric: the mass of communications – educational texts, reports, forms, guide books, reference books, diagrams, dictionaries and manuals – that fall outside the literary and artistic categories of design that it usually prefers to address. This does not, of course, necessarily invalidate its uses in these 'privileged' spheres, though it does set a limit on the application of the 'active participant' approach. However, some critics question the usefulness of deconstructed design in any sphere. 'The idea that design should act out the indeterminacy of reading is a folly ...'

writes Robin Kinross in a self-published polemical pamphlet, *Fellow Readers*. 'Far from giving freedom of interpretation to the reader, deconstructionist design imposes the designer's reading of the text onto the rest of us.'[9] But which texts and which types of reader is Kinross talking about? Nowhere in his discussion does he analyze specific examples and demonstrate the ways in which they fail as communication within their own particular contexts.

What such criticisms also ignore is the degree to which postmodern design might function as a critical practice. In 1983, Hal Foster advanced the idea that there are two kinds of postmodernism, a neo-conservative postmodernism of reaction and a poststructuralist postmodernism of resistance.[10] The postmodernism of reaction repudiates modernism and its radical critique, seeing this as elitist, and in Foster's view, this form is therapeutic and cosmetic. It reduces modernism to a series of styles (which can then be freely plundered), reasserts the verities of tradition and reaffirms the political and economic status quo. Against this, Foster posits the idea of an oppositional postmodernism, which resists both the official culture of modernism and reactionary postmodernism. As always with discussions of postmodernism, there are alternative interpretations. In her book *The Politics of Postmodernism*, Linda Hutcheon modifies Foster's proposal by arguing that separation of the two strands is not possible and that the postmodern enterprise includes both of Foster's types.[11] Postmodernism is engaged in a 'complicitous critique' squarely situated within both economic capitalism and cultural humanism; it is part of the thing it seeks to criticize and, as a result, it cannot be committed to radical change of a utopian modernist kind.

This duality or tension can be seen in the work of a number of designers who, in the 1980s, came to epitomize a postmodern approach to graphic communication. As designer of, first, *The Face* and then of *Arena* magazine, Neville Brody was one of the decade's most visible and influential design figures and his prolific output helped to define the preoccupations of 1980s 'style culture'. Brody intended his stylistic inventions at *The Face* to encourage a closer engagement with the content, which he insisted was the priority,

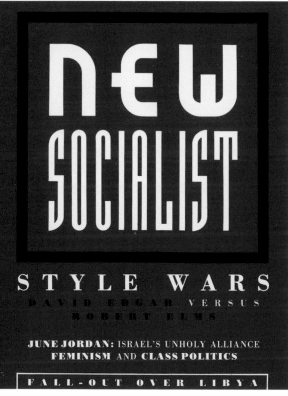

[Top] **Neville Brody. The Face**, no. 49, magazine cover, UK, 1984

[Above] **Neville Brody. New Socialist**, no. 38, magazine cover, UK, 1986

and he rejected the idea that design was about fashion. His public statements at this time were consistently outspoken in their humanism; during a period of Conservative government, he explicitly allied himself with left-wing convictions and causes. A 1986 issue of *New Socialist* magazine, which Brody redesigned at the height of his success, makes this positioning clear. Brody announces the issue's main theme, 'Style Wars', using a graphic language instantly familiar from *The Face*. Inside, Robert Elms, then associate editor of *The Face*, takes the traditional left to task for failing to update its drab, anachronistic image to reflect the new national consciousness of appearances and style. 'Style should be one of our most powerful weapons,' he advises, 'it is one of the mediums that money can never control.'[12] The statement is typical of the confusion that permeated *The Face*, which, in 1985, appeared to proclaim 'The End of Politics'.[13] (Possibly this was meant to be ironic; it can be read either way.) By then it was clear to Brody that money could indeed control style as he watched marketing, advertising and fellow designers assimilate his inventions, stripped of any deeper critical content, as signifiers of fashionable youth culture. At *Arena*, which he art directed from 1986, he responded by switching to simple Helvetica layouts. In 1988, he collaborated with Jon Wozencroft on a front-page feature for *The Guardian*'s review section, which castigated the 'virus' of style and the emptiness of the 'style revolution' and saw design, too, as equally suspect: 'Design is an animal hungry for "fresh" supplies. The process is reductive and the design world faces an abyss of its own making. In the end, design will eat itself. Culture is not a bottomless pit that can be infinitely ransacked – it needs a purposeful present, *lived* experience with which to nourish its context and vocabulary.'[14]

Brody and Wozencroft conclude with a call for *Guardian* readers to 'decode and deconstruct what is presented to you' and for design to encourage a critical perspective.

In the United States, Dan Friedman sought a way of reconciling the positive aspects of modernism and postmodernism. While he was uncomfortable with what he termed the 'darker side' of postmodern philosophy – its cynicism, nihilism and pessimism –

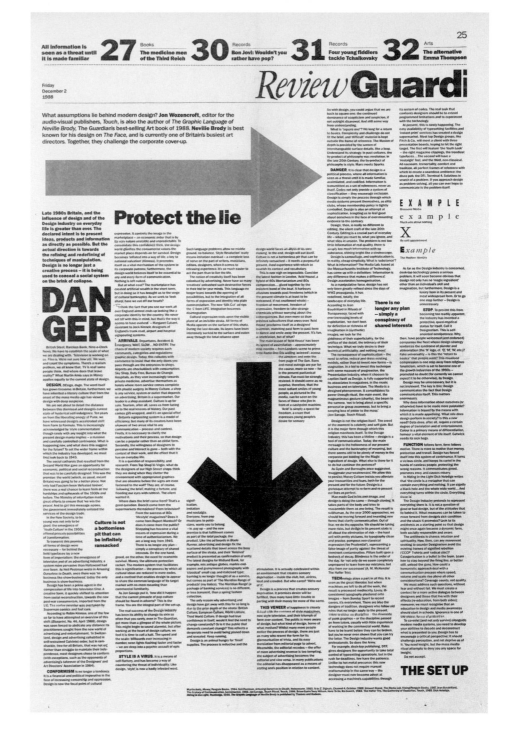

Neville Brody and Jon Wozencroft.
The Guardian, front page of review
section, UK, 1988

he embraced the 'radical insights' and 'multiple realities' that it
also suggested. For Friedman, it was premature and reactionary to
pronounce the end of modernism. In the early 1990s, he termed his
own way of thinking and designing 'Radical Modernism', which he
defined as 'a reaffirmation of the idealistic roots of our modernity,
adjusted to include more of our diverse culture, history, research,
and fantasy'.[15] Friedman, like others, questioned whether
postmodernism represented a decisive break with modernism, or
whether it was a logical continuation, as the word could be taken
to imply. He believed it might somehow be possible to embrace
modernism's heritage, while also accepting the 'new reality of our
cultural pastiche', and yet still hold to a more humanistic purpose.[16]

ΠΟΛΙΤΙΣΜΙΚΗ ΓΕΩΜΕΤΡΙΑ

Dan Friedman. Cultural Geometry,
catalogue cover, Deste Foundation for
Contemporary Art Athens, USA, 1988

Dan Friedman. 'Radical Modernism'
logo, USA, early 1990s

This attempt to have it both ways inevitably suggests Hutcheon's
notion of postmodernism's complicitous critique. In the 1980s,
Friedman devoted his energies to furniture design and to working
on the ever-evolving interior design of his Manhattan apartment,
which in stylistic terms looked emphatically postmodern. At the
end of the decade, inspired by new developments in graphic design,
he became more involved in it again, designing a series of widely
discussed catalogues for exhibitions curated by the art critic Jeffrey
Deitch: *Cultural Geometry* (1988), *Artificial Nature* (1990) and *Post Human*
(1992). Compared to the hallucinogenic exuberance of his three-
dimensional design projects, these pieces are formally restrained.
Friedman juxtaposes words and phrases selected from Dietch's
essays with well-chosen archival photographs to illuminate
recurrent postmodern themes. *Post Human*, for instance, examines
our attempts to construct new selves by altering our appearance,
behaviour and consciousness. In one spread, Friedman floats
the phrase 'We are already experiencing a new kind of electronic
space' across five images of people using bulky mobile phones.
The unreality of these posed stock shots offers an ironic
commentary on the artificiality and strangeness of a new form
of cyberspace that was universally taken for granted within a
matter of years, as handsets shrunk to a fraction of their
original size. Friedman received criticism for deriving his visual
approach from the artist Barbara Kruger and some apologists
of postmodern complexity expressed dismay at his constrained
typographic palette.[17] Nevertheless, his visual essays communicate
their arguments with precision and wit.

Dan Friedman. Artificial Nature, exhibition poster (reverse side), Deste Foundation for Contemporary Art Athens, USA, 1990

Dan Friedman. Post Human, catalogue spread, Deste Foundation for Contemporary Art Athens, USA, 1992

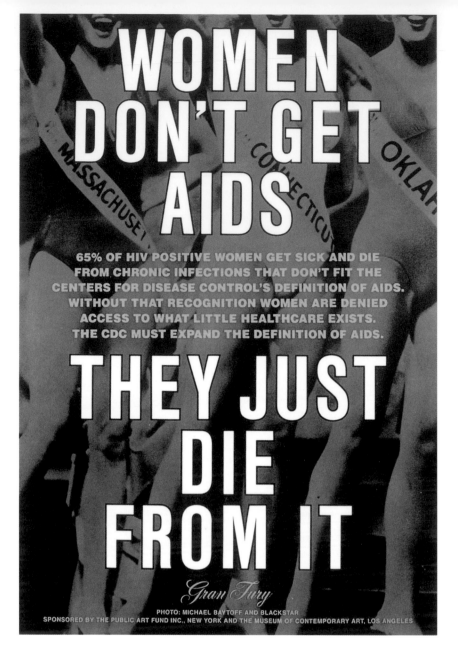

WOMEN DON'T GET AIDS

65% OF HIV POSITIVE WOMEN GET SICK AND DIE
FROM CHRONIC INFECTIONS THAT DON'T FIT THE
CENTERS FOR DISEASE CONTROL'S DEFINITION OF AIDS.
WITHOUT THAT RECOGNITION WOMEN ARE DENIED
ACCESS TO WHAT LITTLE HEALTHCARE EXISTS.
THE CDC MUST EXPAND THE DEFINITION OF AIDS.

THEY JUST DIE FROM IT

Gran Fury

PHOTO: MICHAEL BAYTOFF AND BLACKSTAR
SPONSORED BY THE PUBLIC ART FUND INC., NEW YORK AND THE MUSEUM OF CONTEMPORARY ART, LOS ANGELES

Gran Fury. Women don't get AIDS,
poster, USA, 1991

While Friedman's idea of 'Radical Modernism' was perhaps too personal, too much bound up in his own practice as designer and artist, to catch on with other designers, his visual strategies were often seen at this time in the work of those who sought to contest, in Fredric Jameson's phrase, 'the cultural logic of late capitalism'. The most telling appropriation in this kind of message-making was not from art but from advertising. With urgent messages to impart and no room for ambiguity, politically motivated designers opted for straightforward visual formats of a type familiar to all kinds of viewer from a daily diet of posters, billboards and print ads. Gran Fury, a New York collective of artists and designers founded in 1988 to combat the AIDS crisis, favoured forceful statements in combination with a single memorable image.[18] In one illuminated poster used in a bus shelter in 1991, the copyline 'Women don't get AIDS|They just die from it' is illustrated by a beauty pageant photograph, showing three women wearing

THE ADVANTAGES OF BEING A WOMAN ARTIST:

Working without the pressure of success.
Not having to be in shows with men.
Having an escape from the art world in your 4 free-lance jobs.
Knowing your career might pick up after you're eighty.
Being reassured that whatever kind of art you make it will be labeled feminine.
Not being stuck in a tenured teaching position.
Seeing your ideas live on in the work of others.
Having the opportunity to choose between career and motherhood.
Not having to choke on those big cigars or paint in Italian suits.
Having more time to work after your mate dumps you for someone younger.
Being included in revised versions of art history.
Not having to undergo the embarrassment of being called a genius.
Getting your picture in the art magazines wearing a gorilla suit.

Please send $ and comments to:
Box 1056 Cooper Sta. NY, NY 10276 **GUERRILLA GIRLS** CONSCIENCE OF THE ART WORLD

Guerrilla Girls. The Advantages of Being a Woman Artist, poster, USA, 1988

sashes representing American states. The message is emphatic in its condemnation of a then inadequate definition of AIDS, but positive in its visual mood. The closely cropped swimsuit line-up, rendered in purple, makes an understated appeal to the contemporary taste for ironic retro imagery. Another highly organized and effective protest group, the anonymous Guerrilla Girls, made equally pointed use of the communicative techniques and codes of advertising design to challenge the American art world's sexist exclusion of women from positions of power.[19] In their many street posters, marked 'Guerrilla Girls Conscience of the art world', they developed a black and white signature style, often without images, based on a headline in heavy sanserif capitals. Trenchant facts, statistics, artists' names and signatures were presented below in a standard body copy typeface. The campaign was arguably postmodern in the way that it disregarded distinctions between high and low culture that would once have confined such a critique to specialized art and cultural magazines and the arts pages of the broadsheets. It used a commercial medium to amplify its arguments to the point where they became highly uncomfortable for its targets and, by occupying public space usually monopolized by advertising, it achieved exceptional public presence and persuasive power. What it

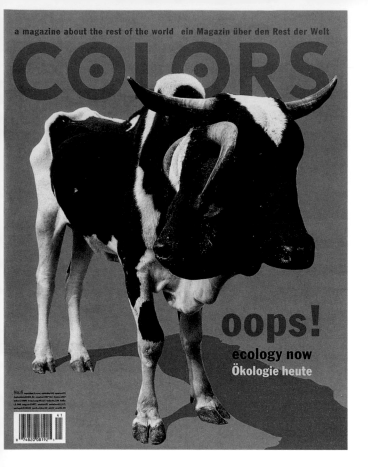

a magazine about the rest of the world   ein Magazin über den Rest der Welt

COLORS

oops!
ecology now
Ökologie heute

a magazine about the rest of the world un magazine qui parle du reste du monde

COLORS 9

Shopping

Defend yourself in style with a designer handgun from Bijan of Beverly Hills. Fashioned from 18-carat gold and studded with diamonds, this .22-caliber revolver is for people with a lot to protect.

us **$98,000**

Défends-toi en style avec un revolver à main griffé signé Bijan de Beverly Hills. Façonné dans de l'or 18 carats et serti de diamants, ce revolver calibre .22 est pour les personnes qui ont beaucoup à protéger.

Dec 94–Feb 95

Tibor Kalman and Scott Stowell. Colors, no. 6, magazine cover, Benetton, Italy, 1994

[Right & opposite] **Tibor Kalman and Mark Porter.** Colors, no. 9, magazine cover and spread, Benetton, Italy, 1994

did not do was treat the communication process as an opportunity for any kind of stylistic 'deconstruction'.

In the work of Tibor Kalman, this plain-speaking design approach found one of its most determined, articulate and influential exponents. If M&Co's output in the 1980s had been the epitome of wise-cracking, game-playing, reference-making postmodernism, in 1993 Kalman repudiated this way of working in the most decisive way: he shut down his company. He proposed instead to 'kidnap' advertising's techniques and apply them to 'issues that matter – ecology and racism, for instance – to change people's perception of the world'.[20] Openly didactic, he argued that it should be possible to apply commercial conventions to make ideas interesting and attractive – 'like candy or canapés' – for readers reluctant to spend time working at longer texts. Kalman's most sustained and controversial attempt to explore these possibilities was the 13 issues of Benetton's *Colors* magazine, which he edited from 1990 to 1996.[21] Like Brody (in his *Arena* phase), Friedman and the Guerrilla Girls, Kalman and his designers employed a typographic language stripped of complexities and frills. Issues of *Colors* were picture-led, with the text usually confined to captions and short passages. Pages had a simplicity, clarity and confidence in the communicative power of the relatively unmediated photographic image that was the opposite of the fractured collage-layouts being created in *Ray Gun* during the same period. Kalman explicitly rejected such mannerisms, regarding them as masks for a lack of meaningful content. Yet *Colors*, as the creation of a multinational company, was a potent example of complicitous critique – humanistic in intention, but still capitalist in essence. As with Oliviero Toscani's related advertising for Benetton, *Colors* raised awkward questions about the degree to which it was appropriate for a commercial oganization to blur once distinct dividing lines between promotion of its wares (if only by association) and matters of deep social and political concern. For some observers, this was a disturbing instance of the postmodern tendency to collapse established boundaries taken a step too far.

Other designers tried to find ways of reconciling postmodern approaches to graphic communication with the expression of oppositional messages. The British designer David Crow belonged to a generation inspired, in the 1980s, by the example of designers such as Brody, Malcolm Garrett and Peter Saville. An interest in punk music led Crow to Dada and Surrealism, while the punk graphics of Jamie Reid introduced him to Situationist ideas about art, culture and politics. Crow could see a clear link between the Situationist Guy Debord's argument that we live in a 'Society of the Spectacle' and changes designers were making in the high streets of Britain, where design was enjoying a new prominence and glamour.[22] In 1986, while working at Garrett's company, Assorted Images, Crow launched the first issue of his own 'magazine', *Trouble*, which took the form of a poster. He changed themes and formats with each issue, delivering his thoughts on

David Crow. Trouble, no. 4,
published as a T-shirt, UK, 1990

[Right] **David Crow. Trouble,** no. 1,
published as a poster, UK, 1986

the 1987 general election as a pack of scratch cards; the meaning of play as a T-shirt; and supermarkets and consumerism as a relatively conventional booklet. All were distinctive for the way in which they applied the Brody-esque graphic style of 1980s consumer culture to political themes that would once have been handled with much less visual sophistication. Their seductive appearance would make them instantly familiar and accessible to a reader of *The Face*, or a buyer of one of Garrett's or Crow's album designs, though small runs meant that *Trouble* had only a limited distribution and audience.

In the early 1990s, Brody and Wozencroft's digital type publication, *Fuse*, launched in 1991, was a significant outlet for designers with experimental inclinations. Its many contributors included Brody himself, Barry Deck, Jeffery Keedy, David Carson, Peter Saville, and Ian Anderson of The Designers Republic. In 1993, Kalman and Crow both devised 'typefaces' for *Fuse* no. 8 on the theme of religion. Kalman's, titled What the Hell, is a series of opposites accessed by typing upper- or lower-case versions of a given

[Top] **Tibor Kalman and Scott Stowell.**
What the Hell, font published in
Fuse, no. 8, UK, 1993

[Above] **David Crow. Creation 6,** font
published in **Fuse,** no. 8, UK, 1993

letter: good|evil, true|false, order|chaos, clean|dirty, right|wrong.
Their proximity within a single key suggests the dependence of
each concept on its binary partner and invites users to decide
which option they prefer. Crow's contribution, Creation 6, is a
series of symbols intended to form the basis of a creation myth.
The area above the baseline represents good, the area below evil.
Different letters stand for such things as boy, girl, god, devil,
conflict, harmony, the great flood, retribution, and death, and
characters can be modified or added in accordance with the user's
beliefs. Creation 6 offers rich possibilities for graphic play, but its
symbols – bolts, a spanner, a washing machine with a lightning
flash – signify little to viewers who do not know the graphic code.

A later *Fuse* project, presented in 1995, challenged the
tendency, often seen in *Fuse* itself, for typographic experiments to
concentrate on communication for a visual elite at the expense of
a broader public discourse. Pussy Galore, created by Teal Triggs,
Liz McQuiston and Siân Cook, members of the Women's Design

Teal Triggs, Liz McQuiston and Siân Cook, WD+RU. Pussy Galore, font published in *Fuse*, no. 12, UK, 1995

and Research Unit (WD+RU), is a conceptual typeface intended to allow interaction and to encourage users to challenge and reassess how women have been represented by language and to consider the structure of language itself. 'In real life, "women's voices" – their politics, culture, and means of expression – have been constructed and filtered through male visions for too long,' write McQuiston and Triggs. 'The new digital revolution affords opportunities to tear away these and other constraints (both political and creative) and model new structures and languages. We can begin to explore new possibilities, alternative perspectives and ideologies.'[23] In Pussy Galore, four levels can be accessed through the keyboard: normal typing = empowerment of women; shift = ugly stereotypes; option = personal choices; shift + option = vulgar and sexual language. Keyboarding at the first level produces strings of icons containing words such as 'mother', 'home maker', 'career', 'she devil' and 'grrrls', while ugly stereotypes include 'tart', 'dumb blonde', 'lolita' and 'the weaker sex'. Asterisks on selected icons reveal the presence of an additional layer of information, such as quotations and image sequences. Individual characters take on new implications depending on the characters next to them, giving rise to random sequences and pathways charged with adventitious meaning – a further encouragement for the user to engage, explore and respond.

The same desire to interact with and resist public speech can be seen in designers' appropriations of corporate logos. David

Shawn Wolfe. *Dispepsi* by Negativland, CD cover, Seeland Records, USA, 1997

Crow's Creation 6, for instance, features a symbol representing conflict composed of mangled versions of the Coca-Cola and Pepsi-Cola logos. Designers Republic have also hijacked and modified the Pepsi logo for use on a record sleeve by the band Pop Will Eat Itself. Ian Anderson argued that if a company succeeds in making its logo ubiquitous in both the environment and viewers' minds, then it has to accept that people will treat it as part of the scenery and perhaps answer back.[24] This was certainly the case when the American experimental musicians and culture jammers Negativland released a satirical CD titled *Dispepsi* (1997), an audio-collage made from fragments of cola advertising. The cover by Seattle artist and designer Shawn Wolfe shows a red and blue yin and yang symbol, clearly modelled on the Pepsi logo, surrounded by the scrambled letters of the title.

Designers Republic offered consumers the chance to 'buy nothing' and other satirically minded designers have taken the idea of nothingness – the hollow promise at the core of so much postmodern consumer culture – even further. In 1991, John Bielenberg, a designer based in San Francisco, invented a fictitious company, Virtual Telemetrix Inc, to explore the idea of 'design as means of propagating corporate myth to infiltrate consumer psychology'. The phantom organization produced an annual report which declined to give readers any financial information, a catalogue full of absurd products such as the 'Liver on a Stalk' ('point out the realistic cirrhosis lesions to your dinner guests'), a web site and a case study for a Las Vegas Casino. The 'dark nature of consumerism' was also the target of Shawn Wolfe's enigmatic anti-brand, Beatkit, which began life in 1984 and expired according to plan in the year 2000.[25] Professional-looking advertisements and promotional materials proclaimed the virtues of a product line that had no clear function and did not actually exist. The most enigmatic of these items, the 'Remover Installer', resembles a machine part or a sealed electronic component. According to a poster, the device 'Makes any lifestyle choice easy to dispense. Represents every detail of your life in full dimension, even when you're away.' The ultimate incomprehensibility of the Remover Installer, even though it appears in some images to exist in solid form, satirizes the abstract

Bielenberg Design. Virtual Telemetrix
1993 Annual Report, spread, USA, 1993

Shawn Wolfe. Uncanny!, poster, USA, 1997

nature of branding's transcendent calls to the consumer. Wolfe was
aiming not at the imperialistic ambitions, omnipresence or failings
of a particular brand, but at an entire system of production and
consumption. As Beatkit freely admits, 'The general gloss of falsity
is our only product.'

The most striking and, in some ways, problematic attempt
to use a postmodern design language to express humanist political
views can be seen in the work of Jonathan Barnbrook. The British
designer's output is so lavish and spectacular in form and, in this
regard, so closely in step with the needs and values of postmodern
commercial culture, that some refuse to accept it can have any
critical content at all. On the other hand, for WD+RU's Teal Triggs,
Barnbrook's 'belief in the socialist construct of Modernism is
housed perfectly in the contemporary language of postmodernist
forms'.[26] Barnbrook, for his part, rejects the idea that his work
belongs in any sense to postmodernism – 'I hate being called a
postmodernist'[27] – precisely because he sees it as signifying the
failure of modernism's idealistic socialist intent. This dichotomy
has been apparent from his earliest commissioned projects.

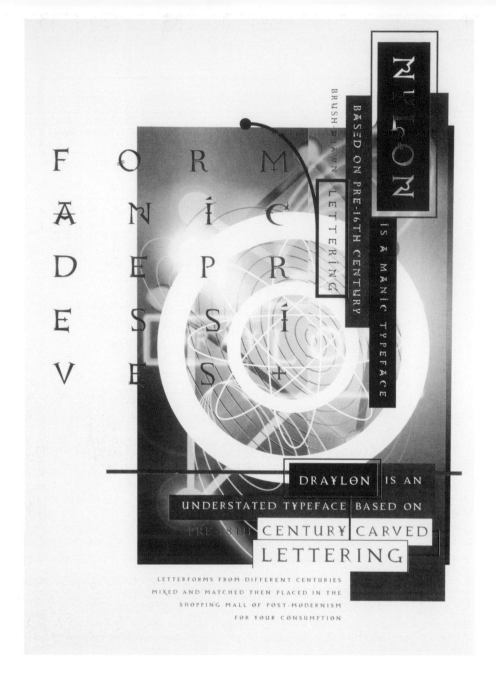

Jonathan Barnbrook. Welcome to the Cult of Virus, brochure page showing Nylon and Draylon typefaces, UK, 1997

Divider pages created in 1993 for the book *Illustration Now* show his preoccupation with consumerism and the military industrial complex. In one page design, a small image of an aeroplane dropping bombs is set into an elaborate graphic frame also containing the words 'we reap as we sow'. Barnbrook gives greater prominence to a second photograph of a hand sowing seeds, but the image's optimism is undercut by the destruction raining down from above, which will obliterate the sower on the ground. He went on to use his carefully titled typeface designs, released by his own Virus Foundry, as vehicles for delivering his acerbic views on commerce (False Idol), advertising and marketing (Prototype), multinational corporations (Bastard), mood-modifying drugs (Prozac), religion (Drone), and postmodernism (Nylon and Draylon). Once purchased, any of these typefaces could, of course, be put to uses at variance with his intentions.

Jonathan Barnbrook. Virus Says Stop
American Cultural Imperialism, poster,
Japan, 1999

While Barnbrook's convictions were evidently sincere, interpretation was complicated by the fact that his work for commercial clients, though devoid of explicit political references, was no different from his personal projects in its formal manipulations. Moreover, he sometimes worked for clients in advertising and the art world who seemed to represent the kind of values he rejected. Does the critical meaning of a Barnbrook design then rest on the presence of artless copylines such as 'Virus says stop American cultural imperialism' – even when the design itself embodies a seductive spectacular excess characteristic of that colonizing process? Any attempt to argue that this poster design enacts its subject matter ironically to strengthen its case is circumvented by the fact that all of Barnbrook's work has this same recognizable look. His complicitous critique would appear to be thoroughly postmodern: he means what he says, but at the same time he cannot escape the prevailing cultural condition.

In 1999, the Canadian anti-corporate magazine *Adbusters* commissioned Barnbrook to create a poster posing the question 'Is economic progress killing the planet?' It was the start of a fruitful collaboration and signalled an increased emphasis on design, as tool and subject matter, in a publication that consistently challenged postmodernism's assumptions and axioms. 'Postmodernism celebrates evanescent flows, a state of no boundaries, the transgressive,' writes John Zerzan, an *Adbusters* contributor. 'If this sounds familiar, it's because these values are shared by the most ardent architects of both consumerism and capitalist globalization.'[28] Postmodernism, Zerzan concludes, 'is the culture of *no resistance*'. In a poster-like spread titled 'Toxic Culture: An Iconography for the Mental Environment', published in an issue devoted to the theme of 'Design Anarchy', *Adbusters* presents a series of icons based on the outline of a human head, graphically depicting noise, erosion of empathy, consumerism, viral marketing, and so on.[29] When it comes to representing postmodernism as an icon, the head contains only an empty space. Elsewhere, a spread written by *Adbusters* and designed by Barnbrook, guest art director of the issue, recycles the received wisdom and clichés of postmodern graphic design rhetoric to scathing effect,

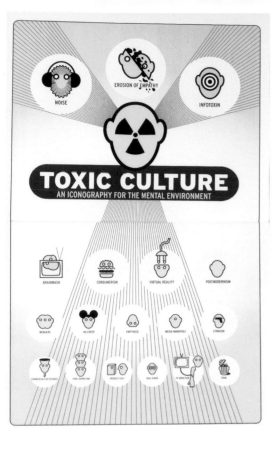

Bill Texas. Adbusters, no.37, 'Design Anarchy'
issue, magazine spread, Canada, 2001

sometimes lifting phrases wholesale from published texts on design:
meaning is arbitrary and without foundation; to impose a unitary
text on readers is authoritarian and oppressive; making texts
visually ambiguous is a way of respecting the reader. 'What if
this subterfuge, irony and disruption is just a postmodern bag
of tricks?' asks Adbusters.[30] Here again, though, Barnbrook's design
is ambiguous. It is certainly legible with a little effort for those
familiar with contemporary design's formal repertoire – its 'bag
of tricks' – but the degree of graphic noise might be seen as a
symptom of the very malaise it seeks to condemn, or is that the
point of the design?

In the mid-1990s, Adbusters' use of design was comparatively
restrained. Its pages were conventional in editorial structure and
layout and its visual commentary was largely confined to the
creation of parody ads – 'subvertisements' – aimed at global
brands such as Calvin Klein, Marlboro and Camel cigarettes.
In 1998, the magazine published an interview with Tibor Kalman
and the following year, with Kalman's encouragement, it launched
a design manifesto, First Things First 2000, attacking consumerist uses
of graphic design.[31] It also introduced a 'Creative Resistance'
competition to encourage young designers to apply their skills to
radical causes. As Adbusters became more visual and gave more space
to design issues, it became more appealing to graphic designers.
By the time the 'Design Anarchy' issue appeared, the magazine
had abandoned its earlier editorial structure, familiar from a
thousand news-stand publications, in favour of a loose, open-
ended structure that flowed from one page to the next without
obvious signposting or a clear sense of orientation. These changes
appeared to reflect the view, often expressed by postmodern
designers in the 1990s, that younger readers require a high degree
of visual stimulation to capture their interest and motivate them
to start reading at all. While it was clearly not Adbusters' intention
to embrace indeterminacy and jump into the poststructural flow,
'Design Anarchy' showed the difficulty of arriving at a persuasive
contemporary graphic language that is not already tainted
in some way by its association with the forces of capitalist
consumerism and with what Foster calls the postmodernism

this page is a living surface.

ALL THE WORLD'S A TEXT.   Can you feel it?

Don't be afraid! Jump right into the multicul ural, poststructural, electronic flow.

Let's Face It! Meaning Is Arbitrary And Without Foundation.

to impose a single text on readers is authoritarian and oppressive

Making texts visually ambiguous and difficult to fathom is a way of respecting our readers. Let's lay obstacles, diversions and false trails. Let's halt and disrupt the discourse in devious ways. Use Schmelvetica, Beowolf, Exocet, Pussy Galore...

WE'LL MIX UP

HIGH AND LOW *Culture*

IN THE BLENDER

EMBRACE THE VERNACULAR. MAKE MOVIE TRAILERS SO FAST AND FURIOUS THAT THE VIEWER DOESN'T HAVE TIME TO THINK.

sometimes the viewer will feel sick to their stomach,

but that's an appropriate reaction to much of the 20th century.

BUT WHAT IF THIS SUBTERFUGE, IRONY AND DISRUPTION IS JUST A POSTMODERN BAG OF TRICKS? ARE WE FOLLOWING OUR OWN FOOTPRINTS IN A

HALL OF MIRRORS?

WHY DO WE DISGUISE OUR OPINIONS — WHY DO WE THROW THE RESPONSIBILITY OF UNDERSTANDING BACK ON OUR READERS?

ARE WE JUST CHICKEN — AFRAID TO TAKE A STAND?

how can we hold fast to any vision, any optimism in a world moving towards complacency, cultural conformity and corporate control?

of reaction. Not for the first time it seemed that the only way forward might be to go back, as Rudy VanderLans suggested in 1991 at the height of postmodern experimentation. 'Does all experimentation in graphic design lead to the simplification of graphic design? Are the graphic designers who concern themselves with complex solutions merely slow learners who try out the wildest schemes only to come to one conclusion, that less is more?'[32]

Yet to go back in any stylistic sense, to imitate for instance the typographic language of modernism, also runs the risk of tumbling into the abyss of postmodern pastiche. The problem goes to the heart of the purpose and meaning of graphic design. As it is now understood by most designers, and perhaps especially by those who are not committed to experimental practice, design's purpose is to help business to sell things. This locates even the most unassuming forms of commercial design activity in a complicitous relationship with postmodern consumer culture, which prioritizes the needs of marketing over other kinds of value. It may be possible to resist this to some degree by working on the inside, as Kalman tried to do at Benetton, but any inroads will be provisional until such time as there is a larger political and cultural transformation. After 13 issues of *Colors*, neither Benetton nor the world had changed, though it is certainly the case that individual readers might have done so. If fundamental systemic change feels unlikely, then this tends to suggest that the postmodern condition will be our reality for the foreseeable future, imposing operational constraints or 'rules' of its own, whether we like it or not. Three pressing questions then arise for designers. To what sustained uses, other than its familiar and largely unquestioned commercial uses, might graphic design be applied? How, and even more to the point, where should designers who wish to engage in a rule-breaking postmodernism of resistance position themselves? And finally, given some of the problems of postmodern visual communication discussed in this book, what forms, in terms of style, might an oppositional graphic design assume at this point?

Notes

Introduction

1. See Gerry Beegan, 'An Interview with Judith Williamson', *Dot Dot Dot*, no. 4, winter 2001|2002, p. 32.

2. Richard Kostelanetz, *A Dictionary of the Avant-Gardes*, London and New York: Routledge, 2001 (second edition), p. 488.

3. See, for instance, Angela McRobbie, *Postmodernism and Popular Culture*, London and New York: Routledge, 1994, and Nigel Wheale (ed.), *The Postmodern Arts: An Introductory Reader*, London and New York: Routledge, 1995.

4. David Harvey, *The Condition of Postmodernity: An Enquiry into the Origins of Cultural Change*, Cambridge, MA and Oxford: Blackwell, 1990, p. 27.

5. Jean-François Lyotard, *The Postmodern Condition: A Report on Knowledge*, Manchester: Manchester University Press, 1984 (first published in French 1977).

6. Interviewed in George Plimpton (ed.), *Writers at Work*, second series, 1963.

7. John Lewis, *Typography: Basic Principles: Influences and Trends since the 19th Century*, London: Studio Books, 1963, p. 70.

8. Ibid., p. 70. Fifteen years later, Lewis had revised his earlier, absolutist view. In *Typography: Design and Practice*, London: Barrie & Jenkins, 1978, p. 135, he writes: 'The book page is rarely a medium for self expression' – a significant concession.

9. Bob Gill, *Forget All the Rules about Graphic Design. Including the Ones in this Book.*, New York: Watson-Guptill Publications, 1985 (first published 1981).

10. Peter Hall and Michael Bierut (eds.), *Tibor Kalman: Perverse Optimist*, London: Booth-Clibborn Editions, 1998, p. 14.

11. Quoted in Roger Tredre, 'Typeout!', *Observer Life* magazine, 12 November 1995, p. 46.

12. Kodwo Eshun, 'Universal Magnetic', *i-D*, no. 171, December 1997, p. 52.

13. Fredric Jameson, 'Postmodernism and Consumer Society' in Hal Foster (ed.), *Postmodern Culture*, London and Sydney: Pluto Press, 1985 (published in the US as *The Anti-Æsthetic*, 1983), p. 120.

14. Peter Dormer, *The Art of the Maker: Skill and its Meaning in Art, Craft and Design*, London: Thames & Hudson, 1994. In particular, see chapter 5, 'Do Experts follow Rules?'.

15. David Jury, *About Face: Reviving the Rules of Typography*, Mies, Switzerland: RotoVision, 2002.

16. Ibid., p. 152.

1 Origins

1. Corin Hughes-Stanton, 'What Comes after Carnaby Street?', *Design*, no. 230, February 1968, pp. 42–3.

2. Ibid., p. 43.

3. Charles Jencks, *The Language of Post-Modern Architecture*, London: Academy Editions, 1984 (fourth edition; first published 1977), p. 5.

4. Ibid., p. 7.

5. Wolfgang Weingart, *Typography*, Baden: Lars Müller Publishers, 2000, p. 112.

6. Ibid., p. 112.

7. For the text of Weingart's lecture, see 'How Can One Make Swiss Typography?', *Octavo*, no. 4, 1987. Reprinted in Michael Bierut et al. (eds.), *Looking Closer 3: Classic Writings on Graphic Design*, New York: Allworth Press, 1999, pp. 219–37.

8. Dan Friedman, *Dan Friedman: Radical Modernism*,

New Haven and London: Yale University Press, 1994, p. 34.

9. Ibid., p. 35.

10. See J. Abbott Miller, 'The 1980s: Postmodern, Postmerger, PostScript', *Print*, XLIII:VI, November|December 1989, p. 163.

11. Quoted in Valerie Alexander, 'April Greiman', *The Magazine of Kansas City Art Institute*, summer 1982, p. 16.

12. Willi Kunz, *Typography: Macro- and Microœsthetics*, Sulgen: Verlag Niggli, 1998, p. 98.

13. Valerie F. Brooks, 'Triumph of the Corporate Style: Communications Design in the 1970s', *Print*, XXXIV:I, January|February 1980, pp. 30–1.

14. Ivan Chermayeff quoted in 'Play and Dismay in Post-Modern Graphics', *I.D.*, March|April 1980, p. 47.

15. Marc Treib, 'Blips, Slits, Zits and Dots: Some (Sour) Notes on Recent Trends in Graphic Design', *Print*, XXXV:I, January|February 1981, p. 30.

16. Robert Venturi, *Complexity and Contradiction in Architecture*, London: Architectural Press, 1977 (second edition; first published 1966), p. 16.

17. Robert Venturi, Denise Scott Brown and Steven Izenour, *Learning from Las Vegas: The Forgotten Symbolism of Architectural Form*, Cambridge, MA and London: MIT Press, 1977 (revised edition; first published 1972).

18. Barbara Radice, *Memphis: Research, Experiences, Results, Failures and Successes of New Design* (trans. Paul Blanchard), London: Thames & Hudson, 1984, p. 88.

19. Ibid., p. 186.

20. For a mid-1980s use of the term 'new wave' in relation to British graphic design, see Catherine McDermott, *Street Style: British Design in the 80s*, London: Design Council, 1987, pp. 57–88.

21. For a discussion of youth subcultures, see Dick Hebdige, *Subculture: The Meaning of Style*, London: Methuen, 1979.

22. See, for instance, Philip B. Meggs, *A History of Graphic Design*, New York and Chichester: John Wiley, 1998 (third edition; first published 1983); and Steven Heller and Seymour Chwast, *Graphic Style: From Victorian to Post-Modern*, London: Thames & Hudson, 1988 (second edition: *Graphic Style:*

From Victorian to Digital, 2000).

23. Quoted in Rick Poynor, 'Peter Saville', *Eye*, vol. 5 no. 17, summer 1995, p. 14. Reprinted in Rick Poynor, *Design Without Boundaries: Visual Communication in Transition*, London: Booth-Clibborn Editions, 1998, pp. 117–23.

2 Deconstruction

1. Paul Feyerabend, *Against Method*, London and New York: Verso, 1993 (third edition; first published 1975), p. 5.

2. Jamie Reid, *Up They Rise: The Incomplete Works of Jamie Reid*, London: Faber and Faber, 1987, p. 105.

3. Art Chantry, *Instant Litter: Concert Posters from Seattle Punk Culture*, Seattle: Real Comet Press, 1985, p. 4.

4. Quoted in Rick Poynor, 'The State of British Graphics', *Blueprint*, no. 46, April 1988, p. 49.

5. Quoted in Kees Broos, 'Hard Werken', *Dutch Art and Architecture Today*, no. 17, May 1985, p. 30.

6. Jacques Derrida, *Of Grammatology*, Baltimore and London: Johns Hopkins University Press, 1997 (corrected edition; first published in English 1976).

7. See Ellen Lupton and J. Abbott Miller, 'Deconstruction and Graphic Design' in *Design Writing Research: Writing on Graphic Design*, New York: Kiosk, 1996, pp. 3–23.

8. Jonathan Culler, *Literary Theory: A Very Short Introduction*, Oxford: Oxford University Press, 1997, p. 126.

9. Christopher Norris, *Deconstruction: Theory and Practice*, London and New York: Routledge, 1991 (revised edition; first published 1982), p. 31.

10. Stuart Sim, *Derrida and the End of History*, London: Icon Books|New York: Totem Books, 1999, p. 31.

11. Philip Johnson and Mark Wigley, *Deconstructivist Architecture*, Boston: Little, Brown, 1988, p. 10.

12. 'Deconstruction at the Tate Gallery', *Architectural Design*, vol. 58 no. 3|4, 1988, p. 7.

13. Philip Meggs, 'De-constructing Typography', *Step-by-Step Graphics*, February 1990. Reprinted in Nancy Aldrich-Ruenzel and John Fennell (eds.), *Designer's Guide to Typography*, Oxford: Phaidon, 1991, p. 135.

14. Chuck Byrne and Martha Witte, 'A Brave New World: Understanding Deconstruction', *Print*, XLIV:VI, November|December 1990, p. 82.

15. Meggs, 'De-constructing Tyography', p. 136.

16. Byrne and Witte, 'A Brave New World', p. 83.

17. Katherine McCoy and Michael McCoy, 'The New Discourse' in Hugh Aldersey-Williams *et al.*, *Cranbrook Design: The New Discourse*, New York: Rizzoli, 1990, p. 16.

18. Quoted in Rudy VanderLans, interview with Jeffery Keedy, *Emigre*, no. 15, 1990, p. 15.

19. Quoted in Jeffery Keedy, 'A Conversation with Edward Fella', *Emigre*, no. 17, 1991, unpaginated.

20. Jeffery Keedy, 'Everything has Changed, Nothing is Different', lecture delivered at 'Fuse 95' conference, Berlin, November 1995.

21. Quoted in Rudy VanderLans, interview with Barry Deck, *Emigre*, no. 15, 1990, p. 21.

22. For a fuller account of these issues, see Rick Poynor, 'Paganini Unplugged' in *Design Without Boundaries: Visual Communication in Transition*, London: Booth-Clibborn Editions, 1998, pp. 219–25.

23. Lewis Blackwell, 'A Hero of Deconstruction', *Independent Saturday Magazine*, 6 December 1997, p. 57.

24. Quoted in Lewis Blackwell, *The End of Print: The Graphic Design of David Carson*, London: Laurence King Publishing, 1995, unpaginated.

25. Ibid., unpaginated.

26. Joshua Berger, 'Regarding the Design, Typography and Legibility of this Publication', *Plazm*, no. 6, 1994, p. 1.

27. Tobias Frere-Jones, 'Towards the Cause of Grunge', *Zed*, no. 1, 1994, p. 32. Reprinted in *Looking Closer 2: Critical Writings on Graphic Design*, pp. 16–8.

28. Jon Wiener, 'Deconstruction goes Pop', *The Nation*, 7 April 1997, pp. 43–4.

29. Quoted in Rick Poynor, 'Katherine McCoy', *Eye*, vol. 4 no. 16, spring 1995, p. 14.

30. Lupton and Miller, 'Deconstruction and Graphic Design', p. 9.

31. Ibid., p. 17.

32. 'A User's Manual' in Avital Ronell, *The Telephone Book: Technology, Schizophrenia, Electric Speech*, Lincoln: University of Nebraska Press, 1989, p. xv.

33. For further discussion, see Gérard Mermoz, 'Deconstruction and the Typography of Books', *Baseline*, no. 25, 1998, pp. 41–4, and Carl Francis DiSalvo, 'Towards an Æsthetics of Intellectual Discourse', *Emigre*, no. 39, summer 1996, pp. 74–8.

3 Appropriation

1. Fredric Jameson, 'Postmodernism and Consumer Society' in Hal Foster (ed.), *Postmodern Culture*, London and Sydney: Pluto Press, 1985 (published in the US as *The Anti-Æsthetic*, 1983), pp. 115–6.

2. Ibid., p. 114.

3. Jessamy Calkin, 'Image Maker', *The Face*, no. 23, March 1982, pp. 44–5.

4. Quoted in Jon Wozencroft, *The Graphic Language of Neville Brody*, London: Thames & Hudson, 1988, p. 8.

5. Malcolm Garrett, 'A Dearth of Typography', *Baseline*, no. 13, 1990, p. 41.

6. Jon Savage, 'The Age of Plunder', *The Face*, no. 33, January 1983, p. 49. Reprinted in Michael Bierut *et al.* (eds.), *Looking Closer 3: Classic Writings on Graphic Design*, New York: Allworth Press, 1999, pp. 267–72.

7. Quoted in Rick Poynor, 'Peter Saville', *Eye*, vol. 5 no. 17, summer 1995, pp. 13–4. Reprinted in Rick Poynor, *Design Without Boundaries: Visual Communication in Transition*, London: Booth-Clibborn Editions, 1998, pp. 117–23.

8. Tibor Kalman, J. Abbott Miller and Karrie Jacobs, 'Good History|Bad History', *Print*, XLV:II, March|April 1991, p. 120. Reprinted in Peter Hall and Michael Bierut (eds.), *Tibor Kalman: Perverse Optimist*, London: Booth-Clibborn Editions, 1998, pp. 76–81.

9. For Scher's reflections on the Swatch poster and surrounding controversy, see Paula Scher, *Make it Bigger*, New York: Princeton Architectural Press, 2002, p. 98.

10. Tibor Kalman, 'Tibor's Typo Tips!', *Baseline*, no. 11, 1989,
p. 5. See also Kalman's and Karrie Jacobs' observations on
the vernacular in 'We're Here to be Bad', *Print*, XLIV: I,
January|February 1990, pp. 122–5. Reprinted in Hall and
Bierut, *Tibor Kalman: Perverse Optimist*, pp. 129–31.

11. Paula Scher, 'Lubevitch & Moscowitz: Forgotten Doyens of
Deli Design', *Print*, XXXIX: VI, November|December 1985, p. 67.

12. For further discussion, see Ellen Lupton, 'High and Low
(A Strange Case of Us and Them?)', *Eye*, vol. 2 no. 7, 1992,
pp. 72–7. A revised version, 'Low and High', is reprinted in
Ellen Lupton and J. Abbott Miller, *Design Writing Research:
Writing on Graphic Design*, New York: Kiosk, 1996, pp. 156–66.
See also Jeffery Keedy, 'I Like the Vernacular... Not!' in
Barbara Glauber (ed.), *Lift and Separate: Graphic Design and
the Quote Vernacular Unquote*, New York: Cooper Union, 1993,
pp. 6–11. Reprinted in Michael Bierut et al. (eds.) *Looking Closer:
Critical Writings on Graphic Design*, New York: Allworth Press,
1994, pp. 101–3.

13. 'Tibor Kalman vs. Joe Duffy', *Print*, XLIV:II, March|April
1990, pp. 68–75, 158–68. See also responses by Michael Rock
and Marc Treib, *Print*, XLV:I, January|February 1991,
pp. 123–4, 129–31.

14. Quoted in Julie Lasky, *Some People Can't Surf: The Graphic
Design of Art Chantry*, San Francisco: Chronicle Books,
2001, p. 100.

15. Margaret Richardson, 'Buy This', *Print*, LII:VI,
November|December 1998, pp. 62–8.

16. Ibid., p. 64.

17. Bruce Handy, 'A Spy Guide to Postmodern Everything',
Spy, April 1988, p. 104.

18. Karen Moss in Kim Abeles, *Encyclopedia Persona*,
Santa Monica: Santa Monica Museum of Art, 1993, p. 10.

4 Techno

1. April Greiman, *Hybrid Imagery: The Fusion of Technology
and Graphic Design*, London: Architecture Design and
Technology Press, 1990, p. 55.

2. Ibid., p. 55.

3. Eric Martin in Greiman, *Hybrid Imagery*, p. 57.

4. Rudy VanderLans and Zuzana Licko, 'The New Primitives',
I.D., vol. 35 no. 2, March|April 1988, pp. 58–61.

5. Ibid., pp. 60–1.

6. Chuck Byrne, 'Miss April', *Print*, XLI:V,
September|October 1987, p. 144.

7. Jean Baudrillard, 'The Ecstasy of Communication' (trans.
John Johnston) in Hal Foster (ed.), *Postmodern Culture*, London
and Sydney: Pluto Press, 1985 (published in the US as *The Anti-
Æsthetic*, 1983), p. 130.

8. Ibid., p. 131.

9. Ibid., p. 133.

10. See P. Scott Makela, '100% Digital Design', *I.D.*, vol. 39
no. 3, May|June 1992, pp. 89–90.

11. P. Scott Makela, 'Redefining Display', *Design Quarterly*,
no. 58, winter 1993, p. 16–7.

12. Rudy VanderLans, interview with P. Scott Makela,
Emigre, no. 23, 1992, unpaginated.

13. Ian Anderson, 'Notes on What Button to Push Next'
in Martin Pesch and Markus Weisbeck, *Discstyle:
The Graphic Arts of Electronic Music and Club Culture*,
London: Collins & Brown, 1999, p. 7.

14. Rudy VanderLans, interview with Ian Anderson,
Emigre, no. 29, winter 1994, p. 19.

15. Ibid., p. 19.

16. Donna J. Haraway, 'A Cyborg Manifesto' in *Simians,
Cyborgs, and Women: The Reinvention of Nature*, London:
Free Association Books, 1991, p. 176.

17. Ibid., p. 178.

18. Marshall McLuhan and Quentin Fiore, *War and Peace
in the Global Village*, Corte Madera, CA: Gingko Press, 2001
(first published 1968), p. 18.

19. J. Abbott Miller, *Dimensional Typography: Case Studies
on the Shape of Letters in Virtual Environments*, New York:
Princeton Architectural Press, 1996, p. 45.

20. See Gilles Deleuze and Félix Guattari, 'A Rhizome
has no Beginning' in *A Thousand Plateaus: Capitalism and
Schizophrenia*, London: Athlone, 1988.

21. Erik Davies, *TechGnosis: Myth, Magic and Mysticism in the Age of Information*, London: Serpent's Tail, 1999, p. 329.

22. Eric Martin in Greiman, *Hybrid Imagery*, p. 57.

23. Jeffery Keedy in *Fast Forward*, Valencia, CA: California Institute of the Arts, 1993, p. 62.

24. Ibid., p. 62.

25. Marshall McLuhan and Quentin Fiore, *The Medium is the Massage: An Inventory of Effects*, Corte Madera, CA: Gingko Press, 2001 (first published 1967), unpaginated.

26. Brenda Laurel, 'Immersive Technogy', *Wired*, 1.6, December 1993, p. 107.

27. Aaron Betsky and Erik Adigard, *Architecture Must Burn: A Manifesto for an Architecture beyond Building*, London: Thames & Hudson, 2000.

28. Ibid., unpaginated.

29. Ibid., unpaginated.

30. See, for instance, Tomato, *Process; A Tomato Project*, London: Thames & Hudson, 1996.

31. See *Büro Destruct*, Berlin: Die Gestalten Verlag, 1999, and Robert Klanten, Hendrik Hellige and Mika Mischler (eds.), *Swiss Graphic Design*, Berlin: Die Gestalten Verlag, 2000.

32. Raphael Urweider in Thomas Bruggisser and Michel Fries (eds.), *Benzin: Young Swiss Graphic Design*, Baden: Lars Müller Publishers, 2001, p. 82. See also Martin Woodtli, *Woodtli*, Berlin: Die Gestalten Verlag, 2001.

33. Ruedi Widmer, interview with Manuel Krebs of Norm, *Benzin*, p. 13.

34. Ibid., p. 13.

5 Authorship

1. Roland Barthes, 'The Death of the Author' in *Image-Music-Text* (trans. Stephen Heath), London: Fontana, 1977, p. 146.

2. Ibid., p. 147.

3. Ibid., p. 148.

4. See Robin Kinross, 'The Rhetoric of Neutrality', in Victor Margolin (ed.), *Design Discourse: History, Theory, Criticism*, Chicago and London: University of Chicago Press, 1989, pp. 131–43.

5. See Walter Benjamin, 'The Author as Producer', in *Reflections: Essays, Aphorisms, Autobiographical Writings*, New York: Schocken Books, 1978, pp. 220–38.

6. Quoted in Will Novosedlik, 'The Producer as Author', *Eye*, vol. 4 no. 15, spring 1996, p. 45.

7. Bruce Mau, *Life Style*, London: Phaidon, 2000, p. 327.

8. OMA, Rem Koolhaas and Bruce Mau, *S,M,L,XL*, Rotterdam: 010|New York: Monacelli Press, 1995.

9. Mau, *Life Style*, p. 322.

10. Ellen Lupton in Ellen Lupton and J. Abbott Miller (eds.), *The ABCs of ▲ ■ ● : The Bauhaus and Design Theory*, New York: The Cooper Union, 1991, p. 23.

11. Ellen Lupton and J. Abbott Miller, *Design Writing Research: Writing on Graphic Design*, New York: Kiosk, 1996.

12. For an ambitious American example, see Andrew Blauvelt (ed.), *Visible Language*, 'New Perspectives: Critical Histories of Graphic Design', parts 1–3, vol. 28 no. 3, July 1994; vol. 28 no. 4, October 1994; vol. 29 no. 1, January 1995.

13. Anne Burdick, 'What has Writing got to do with Design?', *Eye*, vol. 3 no. 9, 1993, p. 4.

14. Ibid., p. 5.

15. *Emigre*, no. 35, summer 1995, and *Emigre*, no. 36, fall 1995.

16. Anne Burdick, 'Introduction|Inscription', *Emigre*, no. 36, fall 1995, unpaginated.

17. Steven McCarthy, 'What is "Self-authored Graphic Design" Anyway?', text for 'Designer as Author: Voices and Visions' exhibition leaflet, Northern Kentucky University, 8 February to 8 March, 1996.

18. Nigel Smith quoted in Novosedlik, 'The Producer as Author', p. 53.

19. Johanna Drucker, *Figuring the Word: Essays on Books, Writing and Visual Practice*, New York: Granary Books, 1998, pp. 275–6.

20. Quoted in Philip B. Meggs, 'Performing Art', *Print*, XLVII:III, May|June 1993, p. 82.

21. See Nancy Solomon, 'Bon Appétite', *Afterimage*, February 1986, p. 16.

22. John Warwicker, untitled text in Tomato, *Process; A Tomato*

Project, London: Thames & Hudson, 1996, unpaginated.

23. Tomato, *Bareback. A Tomato Project*, London:
Laurence King Publishing, 1999.

24. Graham Wood, *Tycho's Nova*, London: Tomato, 2001.

25. Peter Miles, Damon Murray and Stephen Sorrell (Fuel),
Pure Fuel, London: Booth-Clibborn Editions, 1996.

26. Peter Miles, Damon Murray and Stephen Sorrell (Fuel),
Fuel Three Thousand, London: Laurence King Publishing, 2000.

27. For discussion in the context of industrial design, see,
for instance, Anthony Dunne, 'Design Noir', *Blueprint*,
no. 155, November 1998, pp. 24–5.

28. El Lissitzky, 'Topography of Typography', 1923.
Reprinted in Michael Bierut et al., *Looking Closer 3: Classic
Writings on Graphic Design*, New York: Allworth Press, 1999, p. 23.

29. Graham Rawle, *Diary of an Amateur Photographer*,
London: Picador, 1998.

30. Chris Ware, *Jimmy Corrigan: The Smartest Kid on Earth*,
New York: Pantheon, 2000.

31. Mark Z. Danielewski, *House of Leaves*, London:
Doubleday, 2000.

32. Quoted in Gary Groth, 'Understanding (Chris Ware's)
Comics', *The Comics Journal*, December 1997, no. 200, p. 143.

33. For an example of the auteur theory applied to the
work of a graphic designer, see Rick Poynor, *Vaughan Oliver:
Visceral Pleasures*, London: Booth-Clibborn Editions, 2000.

34. Steven Heller and Lita Talarico, mission statement
on the School of Visual Arts website, 2002. See also
Steven Heller (ed.), *The Education of a Design Entrepreneur*,
New York: Allworth Press, 2002.

35. Ellen Lupton, 'The Designer as Producer' in Steven
Heller (ed.), *The Education of a Graphic Designer*, New York:
Allworth Press, 1998, p. 159.

36. Ibid., p. 161.

37. On the auteur theory as applied to film, see Andrew
Sarris, 'Notes on the Auteur Theory in 1962' in Gerald Mast
and Marshall Cohen (eds.), *Film Theory and Criticism: Introductory
Readings*, New York: Oxford University Press, 1974, and
Peter Wollen, *Signs and Meaning in the Cinema*, London:
Secker & Warburg, 1972 (revised edition; first published 1969).

38. See Michel Foucault, 'What is an Author?' in Paul
Rabinow (ed.), *Foucault Reader*, New York: Random House, 1984.

39. Michael Rock, 'Graphic Authorship' in Heller, *The Education of
a Graphic Designer*, p. 155. An earlier, illustrated version of Rock's
essay was published as 'The Designer as Author', *Eye*, vol. 5
no. 20, spring 1996, pp. 44–53.

6 Opposition

1. Quoted in 'Massimo Vignelli vs. Ed Benguiat (Sort Of)',
Print, XLV:V, September|October 1991, p. 91.

2. Paul Rand, 'Confusion and Chaos: The Seduction of
Contemporary Graphic Design', *AIGA Journal of Graphic Design*,
vol. 10 no. 1, 1992. Reprinted as 'From Cassandra to Chaos'
in Paul Rand, *Design Form and Chaos*, New Haven and London:
Yale University Press, 1993.

3. Rand, *Design Form and Chaos*, p. 209.

4. Steven Heller, 'Cult of the Ugly', *Eye*, vol. 3 no. 9, 1993,
p. 53. Reprinted in Michael Bierut et al. (eds), *Looking Closer:
Critical Writings on Graphic Design*, New York: Allworth Press,
1994, pp. 155–9.

5. Ibid., p. 59.

6. *New York Times*, 6 June 1999. The Fella and Vignelli event
was organized by the American Institute of Graphic Arts,
New York, 10 March 1999.

7. Paul Stiff, 'Stop Sitting around and Start Reading', *Eye*,
vol. 3 no. 11, 1993, p. 5. Reprinted as 'Look at Me! Look at Me!
What Designers Want' in Michael Bierut et al. (eds), *Looking
Closer 2: Critical Writings on Graphic Design*, New York: Allworth
Press, 1997, pp. 34–7.

8. Ibid., p. 4.

9. Robin Kinross, *Fellow Readers: Notes on Multiplied Language*,
London: Hyphen Press, 1994, p. 11.

10. Hal Foster, 'Postmodernism: A Preface' in Hal Foster (ed.),
Postmodern Culture, London and Sydney: Pluto Press, 1985
(published in the US as *The Anti-Æsthetic*, 1983), pp. ix–xvi.

11. Linda Hutcheon, *The Politics of Postmodernism*, London and New
York: Routledge, 2002 (second edition; first published 1989).

12. Robert Elms, 'Ditching the Drabbies: A Style for Socialism', *New Socialist*, no. 38, May 1986, p. 14.

13. 'Disinfo Special: The End of Politics', *The Face*, no. 61, May 1985, pp. 124–5. For a detailed discussion of *The Face* in relation to postmodernism, see Dick Hebdige, 'The Bottom Line on Planet One: Squaring Up to The Face' in *Hiding in the Light: On Images and Things*, London and New York: Routledge, 1988, pp. 155–76.

14. Jon Wozencroft and Neville Brody, 'Protect the Lie', *The Guardian*, 2 December 1988, p. 25. See also Neville Brody and Stuart Ewen, 'Design Insurgency', *Print*, XLIV:I, January|February 1990, pp. 118–21.

15. Dan Friedman, *Dan Friedman: Radical Modernism*, New Haven and London: Yale University Press, 1994, p. 11.

16. Ibid., p. 115.

17. See Jeffery Keedy, 'Some Kind of Joke?' (letter), *Eye*, vol. 3 no. 10, 1993, p. 4.

18. See Douglas Crimp and Adam Rolston, *AIDS Demo Graphics*, Seattle: Bay Press, 1990.

19. See The Guerrilla Girls, *Confessions of The Guerrilla Girls*, New York and London: HarperCollins, 1995.

20. Quoted in Moira Cullen, 'Tibor Kalman', *Eye*, no. 20 vol. 5, spring 1996, p. 15.

21. See Maira Kalman and Ruth Peltason (eds.), *Colors: Issues 1–13 The Tibor Kalman Years*, London: Thames & Hudson, 2002.

22. Guy Debord, *The Society of the Spectacle*, New York: Zone Books, 1995 (first published 1967).

23. Liz McQuiston and Teal Triggs, 'A Femme Fatale Font with a Mission', *AIGA Journal of Graphic Design*, vol. 14 no. 3, 1996, p. 40. See also Teal Triggs, 'The Making of Pussy Galore', *Baseline*, no. 20, 1995, pp. 25–8.

24. Rudy VanderLans, interview with Ian Anderson, *Emigre*, no. 29, winter 1994.

25. See Shawn Wolfe, 'My Life at the Point of Sale' in *Uncanny: The Art & Design of Shawn Wolfe*, Seattle: Houston, 2000, unpaginated.

26. Teal Triggs and Jonathan Barnbrook, 'The Typo|Language of Jonathan Barnbrook', London College of Printing Design Open Pamphlet Series, no. 1, autumn 1997, p. 1.

27. Ibid., p. 1.

28. John Zerzan, 'Greasing the Rails to a Cyborg Future', *Adbusters*, no. 35, May|June 2001, p. 88.

29. 'Design Anarchy', *Adbusters*, no. 37, September|October 2001, unpaginated.

30. Ibid., unpaginated.

31. Allan Casey, 'Tibor Kalman', *Adbusters*, no. 23, autumn 1998, pp. 24–31. 'First Things First 2000: A Design Manifesto', *Adbusters*, no. 27, autumn 1999, pp. 56–7.

32. Rudy VanderLans, 'Introduction', *Emigre*, no. 19, 1991, unpaginated.

Selected Bibliography

Adair, Gilbert, *The Postmodernist Always Rings Twice: Reflections on Culture in the 90s,* London: Fourth Estate, 1992.

Aldersey-Williams, Hugh, *New American Design: Products and Graphics for a Post-Industrial Age,* New York: Rizzoli, 1988.

—— **et al.,** *Cranbrook Design: The New Discourse,* New York: Rizzoli, 1990.

Aldrich-Ruenzel, Nancy and Fennell, John (eds.), *Designer's Guide to Typography,* Oxford: Phaidon, 1991.

Aynsley, Jeremy. *A Century of Graphic Design: Graphic Design Pioneers of the 20th Century,* London: Mitchell Beazley, 2001.

Barthes, Roland, *Mythologies,* St. Albans, Herts.: Paladin, 1973 (first published 1957).

—— , *Image-Music-Text,* London: Fontana, 1977.

Belsey, Catherine, *Poststructuralism: A Very Short Introduction,* Oxford and New York: Oxford University Press, 2002.

Benjamin, Walter, *Reflections: Essays, Aphorisms, Autobiographical Writings,* New York: Schocken Books, 1978.

Betsky, Aaron and Adigard, Erik, *Architecture Must Burn: A Manifesto for an Architecture Beyond Building,* London: Thames & Hudson, 2000.

Bierut, Michael, Drenttel, William, Heller, Steven and Holland, D.K. (eds.), *Looking Closer: Critical Writings on Graphic Design,* New York: Allworth Press, 1994.

—— **(eds.),** *Looking Closer 2: Critical Writings on Graphic Design,* New York: Allworth Press, 1997.

Bierut, Michael, Helfand, Jessica, Heller, Steven and Poynor, Rick (eds.), *Looking Closer 3: Classic Writings on Graphic Design,* New York: Allworth Press, 1999.

Blackwell, Lewis, *The End of Print: The Graphic Design of David Carson,* London: Laurence King Publishing, 1995.

Bruggisser, Thomas and Fries, Michael (eds.), *Benzin: Young Swiss Graphic Design,* Baden: Lars Müller Publishers, 2001.

Büro Destruct, *Büro Destruct,* Berlin: Die Gestalten Verlag, 1999.

Chantry, Art, *Instant Litter: Concert Posters from Seattle Punk Culture,* Seattle: Real Comet Press, 1985.

Crimp, Douglas and Rolston, Adam, *AIDS Demo Graphics,* Seattle: Bay Press, 1990.

Culler, Jonathan, *Literary Theory: A Very Short Introduction,* Oxford and New York: Oxford University Press, 1997.

Davies, Erik, *TechGnosis: Myth, Magic and Mysticism in the Age of Information,* London: Serpent's Tail, 1999.

Debord, Guy, *The Society of the Spectacle,* New York: Zone Books, 1995 (first published 1967).

Deleuze, Gilles and Guattari, Félix, *A Thousand Plateaus: Capitalism and Schizophrenia,* London: Athlone, 1988.

Derrida, Jacques, *Of Grammatology,* Baltimore and London: John Hopkins University Press, 1997 (corrected edition; first published in English 1976).

Dormer, Peter, *The Art of the Maker: Skill and its Meaning in Art, Craft and Design,* London: Thames & Hudson, 1994.

Drucker, Johanna, *Figuring the Word: Essays on Books, Writing and Visual Practice,* New York: Granary Books, 1998.

Fella, Edward, *Edward Fella: Letters on America,* London: Laurence King Publishing, 2000.

Feyerabend, Paul, *Against Method,* London and New York: Verso, 1993 (third edition; first published 1975).

Foster, Hal (ed.), *Postmodern Culture,* London and Sydney: Pluto Press, 1985 (first published in the US as *The Anti-Æsthetic,* 1983).

Friedman, Dan, *Dan Friedman: Radical Modernism*, New Haven and London: Yale University Press, 1994.

Gill, Bob, *Forget All the Rules about Graphic Design. Including the Ones in this Book.*, New York: Watson-Guptill Publications, 1985 (first published 1981).

Glauber, Barbara (ed.), *Lift and Separate: Graphic Design and the Quote Vernacular Unquote*, New York: Cooper Union, 1993.

Greiman, April, *Hybrid Imagery: The Fusion of Technology and Graphic Design*, London: Architecture Design and Technology Press, 1990.

Guerrilla Girls, The, *Confessions of The Guerrilla Girls*, New York and London: HarperCollins, 1995.

Hall, Peter and Bierut, Michael (eds.), *Tibor Kalman: Perverse Optimist*, London: Booth-Clibborn Editions, 1998.

Haraway, Donna, *Simians, Cyborgs, and Women: The Reinvention of Nature*, London: Free Association Books, 1991.

Harper, Laurel, *Radical Graphics|Graphic Radicals*, San Francisco: Chronicle Books, 1999.

Harvey, David, *The Condition of Postmodernity: An Enquiry into the Origins of Cultural Change*, Cambridge, MA and Oxford: Blackwell, 1990.

Heartney, Eleanor, *Postmodernism*, London: Tate Publishing, 2001.

Hebdige, Dick, *Subculture: The Meaning of Style*, London: Methuen, 1979.

———, *Hiding in the Light: On Images and Things*, London and New York: Routledge, 1988.

Heller, Steven, *The Education of a Graphic Designer*, New York: Allworth Press, 1998.

———, *The Education of a Design Entrepreneur*, New York: Allworth Press, 2002.

Heller, Steven and Chwast, Seymour, *Graphic Style: From Victorian to Post-Modern*, London: Thames & Hudson, 1988 (second edition: *Graphic Style: From Victorian to Digital*, 2000).

Heller, Steven and Lasky, Julie, *Borrowed Design: Use and Abuse of Historical Form*, New York: Van Nostrand Reinhold, 1993.

Heller, Steven and Fink, Anne, *Faces on the Edge: Type in the Digital Age*, New York: Van Nostrand Reinhold, 1997.

Hollis, Richard, *Graphic Design: A Concise History*, London: Thames & Hudson, 2001 (second edition; first published 1994).

Hopkins, David, *After Modern Art 1945–2000*, Oxford and New York: Oxford University Press, 2000.

Hutcheon, Linda, *The Politics of Postmodernism*, London and New York: Routledge, 2002 (second edition; first published 1989).

Jameson, Fredric, *Postmodernism, or, The Cultural Logic of Late Capitalism*, London and New York: Verso, 1991.

Jencks, Charles, *The Language of Post-Modern Architecture*, London: Academy Editions, 1984 (fourth edition; first published 1977).

———, *What is Post-Modernism?*, Academy Editions, 1996 (fourth edition; first published 1986).

Jobling, Paul and Crowley, David, *Graphic Design: Reproduction and Representation since 1800*, Manchester and New York: Manchester University Press, 1996.

Johnson, Philip and Wigley, Mark, *Deconstructivist Architecture*, Boston: Little, Brown, 1988.

Jordan, Joel T. , Hoeckel, Summer Forest and Jordan, Jason A. (eds.), *Searching for the Perfect Beat: Flyer Designs of the American Rave Scene*, New York: Watson-Guptill Publications, 2000.

Jury, David, *About Face: Reviving the Rules of Typography*, Mies, Switzerland: RotoVision, 2002.

Kalman, Maira and Peltason, Ruth (eds.), *Colors: Issues 1–13 The Tibor Kalman Years*, London: Thames & Hudson, 2002.

Kinross, Robin, *Fellow Readers: Notes on Multiplied Language*, London: Hyphen Press, 1994.

Klanten, Robert, Hellige, Hendrik and Mischler, Mika (eds.), *Swiss Graphic Design*, Berlin: Die Gestalten Verlag, 2000.

Kostelanetz, Richard, *A Dictionary of the Avant-Gardes*, London and New York: Routledge, 2001 (second edition; first published 1993).

Kunz, Willi, *Typography: Macro- and Microæsthetics*, Sulgen: Verlag Niggli, 1998.

Labuz, Ronald, *Contemporary Graphic Design*, New York: Van Nostrand Reinhold, 1991.

Lasky, Julie, *Some People Can't Surf: The Graphic Design of Art Chantry*, San Francisco: Chronicle Books, 2001.

Lewis, John, *Typography: Basic Principles: Influences and Trends since* the 19th Century, London: Studio Books, 1963.

Lupton, Ellen, *Mixing Messages: Contemporary Graphic Design
in America*, London: Thames & Hudson|New York:
Princeton Architectural Press, 1996.

Lupton, Ellen and Miller, J. Abbott, *The ABCs of ▲■●: The
Bauhaus and Design Theory*, New York: The Cooper Union, 1991.

——, *Design Writing Research: Writing on Graphic Design*, New York:
Kiosk, 1996.

Lyotard, Jean-François, *The Postmodern Condition: A Report on
Knowledge*, Manchester: Manchester University Press, 1998
(first published 1977).

Margolin, Victor (ed.), *Design Discourse: History, Theory, Criticism*,
Chicago and London: University of Chicago Press, 1989.

Mast, Gerald and Cohen, Marshall (eds.), *Film Theory and Criticism:
Introductory Readings*, New York: Oxford University Press, 1974.

Mau, Bruce, *Life Style*, London: Phaidon, 2000.

McDermott, Catherine, *Street Style: British Design in the 80s*,
London: Design Council, 1987.

McLuhan, Marshall and Fiore, Quentin, *The Medium is the
Massage: An Inventory of Effects*, Corte Madera, CA: Gingko Press,
2001 (first published 1967).

——, *War and Peace in the Global Village*, Corte Madera,
CA: Gingko Press, 2001 (first published 1968).

McRobbie, Angela, *Postmodernism and Popular Culture*, London
and New York: Routledge, 1994.

Meggs, Philip B., *A History of Graphic Design*, New York and
Chichester: John Wiley, 1998 (third edition; first published 1983).

Miller, J. Abbott, *Dimensional Typography: Case Studies on the Shape
of Letters in Virtual Environments*, New York: Princeton
Architectural Press, 1996.

Norris, Christopher, *Deconstruction: Theory and Practice*, London and
New York: Routledge, 1991 (revised edition; first published 1982).

Pesch, Martin and Weisbeck, Markus *Discstyle: The Graphic
Arts of Electronic Music and Club Culture*, London: Collins &
Brown, 1999.

Plunkett, John and Rossetto, Louis, *Mind Grenades: Manifestos
from the Future*, San Francisco: Hardwired, 1996.

Poynor, Rick (ed.), *The Graphic Edge*, London: Booth-Clibborn
Editions, 1993.

—— (ed.), *Typography Now Two: Implosion*, London: Booth-
Clibborn Editions, 1996.

——, *Design Without Boundaries: Visual Communication in Transition*,
London: Booth-Clibborn Editions, 1998.

Poynor, Rick and Booth-Clibborn, Edward (eds.), *Typography
Now: The Next Wave*, London: Booth-Clibborn Editions, 1991.

Rabinow, Paul (ed.), *Foucault Reader*, New York: Random
House, 1984.

Radice, Barbara, *Memphis: Research, Experiences, Results, Failures
and Successes of New Design*, London: Thames & Hudson, 1984.

Rand, Paul, *Design Form and Chaos*, New Haven and London:
Yale University Press, 1993.

Reid, Jamie, *Up They Rise: The Incomplete Works of Jamie Reid*,
London: Faber and Faber, 1987.

Ronell, Avital, *The Telephone Book: Technology, Schizophrenia,
Electric Speech*, Lincoln: University of Nebraska Press, 1989.

Scher, Paula, *Make it Bigger*, New York: Princeton
Architectural Press, 2002.

Sim, Stuart, *Derrida and the End of History*, London:
Icon Books|New York: Totem Books, 1999.

——, *Irony and Crisis: A Critical History of Postmodern Culture*,
London: Icon Books|New York: Totem Books, 2002.

Stone, Allucquère Rosanne, *The War of Desire and Technology at
the Close of the Mechanical Age*, Cambridge, MA and London: MIT
Press, 1995.

Tomato, *Process; A Tomato Project*, London: Thames & Hudson, 1996.

Turcotte, Bryan Ray and Miller, Christopher T. (eds.),
Fucked Up + Photocopied, Corte Madera, CA: Gingko Press, 1999.

Venturi, Robert, *Complexity and Contradiction in Architecture*,
London: Architectural Press, 1977 (second edition; first
published 1966).

Venturi, Robert, Scott Brown, Denise and Izenour, Steven,
*Learning from Las Vegas: The Forgotten Symbolism of Architectural
Form*, Cambridge MA and London: MIT Press, 1977
(revised edition; first published 1972).

Weingart, Wolfgang, *Typography*, Baden: Lars Müller
Publishers, 2000.

Wheale, Nigel (ed.), *The Postmodern Arts: An Introductory Reader*,
London and New York: Routledge, 1995.

Wolfe, Shawn, *Uncanny: The Art & Design of Shawn Wolfe*,
Seattle: Houston, 2000.

Wollen, Peter, *Signs and Meaning in the Cinema*, London:
Secker & Warburg, 1972 (revised edition; first published 1969).

Woodham, Jonathan M., *Twentieth-Century Design*, Oxford and
New York: Oxford University Press, 1997.

Woods, Tim, *Beginning Postmodernism*, Manchester and New
York: Manchester University Press, 1999.

Woodtli, Martin, *Woodtli*, Berlin: Die Gestalten Verlag, 2001.

Wozencroft, Jon, *The Graphic Language of Neville Brody*,
London: Thames & Hudson, 1988.

Index

Numbers in **bold** refer to illustrations

Picture Credits

Laurence King Publishing Ltd and the author wish to thank the individuals and institutions who have kindly allowed their works to be reproduced in this book. Every effort has been made to contact copyright holders, but should there be any errors or omissions we would be pleased to insert the appropriate acknowledgment in the subsequent edition of this publication. Designers are credited in the captions alongside the illustrations. Additional information is given below. Numbers refer to page numbers (T = top; B = bottom; R = right; L = left).

22L and R Museum für Gestaltung, Zurich
30L photograph courtesy of Studio Michele de Lucchi; 30 R © YELLO; courtesy of Mercury Records, a division of Universal Music Germany
34 reproduced by permission of Andrew King, Temple Mill Music, London
42L Lizzy Tear (cover star); William Faulkner (hair & make-up)
47 Jonathan Barnbrook (design); Indrani (post-production); © 2002 ISO Records|Sony Music Entertainment Inc.
71 reproduced by permission of the British Library Board, London
73 © Sanctuary Records Group, London
74 © Elvis Costello
80L Museum für Gestaltung, Zurich
81 reproduced by permission of Maira Kalman|M&Co
82 reproduced by permission of Maira Kalman|M&Co|Alexander Isley
83T reproduced by permission of Maira Kalman|M&Co; 83B reproduced by permission of Maira Kalman|M&Co|Alexander Isley
89 Alan Disparte (senior art director); Roger Groth (designer illustrator); Anne Buhl (senior editorial director); Helee Hatlestad (senior copywriter)
91T and B © 1988 Spy Publishing Partners, LLP
94 reproduced by permission of the Fellows of Contemporary Art, Los Angeles
101, 102T, 103T reproduced by permission of Laurie Haycock Makela
106R Airline Industries|Todd Baldwin (illustration); Paul Miller (typography)
119 Bob Aufuldish (design); Mark Bartlett (text); Eric Donelan and Bob Aufuldish (ZeitGuys dingbats)
158L reproduced by permission of Maira Kalman|M&Co|Scott Stowell
158R and 159 reproduced by permission of Maira Kalman|Mark Porter
161T reproduced by permission of Maira Kalman|M&Co|Scott Stowell
169 Kalle Lasn (concept); Bill Texas (illustration); courtesy www.adbusters.org
170T Mike Simons; courtesy www.adbusters.org